# IMPERIUM 2

## ARMIES OF THE IMPERIUM

# CONTENTS

## PRODUCED BY GAMES WORKSHOP IN NOTTINGHAM

With thanks to the Mournival for their additional playtesting services

# INTRODUCTION

**Welcome to the second volume of *Index: Imperium*. This book is one of five tomes that contain updated rules for every unit of miniatures in Warhammer 40,000. If you have an army of Astra Militarum, Adeptus Mechanicus, Imperial Knights, Imperial Agents or Talons of the Emperor, this volume allows you to field your models in the new edition of Warhammer 40,000.**

Within these pages are detailed rules entries, known as datasheets, for every Citadel Miniature from the Astra Militarum, Adeptus Mechanicus, Questor Imperialis, Adeptus Ministorum, Astra Telepathica, Officio Assassinorum, Inquisition, Adepta Sororitas, Sisters of Silence and Adeptus Custodes Factions, as well as Imperial Fortifications. When taken together with the *Warhammer 40,000* rulebook, you will have everything you need to field the sledgehammer might of the Imperium of Mankind on the battlefield.

The Astra Militarum is the armoured fist of the Imperium, a sprawling military machine that crushes all before it in a devastating cannonade of heavy munitions and las-fire. In its endless battles, the Imperium can call upon a vast supply of munitions and machines of war, from legions of tanks and thundering mobile artillery, to squadrons of assault aircraft and swift combat walkers. Yet the heart of the Astra Militarum consists of billions upon billions of mortal soldiers, armed

with little more than trusty lasguns and an unshakeable faith in the God-Emperor. But these brave souls do not fight and die alone.

Striding in their midst are the psykers of the Adeptus Astra Telepathica, crackling energies arcing from their raised staffs as they channel the powers of the warp. The Adeptus Mechanicus, masters of ancient technology, unleash their legions of cyber-automata, while the deafening stomp of armoured feet heralds the march of towering Imperial Knights. The Sisters of Silence and the Adeptus Custodes are the Talons of the Emperor, bringing swift retribution to any that defy his rule. The zealous shrieks of Arco-flagellants and the war-hymns of Battle Sisters join in chorus to mark the coming of the Adeptus Ministorum. In the shadows, a lethal game is played as the Officio Assassinorum and the Holy Inquisition stalk their prey. Collectively, these Armies of the Imperium bring the wrath of the Emperor to his foes, defying the corruption of Chaos and the impudence of the alien with roaring guns and keen-edged blades.

## INSIDE YOU WILL FIND:

- **Army Lists:** The first ten sections of this book present all of the datasheets that you will need in order to use your Imperial armies in games of Warhammer 40,000, along with the additional rules and psychic disciplines that make each of these Factions unique.

- **Battle-forged Armies:** This presents a guide on how to organise your miniatures into an army for matched play games, including photocopiable Army Roster sheets.

- **Appendix:** This section contains all of the profiles and rules for the weapons and wargear carried by the units covered in this book, as well as all of the points values you will need to use your army in matched play games.

# DATASHEETS

## 1. Battlefield Role

This is typically used when making a Battle-forged army.

## 2. Power Rating

The higher this is, the more powerful the unit! You can determine the Power Level of your entire army by adding up the Power Ratings of all the units in your army.

## 3. Unit Name

Models move and fight in units, which can have one or more models. Here you'll find the name of the unit.

## 4. Profiles

These contain the following characteristics that tell you how mighty the models in the unit are:

**Move (M):** This is the speed at which a model moves across the battlefield.

**Weapon Skill (WS):** This tells you a model's skill at hand-to-hand fighting. If a model has a Weapon Skill of '-' it is unable to fight in melee and cannot make close combat attacks at all.

**Ballistic Skill (BS):** This shows how accurate a model is when shooting with ranged weapons. If a model has a Ballistic Skill of '-' it has no proficiency with ranged weapons and cannot make shooting attacks at all.

**Strength (S):** This indicates how strong a model is and how likely it is to inflict damage in hand-to-hand combat.

**Toughness (T):** This reflects the model's resilience against physical harm.

**Wounds (W):** Wounds show how much damage a model can sustain before it succumbs to its injuries.

**Attacks (A):** This tells you how many times a model can strike blows in hand-to-hand combat.

**Leadership (Ld):** This reveals how courageous, determined or self-controlled a model is.

**Save (Sv):** This indicates the protection a model's armour gives.

---

### MANTICORE

| NAME | M | WS | BS | S | T | W | A | Ld | Sv |
|---|---|---|---|---|---|---|---|---|---|
| Manticore | * | 6+ | * | 6 | 7 | 11 | * | 7 | 3+ |

A Manticore is a single model equipped with four storm eagle rockets and a heavy bolter.

| WEAPON | RANGE | TYPE | S | AP | D | ABILITIES |
|---|---|---|---|---|---|---|
| Heavy bolter | 36" | Heavy 3 | 5 | -1 | 1 | - |
| Heavy flamer | 8" | Heavy D6 | 5 | -1 | 1 | This weapon automatically hits its target. |
| Heavy stubber | 36" | Heavy 3 | 4 | 0 | 1 | - |
| Hunter-killer missile | 48" | Heavy 1 | 8 | -2 | D6 | Each hunter-killer missile can only be fired once per battle. |
| Storm eagle rockets | 120" | Heavy 2D6 | 10 | -2 | D3 | This weapon can target units that are not visible to the bearer. A model can only fire a single storm eagle rocket per turn. Each storm eagle rocket can only be fired once per battle. |
| Storm bolter | 24" | Rapid Fire 2 | 4 | 0 | 1 | - |

**WARGEAR OPTIONS**
- This model may replace its heavy bolter with a heavy flamer.
- This model may take a heavy stubber or storm bolter.
- This model may take a hunter-killer missile.

**ABILITIES**

**Explodes:** If this model is reduced to 0 wounds, roll a D6 before removing it from the battlefield. On a 6 it explodes, and each unit within 6" suffers D3 mortal wounds.

**Smoke Launchers:** Once per game, instead of shooting any weapons in the Shooting phase, this model can use its smoke launchers; if it does so, until your next Shooting phase your opponent must subtract 1 from any hit rolls that target it.

**FACTION KEYWORDS** IMPERIUM, ASTRA MILITARUM, \<REGIMENT\>

**KEYWORDS** VEHICLE, MANTICORE

---

**DAMAGE**
Some of this model's characteristics change as it suffers damage, as shown below:

| REMAINING W | M | BS | A |
|---|---|---|---|
| 6-11+ | 12" | 4+ | 3 |
| 3-5 | 8" | 5+ | D3 |
| 1-2 | 4" | 6+ | 1 |

---

## 5. Unit Composition & Wargear

This tells you what models are in the unit and covers the basic weapons and equipment the models are armed with.

## 6. Weapons

The weapons that a unit comes equipped with are described using a set of characteristics as follows:

**Range:** How far the weapon can shoot. Weapons with a range of 'Melee' can only be used in hand-to-hand combat. All other weapons are referred to as ranged weapons.

**Type:** These are all explained under the Shooting and Fight phases of the core rules.

**Strength (S):** How likely the weapon is to inflict damage. If a weapon's Strength lists 'User', it is equal to the wielder's current Strength. If a weapon lists a modifier such as '+1' or 'x2', you should modify the user's current Strength characteristic as shown to determine the weapon's Strength. For example, if a weapon's Strength was 'x2', and the user had a Strength characteristic of 6, that weapon has Strength 12.

**Armour Penetration (AP):** How good it is at getting through armour.

**Damage (D):** The amount of damage inflicted by a successful hit.

## 7. Wargear Options

Some units have a number of choices as to which gear they take into battle – this section describes these options. Weapons which a unit may take as an optional choice are typically described in the appendix.

## 8. Abilities

Many units have exciting special abilities that are not covered by the core rules; these will be described here.

## 9. Keywords

All datasheets have a list of keywords, sometimes separated into Faction keywords and other keywords. The former can be used as a guide to help decide which models to include in your army, but otherwise both sets of keywords are functionally the same. Sometimes a rule will say that it applies to models that have a specific keyword. For example, a rule might say that it applies to 'all CADIAN models'. This means it would only apply to models that have the Cadian keyword on their datasheet.

# ASTRA MILITARUM

**The Astra Militarum is the sledgehammer of the Emperor, and its countless armies form the vast majority of the Imperium's military might. Although often outclassed in terms of strength and technological advancement, the warriors and vehicles of the Imperial Guard stand together, relentlessly wearing down their enemies until nothing is left but a cratered wasteland.**

The Astra Militarum is not a precise, swift tool of war like an Adeptus Astartes strike force. Instead it is a heavy assemblage of destruction, used to bludgeon a foe into oblivion over the course of a bloody campaign. Many such conflicts take decades, or even centuries, to complete, but the masters of the Astra Militarum are quite happy to wage costly wars of attrition. In many ways it is their signature style of warfare.

Although an individual Imperial Guardsman can never be the equal of a Space Marine, there are often tens of thousands of men in each regiment. With literally trillions of new recruits tithed to the Astra Militarum each year, their commanders have a functionally infinite amount of manpower to draw upon. Quantity is a vital asset in itself; in essence, the limit of the Imperial Guard's power is not the number of troops it can call upon, but the complex logistics in gathering them for battle, especially when the Imperium is riven by warp tempests. It has been known for unscrupulous commanders to send in so many waves of infantry that the enemy is battered apart by a living tide. Commander Chenkov of Valhalla once took an impregnable fortress by sending his men, the Tundra Wolves, to their deaths in an unending stream. Towards the end of the siege, the corpses of the soldiers sent in the first waves formed a fleshy ramp up to the battlements for their brethren to assault.

Though those conscripted to the Astra Militarum hail from a million different worlds, each Imperial Guard regiment adheres closely to the Tactica Imperium. They are hence largely uniform in their composition, and usually keyed to a particular role. Most infantry regiments, for example, contain no heavy artillery, whilst most armoured regiments contain no infantry. As a result, regiments are usually required to work together in formations known as battle groups or task forces. This practice of institutionalised division dates back to the days following the Horus Heresy, when the Legions of the Space Marines were reduced to far smaller Chapters to prevent them becoming too much of a threat should they be corrupted. At much the same time, it was decreed that Imperial Guard regiments should be separate, yet interdependent, so that any rebellions could be quickly isolated and quashed, leaving the rest of the military machine to continue its duties.

The Tactica Imperium sets down a basic template around which infantry regiments are organised. Each is split into companies, with each company under the command of a senior officer. The number of companies in a regiment varies greatly, but most regiments are comprised of between three and twenty companies. Companies are further divided into platoons, typically between three and six. Platoons consist of a number of ten-man squads, usually two to five, led by a five-man command squad, but they can also include special weapons squads, heavy weapons squads, and conscripts barely out of basic training. A full platoon can number well over a hundred men, and a full-strength regiment can number in the tens of thousands.

Terms and specific rank names vary significantly. While the regimental commander is normally a colonel, the culture from which he is drawn might use an entirely different term, ranging from 'Knight Magnificent' to 'Chief Hetman' to 'Marquis Battalio.' Provided it can fight effectively with standard issue lasguns, bayonets and flak armour, each regiment is allowed to keep its warrior culture and identity, the better to ensure cohesion and bonds of loyalty. In this way entire cultures can be rapidly recruited.

This hierarchy-based structure is maintained in other types of regiment. In a tank regiment, for example, the individual Guardsmen form tank crews, with each tank taking the place of a squad as the basic unit. These are formed into squadrons, led by a command tank, and organised into tank companies, a number of which make up an armoured regiment. In the rare but devastatingly powerful super-heavy tank regiments, each individual tank is the equivalent of a platoon, meaning that such a regiment will usually only number nine to twelve super-heavy tanks in addition to its numerous supply and service vehicles. Such regiments are rarely deployed en masse, but are usually split into smaller squadrons of super-heavy tanks and assigned as armoured support to more conventional regiments.

The basic Astra Militarum regiment is also supported by many specialist units that are part of the wider Departmento Munitorum. These are personnel supplied by auxiliary institutions that have long been a part of the Imperium's military bedrock. Amongst them are the Schola Progenium, source of the iron-willed Commissars and the elite soldiery of the Militarum Tempestus; the Scholastica Psykana, which provides soul-bound psykers reliable enough to serve in the Emperor's armies; and the Abhuman Auxilla, which oversees the military contributions of Ratlings, Ogryns and other such genetic offshoots of Humanity. The regimental specialists from the Departmento Munitorum are further bolstered by elements from the wider Imperium. These include priests of the Adeptus Ministorum, who see to the spiritual reinforcement of the infantry, and the Enginseers and servitors of the Adeptus Mechanicus, who tend to the Imperial Guard's war machines.

## ASTRA MILITARUM BATTLE GROUPS

When a force of combined arms is required, units are drafted from the available regiments and placed under the command of a senior officer, such as a colonel or a captain. These formations are known as battle groups. These can vary in size, from company-level units of a hundred or so men and five or six vehicles, to a force almost as large as a true regiment.

Some battle groups are a balanced mix, likely to be taken from several different regiments from many different worlds. Others, however, are highly specialised, designed to meet very specific battlefield challenges. A battle group might consist only of Chimera-mounted infantry and airborne support if sent to strike an island fortress, for instance. Similarly, a deployment of self-propelled artillery will be assigned to support an armoured breakthrough, or an entire company of Sentinels will be sent to rout a dug-in enemy in a jungle fight. As squads, companies, and entire regiments drop below strength due to the attrition of battle, undersized formations are merged to create composite groups. Few orderly formations survive the journey through the warp to the designated battleground intact, let alone the crucible of war that follows.

## INFANTRY REGIMENTS

An Imperial Guard infantry regiment is a sight to stir the blood of any military commander. Rank after rank of uniformed warriors march in close order drill to the front line, lasguns held tight against their shoulders until the enemy is within range. Filling trenches, manning bastions, hunkering down in the rubble of shattered cities, the infantry regiment becomes a wall of living flesh that bars the path of the tyrant and the fiend. When the enemy comes close the officers at the core of each platoon will bark their orders, each imperative relayed along the line by vox officers and laud-hailer cherubim. A hurricane of las-beams shoots out, blasting back the enemy with sheer weight of fire. Those cunning or stalwart enough to escape the fury of such fusillades find themselves under attack from grizzled veterans proven in the heat of war, special weapons teams that can melt enemy tanks to blackening slag, and snipers that can bullseye an enemy leader from a hundred paces.

## ARMOURED REGIMENTS

The ground shivers at the passage of rugged Astra Militarum tanks, their broad treads chewing the cratered ground to muddy ruin as they trundle to the front line. Even a single squadron of Leman Russ battle tanks can blast apart an enemy strike force. Yet the lords of steel that direct these formidable spearheads have not only the famously deadly Leman Russ at their behest; alongside these iconic war machines come anti-tank Vanquishers, Punishers capable of mowing down alien hordes in a storm of bullets, Hellhound flame tanks and Bane Wolf tanks that send clouds of intensely lethal gas into the ranks of the foe.

## RECON REGIMENTS

The sheer size of the Astra Militarum's armed forces can make for an unwieldy weapon. To ensure it is brought to bear with optimum force, the Imperial Guard's commanders employ elements from reconnaissance regiments. These are largely comprised of Sentinels – bipedal heavy weapons platforms that can pick their way through even the densest terrain – though they also include Rough Riders, cavalry shock troops whose hunting lances can lay low even the power-armoured butchers of the Heretic Astartes.

## ARTILLERY REGIMENTS

Though rarely used in isolation, artillery regiments are perhaps the most devastating of all. As with all Imperial Guard guns they are self-propelled, enabling them to move – albeit slowly – from one war zone to the next under their own steam, or to punish an advancing force with a rolling barrage that does not cease until the enemy is utterly flattened. Such armoured forces are known not only for the iconic earthshaker cannons of their Basilisks, but also Manticore rocket launchers, Hydra autocannons and Wyvern area denial batteries. Even the massive Deathstrike missiles are at the command of the Astra Militarum's artillery commanders. Together these assets can command any battlefield, for as any Imperial artillerist knows, big guns never tire.

# ASTRA MILITARUM ARMY LIST

This section contains all of the datasheets that you will need in order to fight battles with your Astra Militarum miniatures. Each datasheet includes the characteristics profiles of the unit it describes, as well as any wargear and abilities it may have. Some rules are common to several Astra Militarum units – these are described below and referenced on the datasheets.

## KEYWORDS

Throughout this section you will come across a keyword that is within angular brackets, specifically <REGIMENT>. This is shorthand for a keyword of your own choosing, as described below.

### <REGIMENT>

All Astra Militarum belong to a regiment, drawn from one of the many worlds of the Imperium of Man. Each has its own distinct traditions, training regimes and methods of waging war.

Some datasheets specify what regiment the unit is drawn from (e.g. Lord Castellan Creed has the CADIAN keyword, so is from the Cadian Regiment, while a Tempestor Prime has the MILITARUM TEMPESTUS keyword, so is from the Militarum Tempestus Regiment). If an ASTRA MILITARUM datasheet does not specify which regiment it is drawn from, it will typically have the <REGIMENT> keyword. When you include such a unit in your army, you must nominate which regiment that unit is from. You then simply replace the <REGIMENT> keyword in every instance on that unit's datasheet with the name of your chosen regiment. You cannot choose to replace the <REGIMENT> keyword with MILITARUM TEMPESTUS, but you can use any of the other regiments that you have read about, or make up your own.

For example, if you included a Command Squad in your army and wanted them to be from the Vostroyan Firstborn regiment, their <REGIMENT> Faction keyword is changed to VOSTROYAN and their Regimental Standard ability would say: 'All friendly VOSTROYAN units add 1 to their Leadership whilst they are within 6" of any VOSTROYAN Veteran with a regimental standard.'

## ABILITIES

The following ability is common to several Astra Militarum units:

### Voice of Command

This unit may issue one order per turn to the soldiers under their command at the start of their Shooting phase. Orders may only be issued to INFANTRY units within 6" of this unit that have the same <REGIMENT> keyword as this unit. To issue an order, pick a target unit and choose which order you wish to issue from the table below. A unit may only be affected by one order per turn.

| ASTRA MILITARUM ORDERS |
| --- |
| **ORDER** |
| **Take Aim!**<br>Re-roll hit rolls of 1 for all the models in the ordered unit until the end of the phase. |
| **First Rank, Fire! Second Rank, Fire!**<br>All lasguns and all hot-shot lasguns in the ordered unit change their Type to Rapid Fire 2 until the end of the phase. |
| **Bring it Down!**<br>Re-roll wound rolls of 1 for all the models in the ordered unit until the end of the phase. |
| **Forwards, for the Emperor!**<br>The ordered unit can shoot this phase even if it Advanced in its Movement phase. |
| **Get Back in the Fight!**<br>The ordered unit can shoot this phase even if it Fell Back in its Movement phase. |
| **Move! Move! Move!**<br>Instead of shooting this phase the ordered unit immediately moves as if it were the Movement phase. It must Advance as part of this move, and cannot declare a charge during this turn. |
| **Fix Bayonets!**<br>This order can only be issued to units that are within 1" of an enemy unit. The ordered unit immediately fights as if it were the Fight phase. |

# WARGEAR

Many of the units you will find on the following pages reference one or more of the wargear lists below. When this is the case, the unit may take any item from the appropriate list. The profiles for the items in these lists can be found in the appendix (pg 144-146).

## ASTRA MILITARUM RANGED WEAPONS

- Bolt pistol
- Boltgun
- Plasma pistol

## ASTRA MILITARUM SPECIAL WEAPONS

- Sniper rifle [1]
- Flamer
- Grenade launcher
- Meltagun
- Plasma gun

## ASTRA MILITARUM HEAVY WEAPONS

- Mortar
- Autocannon
- Heavy bolter
- Missile launcher
- Lascannon

## ASTRA MILITARUM MELEE WEAPONS

- Power axe
- Power maul
- Power sword
- Power fist

[1] Cannot be taken by Rough Riders.

# COMPANY COMMANDER

**3 POWER**

| NAME | M | WS | BS | S | T | W | A | Ld | Sv |
|---|---|---|---|---|---|---|---|---|---|
| Company Commander | 6" | 3+ | 3+ | 3 | 3 | 4 | 3 | 8 | 5+ |

A Company Commander is a single model armed with a laspistol, chainsword and frag grenades.

| WEAPON | RANGE | TYPE | S | AP | D | ABILITIES |
|---|---|---|---|---|---|---|
| Laspistol | 12" | Pistol 1 | 3 | 0 | 1 | - |
| Shotgun | 12" | Assault 2 | 3 | 0 | 1 | If the target is within half range, add 1 to this weapon's Strength. |
| Chainsword | Melee | Melee | User | 0 | 1 | Each time the bearer fights, it can make 1 additional attack with this weapon. |
| Frag grenade | 6" | Grenade D6 | 3 | 0 | 1 | - |

| WARGEAR OPTIONS | • This model may replace its chainsword with an item from the *Astra Militarum Melee Weapons* list.<br>• This model may replace its laspistol with a shotgun or an item from the *Astra Militarum Ranged Weapons* list. |
|---|---|
| ABILITIES | **Voice of Command** (pg 10)<br><br>**Refractor Field:** This model has a 5+ invulnerable save. | **Senior Officer:** This model may use the Voice of Command ability twice in each of your turns. Resolve the effects of the first order before issuing the second order. |
| FACTION KEYWORDS | IMPERIUM, ASTRA MILITARUM, <REGIMENT> |
| KEYWORDS | CHARACTER, INFANTRY, OFFICER, COMPANY COMMANDER |

Company Commanders lead from the front lines, bellowing orders to their troops amidst hails of enemy fire.

12

## TANK COMMANDER

**13** POWER

### DAMAGE
Some of this model's characteristics change as it suffers damage, as shown below:

| REMAINING W | M | BS | A |
|---|---|---|---|
| 7-12+ | 10" | 3+ | 3 |
| 4-6 | 7" | 4+ | D3 |
| 1-3 | 4" | 5+ | 1 |

| NAME | M | WS | BS | S | T | W | A | Ld | Sv |
|---|---|---|---|---|---|---|---|---|---|
| Tank Commander | * | 6+ | * | 7 | 8 | 12 | * | 7 | 3+ |

A Tank Commander is a single model. He rides to battle from the cupola of a Leman Russ battle tank, which is equipped with a battle cannon and a heavy bolter.

| WEAPON | RANGE | TYPE | S | AP | D | ABILITIES |
|---|---|---|---|---|---|---|
| Battle cannon | 72" | Heavy D6 | 8 | -2 | D3 | - |
| Demolisher cannon | 24" | Heavy D3 | 10 | -3 | D6 | When attacking units with 5 or more models, change this weapon's Type to Heavy D6. |
| Eradicator nova cannon | 36" | Heavy D6 | 6 | -2 | D3 | Units attacked by this weapon do not gain any bonus to their saving throws for being in cover. |
| Executioner plasma cannon | When attacking with this weapon, choose one of the profiles below. | | | | | |
| - Standard | 36" | Heavy D6 | 7 | -3 | 1 | - |
| - Supercharge | 36" | Heavy D6 | 8 | -3 | 2 | If you make one or more hit rolls of 1, the bearer suffers D6 mortal wounds after all of this weapon's shots have been resolved. |
| Exterminator autocannon | 48" | Heavy 4 | 7 | -1 | 2 | - |
| Heavy bolter | 36" | Heavy 3 | 5 | -1 | 1 | - |
| Heavy flamer | 8" | Heavy D6 | 5 | -1 | 1 | This weapon automatically hits its target. |
| Heavy stubber | 36" | Heavy 3 | 4 | 0 | 1 | - |
| Lascannon | 48" | Heavy 1 | 9 | -3 | D6 | - |
| Multi-melta | 24" | Heavy 1 | 8 | -4 | D6 | If the target is within half range of this weapon, roll two dice when inflicting damage with it and discard the lowest result. |
| Plasma cannon | When attacking with this weapon, choose one of the profiles below. | | | | | |
| - Standard | 36" | Heavy D3 | 7 | -3 | 1 | - |
| - Supercharge | 36" | Heavy D3 | 8 | -3 | 2 | On a hit roll of 1, the bearer is slain after all of this weapon's shots have been resolved. |
| Punisher gatling cannon | 24" | Heavy 20 | 5 | 0 | 1 | - |
| Storm bolter | 24" | Rapid Fire 2 | 4 | 0 | 1 | - |
| Vanquisher battle cannon | 72" | Heavy 1 | 8 | -3 | D6 | Roll two dice when inflicting damage with this weapon and discard the lowest result. |

**WARGEAR OPTIONS**
- This model may replace its battle cannon with an exterminator autocannon, vanquisher battle cannon, eradicator nova cannon, demolisher cannon, punisher gatling cannon or executioner plasma cannon.
- This model may replace its heavy bolter with a heavy flamer or a lascannon.
- This model may take two heavy bolters, two heavy flamers, two multi-meltas or two plasma cannons.
- This model may take a heavy stubber or storm bolter.

**ABILITIES**

**Grinding Advance:** This model does not suffer the penalty to turret weapon hit rolls for shooting a Heavy weapon on a turn in which it has moved. The following weapons are turret weapons: battle cannon, eradicator nova cannon, exterminator autocannon, vanquisher battle cannon, demolisher cannon, executioner plasma cannon and punisher gatling cannon.

**Explodes:** If this model is reduced to 0 wounds, roll a D6 before removing it from the battlefield. On a 6 it explodes, and each unit within 6" suffers D3 mortal wounds.

**Smoke Launchers:** Once per game, instead of shooting any weapons in the Shooting phase, this model can use its smoke launchers; until your next Shooting phase your opponent must subtract 1 from all hit rolls for ranged weapons that target this vehicle.

**Tank Orders:** This model can issue an order to a friendly <REGIMENT> LEMAN RUSS at the start of your Shooting phase. To issue a Tank Order, pick a target LEMAN RUSS within 6" of this model (though the unit you pick cannot be a CHARACTER) and choose which order you wish to issue from the table to the right. Each LEMAN RUSS can only be given a single order each turn.

**Emergency Plasma Vents:** If this model fires a supercharged plasma cannon, and you roll one or more hit rolls of 1, it is not automatically destroyed. Instead, it suffers 6 mortal wounds and cannot fire any plasma cannons for the rest of the battle.

### TANK ORDERS

**ORDER**

**Full Throttle!**
Instead of shooting this phase the ordered model immediately moves as if it were the Movement phase. It must Advance as part of this move, and cannot declare a charge during this turn.

**Gunners, Kill on Sight!**
Re-roll hit rolls of 1 for the ordered model until the end of the phase.

**Strike and Shroud!**
This order can only be issued to a model that has not yet used its smoke launchers during the battle. The ordered model can shoot its weapons and launch its smoke launchers during this phase.

| FACTION KEYWORDS | IMPERIUM, ASTRA MILITARUM, <REGIMENT> |
|---|---|
| KEYWORDS | CHARACTER, VEHICLE, LEMAN RUSS, TANK COMMANDER |

## MASTER OF ORDNANCE

**2 POWER**

| NAME | M | WS | BS | S | T | W | A | Ld | Sv |
|------|---|----|----|---|---|---|---|----|----|
| Master of Ordnance | 6" | 4+ | 3+ | 3 | 3 | 3 | 2 | 6 | 5+ |

A Master of Ordnance is a single model armed with a laspistol.

| WEAPON | RANGE | TYPE | S | AP | D | ABILITIES |
|--------|-------|------|---|----|----|-----------|
| Laspistol | 12" | Pistol 1 | 3 | 0 | 1 | - |
| Artillery barrage | 100" | Heavy D6 | 8 | -2 | D3 | This weapon can only be fired once per battle, and cannot be used if the bearer moves. This weapon can target units that are not visible to the bearer (when doing so, subtract 1 from the hit rolls). You may only use one artillery barrage per turn, regardless of how many Masters of Ordnance you have in your army. |

| ABILITIES | **Master of Ballistics:** You can re-roll any hit rolls of 1 made for friendly <REGIMENT> Basilisks, Wyverns, Manticores or Deathstrikes when they target enemy units over 36" away in the Shooting phase, if they are within 3" of this model. |
|-----------|---|
| **FACTION KEYWORDS** | IMPERIUM, ASTRA MILITARUM, <REGIMENT> |
| **KEYWORDS** | CHARACTER, INFANTRY, MASTER OF ORDNANCE |

## PLATOON COMMANDER

**2 POWER**

| NAME | M | WS | BS | S | T | W | A | Ld | Sv |
|------|---|----|----|---|---|---|---|----|----|
| Platoon Commander | 6" | 3+ | 3+ | 3 | 3 | 3 | 3 | 7 | 5+ |

A Platoon Commander is a single model armed with a laspistol, chainsword and frag grenades.

| WEAPON | RANGE | TYPE | S | AP | D | ABILITIES |
|--------|-------|------|---|----|----|-----------|
| Laspistol | 12" | Pistol 1 | 3 | 0 | 1 | - |
| Shotgun | 12" | Assault 2 | 3 | 0 | 1 | If the target is within half range, add 1 to this weapon's Strength. |
| Chainsword | Melee | Melee | User | 0 | 1 | Each time the bearer fights, it can make 1 additional attack with this weapon. |
| Frag grenade | 6" | Grenade D6 | 3 | 0 | 1 | - |

| WARGEAR OPTIONS | • This model may replace its chainsword with an item from the *Astra Militarum Melee Weapons* list.<br>• This model may replace its laspistol with a shotgun or an item from the *Astra Militarum Ranged Weapons* list. |
|-----------------|---|
| ABILITIES | **Voice of Command** (pg 10)<br><br>**Refractor Field:** This model has a 5+ invulnerable save. |
| **FACTION KEYWORDS** | IMPERIUM, ASTRA MILITARUM, <REGIMENT> |
| **KEYWORDS** | CHARACTER, INFANTRY, OFFICER, PLATOON COMMANDER |

# COMMAND SQUAD

**3 POWER**

| NAME | M | WS | BS | S | T | W | A | Ld | Sv |
|---|---|---|---|---|---|---|---|---|---|
| Veteran | 6" | 4+ | 3+ | 3 | 3 | 1 | 1 | 6 | 5+ |
| Veteran Heavy Weapons Team | 6" | 4+ | 3+ | 3 | 3 | 2 | 2 | 6 | 5+ |

This unit contains 4 Veterans. Each model is armed with a lasgun and frag grenades.

| WEAPON | RANGE | TYPE | S | AP | D | ABILITIES |
|---|---|---|---|---|---|---|
| Heavy flamer | 8" | Heavy D6 | 5 | -1 | 1 | This weapon automatically hits its target. |
| Laspistol | 12" | Pistol 1 | 3 | 0 | 1 | - |
| Lasgun | 24" | Rapid Fire 1 | 3 | 0 | 1 | - |
| Chainsword | Melee | Melee | User | 0 | 1 | Each time the bearer fights, it can make 1 additional attack with this weapon. |
| Frag grenade | 6" | Grenade D6 | 3 | 0 | 1 | - |

| WARGEAR OPTIONS | |
|---|---|
| | • Any Veteran may replace their lasgun with a laspistol and a chainsword.<br>• One Veteran may take a vox-caster.<br>• One other Veteran may replace their lasgun with a heavy flamer.<br>• One other Veteran may take a regimental standard.<br>• One other Veteran may take a medi-pack.<br>• Two other Veterans may form a Veteran Heavy Weapons Team which must take an item from the *Astra Militarum Heavy Weapons* list.<br>• Any other Veteran may replace their lasgun with an item from the *Astra Militarum Special Weapons* list. |

| ABILITIES | |
|---|---|
| | **Medi-pack:** At the end of any of your Movement phases, a model with a medi-pack can attempt to heal a single model. Select a friendly **ASTRA MILITARUM INFANTRY** unit within 3" and roll a D6. On a roll of 4+, one model in the unit recovers a wound it lost earlier in the battle (if the unit has a Wounds characteristic of 1, one model slain earlier in the battle is returned to the unit instead). A unit can only be the target of this ability once in each turn.<br><br>**Regimental Standard:** All friendly <REGIMENT> units add 1 to their Leadership whilst they are within 6" of any <REGIMENT> Veteran with a regimental standard.<br><br>**Vox-caster:** If a friendly **OFFICER** is within 3" of a unit with a vox-caster when using their Voice of Command ability, you may extend the range of the order to 18" if the target unit also contains a vox-caster. |

| FACTION KEYWORDS | IMPERIUM, ASTRA MILITARUM, <REGIMENT> |
|---|---|
| KEYWORDS | INFANTRY, VETERANS, COMMAND SQUAD |

The hardened veterans of a Command Squad protect officers on the battlefield whilst inspiring the rank-and-file with their heroics.

## INFANTRY SQUAD

▶ 3 POWER

| NAME | M | WS | BS | S | T | W | A | Ld | Sv |
|---|---|---|---|---|---|---|---|---|---|
| Guardsman | 6" | 4+ | 4+ | 3 | 3 | 1 | 1 | 6 | 5+ |
| Sergeant | 6" | 4+ | 4+ | 3 | 3 | 1 | 2 | 7 | 5+ |
| Heavy Weapons Team | 6" | 4+ | 4+ | 3 | 3 | 2 | 2 | 6 | 5+ |

This unit contains 1 Sergeant and 9 Guardsmen.
• Each Guardsman is armed with a lasgun and frag grenades.
• The Sergeant is armed with a laspistol, chainsword and frag grenades.

| WEAPON | RANGE | TYPE | S | AP | D | ABILITIES |
|---|---|---|---|---|---|---|
| Lasgun | 24" | Rapid Fire 1 | 3 | 0 | 1 | - |
| Laspistol | 12" | Pistol 1 | 3 | 0 | 1 | - |
| Chainsword | Melee | Melee | User | 0 | 1 | Each time the bearer fights, it can make 1 additional attack with this weapon. |
| Power axe | Melee | Melee | +1 | -2 | 1 | - |
| Power maul | Melee | Melee | +2 | -1 | 1 | - |
| Power sword | Melee | Melee | User | -3 | 1 | - |
| Frag grenade | 6" | Grenade D6 | 3 | 0 | 1 | - |

| WARGEAR OPTIONS | • One Guardsman may take a vox-caster.<br>• Two other Guardsmen may form a Heavy Weapons Team who must take an item from the *Astra Militarum Heavy Weapons* list.<br>• One other Guardsman may replace his lasgun with an item from the *Astra Militarum Special Weapons* list.<br>• The Sergeant may replace their laspistol with an item from the *Astra Militarum Ranged Weapons* list.<br>• The Sergeant may replace their chainsword with a power axe, power maul or power sword. |
|---|---|
| ABILITIES | **Vox-caster:** If a friendly **OFFICER** is within 3" of a unit with a vox-caster when using their Voice of Command ability, you may extend the range of the order to 18" if the target unit also contains a vox-caster. |
| FACTION KEYWORDS | IMPERIUM, ASTRA MILITARUM, <REGIMENT> |
| KEYWORDS | INFANTRY, INFANTRY SQUAD |

## SPECIAL WEAPONS SQUAD

3 POWER

| NAME | M | WS | BS | S | T | W | A | Ld | Sv |
|---|---|---|---|---|---|---|---|---|---|
| Guardsman | 6" | 4+ | 4+ | 3 | 3 | 1 | 1 | 6 | 5+ |

This unit contains 6 Guardsmen. Each model is armed with a lasgun and frag grenades.

| WEAPON | RANGE | TYPE | S | AP | D | ABILITIES |
|---|---|---|---|---|---|---|
| Lasgun | 24" | Rapid Fire 1 | 3 | 0 | 1 | - |
| Demolition charge | 6" | Grenade D6 | 8 | -3 | D3 | Each demolition charge can only be used once per battle. |
| Frag grenade | 6" | Grenade D6 | 3 | 0 | 1 | - |

| WARGEAR OPTIONS | • Three models must either take a demolition charge, or replace their lasgun with an item from the *Astra Militarum Special Weapons* list. |
|---|---|
| FACTION KEYWORDS | IMPERIUM, ASTRA MILITARUM, <REGIMENT> |
| KEYWORDS | INFANTRY, SPECIAL WEAPONS SQUAD |

## HEAVY WEAPONS SQUAD

**3** POWER

| NAME | M | WS | BS | S | T | W | A | Ld | Sv |
|---|---|---|---|---|---|---|---|---|---|
| Heavy Weapons Team | 6" | 4+ | 4+ | 3 | 3 | 2 | 2 | 6 | 5+ |

This unit contains 3 Heavy Weapons Teams. Each model is armed with a lasgun and frag grenades.

| WEAPON | RANGE | TYPE | S | AP | D | ABILITIES |
|---|---|---|---|---|---|---|
| Lasgun | 24" | Rapid Fire 1 | 3 | 0 | 1 | - |
| Frag grenade | 6" | Grenade D6 | 3 | 0 | 1 | - |

| WARGEAR OPTIONS | • Each model must take an item from the *Astra Militarum Heavy Weapons* list. |
|---|---|
| FACTION KEYWORDS | IMPERIUM, ASTRA MILITARUM, <REGIMENT> |
| KEYWORDS | INFANTRY, HEAVY WEAPONS SQUAD |

## VETERANS

**6** POWER

| NAME | M | WS | BS | S | T | W | A | Ld | Sv |
|---|---|---|---|---|---|---|---|---|---|
| Veteran | 6" | 4+ | 3+ | 3 | 3 | 1 | 1 | 6 | 5+ |
| Veteran Sergeant | 6" | 4+ | 3+ | 3 | 3 | 1 | 2 | 7 | 5+ |
| Veteran Weapons Team | 6" | 4+ | 3+ | 3 | 3 | 2 | 2 | 6 | 5+ |

This unit contains 1 Veteran Sergeant and 9 Veterans.
• Each Veteran is armed with a lasgun and frag grenades.
• The Veteran Sergeant is armed with a laspistol, chainsword and frag grenades.

| WEAPON | RANGE | TYPE | S | AP | D | ABILITIES |
|---|---|---|---|---|---|---|
| Lasgun | 24" | Rapid Fire 1 | 3 | 0 | 1 | - |
| Laspistol | 12" | Pistol 1 | 3 | 0 | 1 | - |
| Heavy flamer | 8" | Heavy D6 | 5 | -1 | 1 | This weapon automatically hits its target. |
| Shotgun | 12" | Assault 2 | 3 | 0 | 1 | If the target is within half range, add 1 to this weapon's Strength. |
| Chainsword | Melee | Melee | User | 0 | 1 | Each time the bearer fights, it can make 1 additional attack with this weapon. |
| Frag grenade | 6" | Grenade D6 | 3 | 0 | 1 | - |

| WARGEAR OPTIONS | • Any Veteran may replace their lasgun with a shotgun.<br>• One Veteran may take a vox-caster.<br>• One other Veteran may replace their lasgun with a heavy flamer.<br>• Two other Veterans may form a Veteran Weapons Team who must take an item from the *Astra Militarum Heavy Weapons* list.<br>• Up to three other Veterans may replace their lasgun with an item from the *Astra Militarum Special Weapons* list.<br>• The Veteran Sergeant may replace their chainsword with an item from the *Astra Militarum Melee Weapons* list.<br>• The Veteran Sergeant may replace their laspistol with an item from the *Astra Militarum Ranged Weapons* list. |
|---|---|
| ABILITIES | **Vox-caster:** If a friendly **OFFICER** is within 3" of a unit with a vox-caster when using their Voice of Command ability, you may extend the range of the order to 18" if the target unit also contains a vox-caster. |
| FACTION KEYWORDS | IMPERIUM, ASTRA MILITARUM, <REGIMENT> |
| KEYWORDS | INFANTRY, VETERANS |

# CONSCRIPTS

**3** POWER

| NAME | M | WS | BS | S | T | W | A | Ld | Sv |
|------|---|-----|-----|---|---|---|---|-----|-----|
| Conscript | 6" | 5+ | 5+ | 3 | 3 | 1 | 1 | 4 | 5+ |

This unit contains 20 Conscripts. It can include up to 10 additional Conscripts (**Power Rating +1**), up to 20 additional Conscripts (**Power Rating +2**) or up to 30 additional Conscripts (**Power Rating +3**).
• The Conscripts are each equipped with a lasgun and frag grenades.

| WEAPON | RANGE | TYPE | S | AP | D | ABILITIES |
|--------|-------|------|---|-----|---|-----------|
| Lasgun | 24" | Rapid Fire 1 | 3 | 0 | 1 | - |
| Frag grenade | 6" | Grenade D6 | 3 | 0 | 1 | - |

| FACTION KEYWORDS | IMPERIUM, ASTRA MILITARUM, <REGIMENT> |
|------------------|--------------------------------------|
| KEYWORDS | INFANTRY, CONSCRIPTS |

# ROUGH RIDERS

**3** POWER

| NAME | M | WS | BS | S | T | W | A | Ld | Sv |
|------|---|-----|-----|---|---|---|---|-----|-----|
| Rough Rider | 10" | 4+ | 4+ | 3 | 3 | 2 | 1 | 6 | 5+ |
| Rough Rider Sergeant | 10" | 4+ | 4+ | 3 | 3 | 2 | 2 | 7 | 5+ |

This unit contains 1 Rough Rider Sergeant and 4 Rough Riders. It can include up to 5 additional Rough Riders (**Power Rating +2**). Each model is armed with a laspistol, chainsword, hunting lance and frag grenades, and rides a Purebred Steed which attacks with trampling hooves.

| WEAPON | RANGE | TYPE | S | AP | D | ABILITIES |
|--------|-------|------|---|-----|---|-----------|
| **Rough Rider and Rough Rider Sergeant** | | | | | | |
| Laspistol | 12" | Pistol 1 | 3 | 0 | 1 | - |
| Plasma pistol | When attacking with this weapon, choose one of the profiles below. | | | | | |
| - Standard | 12" | Pistol 1 | 7 | -3 | 1 | - |
| - Supercharge | 12" | Pistol 1 | 8 | -3 | 2 | On a hit roll of 1, the bearer is slain. |
| Chainsword | Melee | Melee | User | 0 | 1 | Each time the bearer fights, it can make 1 additional attack with this weapon. |
| Hunting lance | Melee | Melee | +2 | -2 | D3 | A model may only attack with this weapon on a turn in which it has charged. |
| Power axe | Melee | Melee | +1 | -2 | 1 | - |
| Power lance | Melee | Melee | +2 | -1 | 1 | - |
| Power maul | Melee | Melee | +2 | -1 | 1 | - |
| Power sword | Melee | Melee | User | -3 | 1 | - |
| Frag grenade | 6" | Grenade D6 | 3 | 0 | 1 | - |
| **Purebred Steed** | | | | | | |
| Trampling hooves | Melee | Melee | User | 0 | 1 | After a model on this mount makes its close combat attacks, you can attack with its mount. Make 1 additional attack, using this weapon profile. |

| WARGEAR OPTIONS | • The Rough Rider Sergeant may replace their laspistol with a plasma pistol.<br>• The Rough Rider Sergeant may replace their chainsword with a power axe, power lance, power maul or power sword.<br>• Instead of hunting lances, up to two Rough Riders can be equipped with an item from the *Astra Militarum Special Weapons* list. |
|-----------------|-----------------|
| ABILITIES | **Flanking Manoeuvres:** During deployment, you can set up this unit riding around the flanks instead of placing it on the battlefield. At the end of any of your Movement phases the unit can join the battle – set it up so that all models in the unit are within 7" of a battlefield edge of your choice and more than 9" from any enemy models. |
| FACTION KEYWORDS | IMPERIUM, ASTRA MILITARUM, <REGIMENT> |
| KEYWORDS | CAVALRY, ROUGH RIDERS |

# SCOUT SENTINELS

⚡ (2 POWER)

| NAME | M | WS | BS | S | T | W | A | Ld | Sv |
|------|---|----|----|---|---|---|---|----|----|
| Scout Sentinel | 9" | 4+ | 4+ | 5 | 5 | 6 | 1 | 7 | 4+ |

This unit contains 1 Scout Sentinel. It can include 1 additional Scout Sentinel (**Power Rating +2**) or 2 additional Scout Sentinels (**Power Rating +4**). Each model is equipped with a multi-laser.

| WEAPON | RANGE | TYPE | S | AP | D | ABILITIES |
|--------|-------|------|---|----|----|-----------|
| Autocannon | 48" | Heavy 2 | 7 | -1 | 2 | - |
| Heavy flamer | 8" | Heavy D6 | 5 | -1 | 1 | This weapon automatically hits its target. |
| Hunter-killer missile | 48" | Heavy 1 | 8 | -2 | D6 | Each hunter-killer missile can only be fired once per battle. |
| Lascannon | 48" | Heavy 1 | 9 | -3 | D6 | - |
| Missile launcher | When attacking with this weapon, choose one of the profiles below. | | | | | |
| - Frag missile | 48" | Heavy D6 | 4 | 0 | 1 | - |
| - Krak missile | 48" | Heavy 1 | 8 | -2 | D6 | - |
| Multi-laser | 36" | Heavy 3 | 6 | 0 | 1 | - |
| Sentinel chainsaw | Melee | Melee | User | -1 | 1 | - |

| WARGEAR OPTIONS | • Any model may replace its multi-laser with a heavy flamer, autocannon, missile launcher or lascannon.<br>• Any model may take a Sentinel chainsaw.<br>• Any model may take a hunter-killer missile. |
|---|---|
| ABILITIES | **Explodes:** If a model in this unit is reduced to 0 wounds, roll a D6 before removing the model from the battlefield. On a 6 it explodes, and each unit within 3" suffers 1 mortal wound.<br><br>**Scout Vehicle:** At the start of the first battle round but before the first turn begins, you can move this unit up to 9". It cannot end this move within 9" of any enemy models. If both players have units that can do this, the player who is taking the first turn moves their units first.<br><br>**Smoke Launchers:** Once per game, instead of shooting any weapons in the Shooting phase, this unit can use its smoke launchers; until your next Shooting phase your opponent must subtract 1 from all hit rolls for ranged weapons that target it. |
| FACTION KEYWORDS | **IMPERIUM, ASTRA MILITARUM, <REGIMENT>** |
| KEYWORDS | **VEHICLE, SCOUT SENTINELS** |

# ARMOURED SENTINELS

**3 POWER**

| NAME | M | WS | BS | S | T | W | A | Ld | Sv |
|------|---|----|----|---|---|---|---|----|----|
| Armoured Sentinel | 8" | 4+ | 4+ | 5 | 5 | 6 | 1 | 7 | 3+ |

This unit contains 1 Armoured Sentinel. It can include 1 additional Armoured Sentinel (**Power Rating +3**) or 2 additional Armoured Sentinels (**Power Rating +6**). Each model is equipped with a multi-laser.

| WEAPON | RANGE | TYPE | S | AP | D | ABILITIES |
|--------|-------|------|---|----|----|-----------|
| Autocannon | 48" | Heavy 2 | 7 | -1 | 2 | - |
| Heavy flamer | 8" | Heavy D6 | 5 | -1 | 1 | This weapon automatically hits its target. |
| Hunter-killer missile | 48" | Heavy 1 | 8 | -2 | D6 | Each hunter-killer missile can only be fired once per battle. |
| Lascannon | 48" | Heavy 1 | 9 | -3 | D6 | - |
| Missile launcher | When attacking with this weapon, choose one of the profiles below. | | | | | |
| - Frag missile | 48" | Heavy D6 | 4 | 0 | 1 | - |
| - Krak missile | 48" | Heavy 1 | 8 | -2 | D6 | - |
| Multi-laser | 36" | Heavy 3 | 6 | 0 | 1 | - |
| Plasma cannon | When attacking with this weapon, choose one of the profiles below. | | | | | |
| - Standard | 36" | Heavy D3 | 7 | -3 | 1 | - |
| - Supercharge | 36" | Heavy D3 | 8 | -3 | 2 | On a hit roll of 1, the bearer is slain after all of this weapon's shots have been resolved. |
| Sentinel chainsaw | Melee | Melee | User | -1 | 1 | - |

| WARGEAR OPTIONS | |
|---|---|
| | • Any model may replace its multi-laser with a heavy flamer, autocannon, missile launcher, lascannon or plasma cannon.<br>• Any model may take a Sentinel chainsaw.<br>• Any model may take a hunter-killer missile. |

| ABILITIES | |
|---|---|
| | **Explodes:** If a model in this unit is reduced to 0 wounds, roll a D6 before removing the model from the battlefield. On a 6 it explodes, and each unit within 3" suffers 1 mortal wound.<br><br>**Smoke Launchers:** Once per game, instead of shooting its weapons in the Shooting phase, this unit can use its smoke launchers. If it does so, until your next Shooting phase your opponent must subtract 1 from all hit rolls for ranged weapons that target it. |

| FACTION KEYWORDS | **IMPERIUM, ASTRA MILITARUM, <REGIMENT>** |
|---|---|
| **KEYWORDS** | **VEHICLE, ARMOURED SENTINELS** |

Swift and rugged, Armoured Sentinels excel at outflanking and destroying enemy vehicles.

## CHIMERA

**5** POWER

A Chimera is a single model equipped with a multi-laser, a heavy bolter and two lasgun arrays.

| NAME | M | WS | BS | S | T | W | A | Ld | Sv |
|------|---|----|----|---|---|---|---|----|----|
| Chimera | * | 6+ | * | 6 | 7 | 10 | * | 7 | 3+ |

**DAMAGE**

Some of this model's characteristics change as it suffers damage, as shown below:

| REMAINING W | M | BS | A |
|-------------|-----|----|----|
| 6-10+ | 12" | 4+ | 3 |
| 3-5 | 8" | 5+ | D3 |
| 1-2 | 4" | 6+ | 1 |

| WEAPON | RANGE | TYPE | S | AP | D | ABILITIES |
|--------|-------|------|---|----|----|-----------|
| Heavy bolter | 36" | Heavy 3 | 5 | -1 | 1 | - |
| Heavy flamer | 8" | Heavy D6 | 5 | -1 | 1 | This weapon automatically hits its target. |
| Heavy stubber | 36" | Heavy 3 | 4 | 0 | 1 | - |
| Hunter-killer missile | 48" | Heavy 1 | 8 | -2 | D6 | Each hunter-killer missile can only be fired once per battle. |
| Lasgun array | 24" | Rapid Fire 3 | 3 | 0 | 1 | This weapon can only be fired if a unit is embarked upon the vehicle equipped with it. |
| Multi-laser | 36" | Heavy 3 | 6 | 0 | 1 | - |
| Storm bolter | 24" | Rapid Fire 2 | 4 | 0 | 1 | - |

| WARGEAR OPTIONS | |
|---|---|
| | • This model may replace its heavy bolter with a heavy flamer. |
| | • This model may replace its multi-laser with a heavy flamer or a heavy bolter. |
| | • This model may take a hunter-killer missile. |
| | • This model may take a storm bolter or a heavy stubber. |

| ABILITIES | |
|---|---|
| | **Explodes:** If this model is reduced to 0 wounds, roll a D6 before removing it from the battlefield and before any embarked models disembark. On a 6 it explodes, and each unit within 6" suffers D3 mortal wounds. |
| | **Smoke Launchers:** Once per game, instead of shooting any weapons in the Shooting phase, this model can use its smoke launchers; until your next Shooting phase your opponent must subtract 1 from all hit rolls for ranged weapons that target this vehicle. |

| TRANSPORT | |
|---|---|
| | This model can transport 12 **Astra Militarum Infantry** models. Each Heavy Weapons Team or Veteran Heavy Weapons Team takes the space of two other models and each **Ogryn** takes the space of three other models. |

| FACTION KEYWORDS | **Imperium, Astra Militarum, <Regiment>** |
|---|---|
| KEYWORDS | **Vehicle, Transport, Chimera** |

---

## TAUROX

**4** POWER

A Taurox is a single model equipped with two autocannons.

| NAME | M | WS | BS | S | T | W | A | Ld | Sv |
|------|---|----|----|---|---|---|---|----|----|
| Taurox | * | 6+ | * | 6 | 6 | 10 | * | 7 | 3+ |

**DAMAGE**

Some of this model's characteristics change as it suffers damage, as shown below:

| REMAINING W | M | BS | A |
|-------------|-----|----|----|
| 6-10+ | 14" | 4+ | 3 |
| 3-5 | 10" | 5+ | D3 |
| 1-2 | 6" | 6+ | 1 |

| WEAPON | RANGE | TYPE | S | AP | D | ABILITIES |
|--------|-------|------|---|----|----|-----------|
| Autocannon | 48" | Heavy 2 | 7 | -1 | 2 | - |
| Heavy stubber | 36" | Heavy 3 | 4 | 0 | 1 | - |
| Storm bolter | 24" | Rapid Fire 2 | 4 | 0 | 1 | - |

| WARGEAR OPTIONS | |
|---|---|
| | • This model may take a storm bolter or heavy stubber. |

| ABILITIES | |
|---|---|
| | **Explodes:** If this model is reduced to 0 wounds, roll a D6 before removing it from the battlefield and before any embarked models disembark. On a 6 it explodes, and each unit within 6" suffers D3 mortal wounds. |

| TRANSPORT | |
|---|---|
| | This model can transport 10 **Astra Militarum Infantry** models. Each Heavy Weapons Team or Veteran Heavy Weapons Team takes the space of two other models and each **Ogryn** takes the space of three other models. |

| FACTION KEYWORDS | **Imperium, Astra Militarum, <Regiment>** |
|---|---|
| KEYWORDS | **Vehicle, Transport, Taurox** |

# HELLHOUNDS

**5** POWER

| NAME | M | WS | BS | S | T | W | A | Ld | Sv |
|------|---|----|----|---|---|---|---|----|----|
| Hellhound | * | 6+ | * | 6 | 7 | 11 | * | 7 | 3+ |
| Devil Dog | * | 6+ | * | 6 | 7 | 11 | * | 7 | 3+ |
| Bane Wolf | * | 6+ | * | 6 | 7 | 11 | * | 7 | 3+ |

**DAMAGE**
Some of this model's characteristics change as it suffers damage, as shown below:

| REMAINING W | M | BS | A |
|-------------|---|----|----|
| 6-11+ | 12" | 4+ | 3 |
| 3-5 | 8" | 5+ | D3 |
| 1-2 | 4" | 6+ | 1 |

This unit contains 1 Hellhound, Devil Dog or Bane Wolf. It can include 1 additional Hellhound, Devil Dog or Bane Wolf (**Power Rating +5**) or 2 additional Hellhounds, Devil Dogs and/or Bane Wolfs in any combination (**Power Rating +10**).
• Each Hellhound is equipped with a heavy bolter and an inferno cannon.
• Each Devil Dog is equipped with a heavy bolter and a melta cannon.
• Each Bane Wolf is equipped with a heavy bolter and a chem cannon.

| WEAPON | RANGE | TYPE | S | AP | D | ABILITIES |
|--------|-------|------|---|----|----|-----------|
| Chem cannon | 8" | Heavy D6 | * | -3 | 1 | This weapon automatically hits its target. In addition, it wounds on a 2+, unless it is targeting a **VEHICLE**, in which case it wounds on a 6+. |
| Heavy bolter | 36" | Heavy 3 | 5 | -1 | 1 | - |
| Heavy flamer | 8" | Heavy D6 | 5 | -1 | 1 | This weapon automatically hits its target. |
| Inferno cannon | 16" | Heavy D6 | 6 | -1 | 2 | This weapon automatically hits its target. |
| Melta cannon | 24" | Heavy D3 | 8 | -4 | D6 | If the target is within half range of this weapon, roll two dice when inflicting damage with it and discard the lowest result. |
| Multi-melta | 24" | Heavy 1 | 8 | -4 | D6 | If the target is within half range of this weapon, roll two dice when inflicting damage with it and discard the lowest result. |

| WARGEAR OPTIONS | • Any model may replace its heavy bolter with a heavy flamer or a multi-melta. |
|-----------------|---|
| ABILITIES | **Explodes:** If a Hellhound, Devil Dog or Bane Wolf is reduced to 0 wounds, roll a D6 (adding 2 to the result in the case of a Hellhound) before removing it from the battlefield. On a 6+ it explodes, and each unit within 6" suffers D3 mortal wounds.<br><br>**Smoke Launchers:** Once per game, instead of shooting any weapons in the Shooting phase, a Hellhound, Devil Dog or Bane Wolf can use its smoke launchers; until your next Shooting phase your opponent must subtract 1 from all hit rolls for ranged weapons that target it.<br><br>**Vehicle Squadron:** The first time this unit is set up, all models in this unit must be placed within 6" of each other. From that point onwards, each operates independently and is treated as a separate unit for all rules purposes. |
| FACTION KEYWORDS | IMPERIUM, ASTRA MILITARUM, <REGIMENT> |
| KEYWORDS | VEHICLE, HELLHOUNDS |

# BASILISKS

**DAMAGE**
Some of this model's characteristics change as it suffers damage, as shown below:

| REMAINING W | M | BS | A |
|---|---|---|---|
| 6-11+ | 12" | 4+ | 3 |
| 3-5 | 8" | 5+ | D3 |
| 1-2 | 4" | 6+ | 1 |

| NAME | M | WS | BS | S | T | W | A | Ld | Sv |
|---|---|---|---|---|---|---|---|---|---|
| Basilisk | * | 6+ | * | 6 | 6 | 11 | * | 7 | 3+ |

This unit contains 1 Basilisk. It can include 1 additional Basilisk (**Power Rating +6**) or 2 additional Basilisks (**Power Rating +12**) Each model is equipped with an earthshaker cannon and a heavy bolter.

| WEAPON | RANGE | TYPE | S | AP | D | ABILITIES |
|---|---|---|---|---|---|---|
| Earthshaker cannon | 240" | Heavy D6 | 9 | -2 | D3 | Roll two dice for the number of attacks when firing this weapon and discard the lowest result. This weapon can target units that are not visible to the bearer. |
| Heavy bolter | 36" | Heavy 3 | 5 | -1 | 1 | - |
| Heavy flamer | 8" | Heavy D6 | 5 | -1 | 1 | This weapon automatically hits its target. |
| Heavy stubber | 36" | Heavy 3 | 4 | 0 | 1 | - |
| Hunter-killer missile | 48" | Heavy 1 | 8 | -2 | D6 | Each hunter-killer missile can only be fired once per battle. |
| Storm bolter | 24" | Rapid Fire 2 | 4 | 0 | 1 | - |

| WARGEAR OPTIONS | • Any model may replace its heavy bolter with a heavy flamer.<br>• Any model may take a heavy stubber or storm bolter.<br>• Any model may take a hunter-killer missile. |
|---|---|
| ABILITIES | **Vehicle Squadron:** The first time this unit is set up, all models in this unit must be placed within 6" of each other. From that point onwards, each operates independently and is treated as a separate unit for all rules purposes.<br><br>**Explodes:** If this model is reduced to 0 wounds, roll a D6 before removing it from the battlefield. On a 6 it explodes, and each unit within 6" suffers D3 mortal wounds.<br><br>**Smoke Launchers:** Once per game, instead of shooting any weapons in the Shooting phase, this model can use its smoke launchers; until your next Shooting phase your opponent must subtract 1 from all hit rolls for ranged weapons that target this vehicle. |
| FACTION KEYWORDS | **IMPERIUM, ASTRA MILITARUM, <REGIMENT>** |
| KEYWORDS | **VEHICLE, BASILISKS** |

The thunderous roar of Basilisks carries all the way to the front lines as their earthshaker shells rain down upon the enemy.

## 6 POWER

# HYDRAS

### DAMAGE
Some of this model's characteristics change as it suffers damage, as shown below:

| REMAINING W | M | BS | A |
|---|---|---|---|
| 6-11+ | 12" | 4+ | 3 |
| 3-5 | 8" | 5+ | D3 |
| 1-2 | 4" | 6+ | 1 |

| NAME | M | WS | BS | S | T | W | A | Ld | Sv |
|---|---|---|---|---|---|---|---|---|---|
| Hydra | * | 6+ | * | 6 | 6 | 11 | * | 7 | 3+ |

This unit contains 1 Hydra. It can include 1 additional Hydra (**Power Rating +6**) or 2 additional Hydras (**Power Rating +12**). Each model is equipped with a Hydra quad autocannon and a heavy bolter.

| WEAPON | RANGE | TYPE | S | AP | D | ABILITIES |
|---|---|---|---|---|---|---|
| Heavy bolter | 36" | Heavy 3 | 5 | -1 | 1 | - |
| Heavy flamer | 8" | Heavy D6 | 5 | -1 | 1 | This weapon automatically hits its target. |
| Heavy stubber | 36" | Heavy 3 | 4 | 0 | 1 | - |
| Hunter-killer missile | 48" | Heavy 1 | 8 | -2 | D6 | Each hunter-killer missile can only be fired once per battle. |
| Hydra quad autocannon | 72" | Heavy 8 | 7 | -1 | 2 | Add 1 to all hit rolls made for this weapon against targets that can **FLY**. Subtract 1 from the hit rolls made for this weapon against all other targets. |
| Storm bolter | 24" | Rapid Fire 2 | 4 | 0 | 1 | - |

| WARGEAR OPTIONS | • Any model may replace its heavy bolter with a heavy flamer.<br>• Any model may take a heavy stubber or storm bolter.<br>• Any model may take a hunter-killer missile. |
|---|---|
| ABILITIES | **Explodes:** If this model is reduced to 0 wounds, roll a D6 before removing it from the battlefield. On a 6 it explodes, and each unit within 6" suffers D3 mortal wounds.<br><br>**Smoke Launchers:** Once per game, instead of shooting any weapons in the Shooting phase, this model can use its smoke launchers; until your next Shooting phase your opponent must subtract 1 from all hit rolls for ranged weapons that target this vehicle.<br><br>**Vehicle Squadron:** The first time this unit is set up, all models in this unit must be placed within 6" of each other. From that point onwards, each operates independently and is treated as a separate unit for all rules purposes. |
| FACTION KEYWORDS | **IMPERIUM, ASTRA MILITARUM, <REGIMENT>** |
| KEYWORDS | **VEHICLE, HYDRAS** |

# WYVERNS

| NAME | M | WS | BS | S | T | W | A | Ld | Sv |
|------|---|----|----|---|---|---|---|-----|-----|
| Wyvern | * | 6+ | * | 6 | 6 | 11 | * | 7 | 3+ |

**DAMAGE**

Some of this model's characteristics change as it suffers damage, as shown below:

| REMAINING W | M | BS | A |
|-------------|-----|-----|-----|
| 6-11+ | 12" | 4+ | 3 |
| 3-5 | 8" | 5+ | D3 |
| 1-2 | 4" | 6+ | 1 |

This unit contains 1 Wyvern. It can include 1 additional Wyvern (**Power Rating +5**) or 2 additional Wyverns (**Power Rating +10**). Each model is equipped with a Wyvern quad stormshard mortar and a heavy bolter.

| WEAPON | RANGE | TYPE | S | AP | D | ABILITIES |
|--------|-------|------|---|-----|---|-----------|
| Heavy bolter | 36" | Heavy 3 | 5 | -1 | 1 | - |
| Heavy flamer | 8" | Heavy D6 | 5 | -1 | 1 | This weapon automatically hits its target. |
| Heavy stubber | 36" | Heavy 3 | 4 | 0 | 1 | - |
| Hunter-killer missile | 48" | Heavy 1 | 8 | -2 | D6 | Each hunter-killer missile can only be fired once per battle. |
| Storm bolter | 24" | Rapid Fire 2 | 4 | 0 | 1 | - |
| Wyvern quad stormshard mortar | 48" | Heavy 4D6 | 4 | 0 | 1 | This weapon can target units that are not visible to the bearer. You can re-roll failed wound rolls for this weapon. |

| WARGEAR OPTIONS | |
|-----------------|---|
| | • Any model may replace its heavy bolter with a heavy flamer. |
| | • Any model may take a heavy stubber or storm bolter. |
| | • Any model may take a hunter-killer missile. |

| ABILITIES | |
|-----------|---|
| | **Explodes:** If this model is reduced to 0 wounds, roll a D6 before removing it from the battlefield. On a 6 it explodes, and each unit within 6" suffers D3 mortal wounds. |
| | **Smoke Launchers:** Once per game, instead of shooting any weapons in the Shooting phase, this model can use its smoke launchers; until your next Shooting phase your opponent must subtract 1 from all hit rolls for ranged weapons that target this vehicle. |
| | **Vehicle Squadron:** The first time this unit is set up, all models in this unit must be placed within 6" of each other. From that point onwards, each operates independently and is treated as a separate unit for all rules purposes. |

| FACTION KEYWORDS | **IMPERIUM, ASTRA MILITARUM, <REGIMENT>** |
|------------------|-------------------------------------------|

| KEYWORDS | **VEHICLE, WYVERNS** |
|----------|----------------------|

The earth trembles under the colossal tracks and massed footfalls of an Astra Militarum advance. Through weight of numbers, firepower and grit they deliver death to the enemies of the Imperium.

| | 7 POWER | MANTICORE | | | | | | | | | |
|---|---|---|---|---|---|---|---|---|---|---|---|

| NAME | M | WS | BS | S | T | W | A | Ld | Sv |
|---|---|---|---|---|---|---|---|---|---|
| Manticore | ∗ | 6+ | ∗ | 6 | 7 | 11 | ∗ | 7 | 3+ |

**DAMAGE**

Some of this model's characteristics change as it suffers damage, as shown below:

| REMAINING W | M | BS | A |
|---|---|---|---|
| 6-11+ | 12" | 4+ | 3 |
| 3-5 | 8" | 5+ | D3 |
| 1-2 | 4" | 6+ | 1 |

A Manticore is a single model equipped with four storm eagle rockets and a heavy bolter.

| WEAPON | RANGE | TYPE | S | AP | D | ABILITIES |
|---|---|---|---|---|---|---|
| Heavy bolter | 36" | Heavy 3 | 5 | -1 | 1 | - |
| Heavy flamer | 8" | Heavy D6 | 5 | -1 | 1 | This weapon automatically hits its target. |
| Heavy stubber | 36" | Heavy 3 | 4 | 0 | 1 | - |
| Hunter-killer missile | 48" | Heavy 1 | 8 | -2 | D6 | Each hunter-killer missile can only be fired once per battle. |
| Storm eagle rockets | 120" | Heavy 2D6 | 10 | -2 | D3 | This weapon can target units that are not visible to the bearer. A model can only fire a single storm eagle rocket per turn. Each storm eagle rocket can only be fired once per battle. |
| Storm bolter | 24" | Rapid Fire 2 | 4 | 0 | 1 | - |

| WARGEAR OPTIONS | • This model may replace its heavy bolter with a heavy flamer.<br>• This model may take a heavy stubber or storm bolter.<br>• This model may take a hunter-killer missile. |
|---|---|
| ABILITIES | **Explodes:** If this model is reduced to 0 wounds, roll a D6 before removing it from the battlefield. On a 6 it explodes, and each unit within 6" suffers D3 mortal wounds.<br><br>**Smoke Launchers:** Once per game, instead of shooting any weapons in the Shooting phase, this model can use its smoke launchers; until your next Shooting phase your opponent must subtract 1 from all hit rolls for ranged weapons that target this vehicle. |
| FACTION KEYWORDS | IMPERIUM, ASTRA MILITARUM, <REGIMENT> |
| KEYWORDS | VEHICLE, MANTICORE |

# DEATHSTRIKE

| NAME | M | WS | BS | S | T | W | A | Ld | Sv |
|---|---|---|---|---|---|---|---|---|---|
| Deathstrike | * | 6+ | * | 6 | 7 | 11 | * | 7 | 3+ |

A Deathstrike is a single model equipped with a Deathstrike missile and a heavy bolter.

### DAMAGE
Some of this model's characteristics change as it suffers damage, as shown below:

| REMAINING W | M | BS | A |
|---|---|---|---|
| 6-11+ | 12" | 4+ | 3 |
| 3-5 | 8" | 5+ | D3 |
| 1-2 | 4" | 6+ | 1 |

| WEAPON | RANGE | TYPE | S | AP | D | ABILITIES |
|---|---|---|---|---|---|---|
| Deathstrike missile | 200" | Heavy 3D6 | * | * | * | This weapon can only be fired once per battle. This weapon can target units that are not visible to the bearer. Each time you hit the target with this weapon it suffers a mortal wound. After resolving all damage on the unit, roll a D6 for every other unit within 6" of the target unit – on a 4+ that unit also suffers D3 mortal wounds. |
| Heavy bolter | 36" | Heavy 3 | 5 | -1 | 1 | - |
| Heavy flamer | 8" | Heavy D6 | 5 | -1 | 1 | This weapon automatically hits its target. |
| Heavy stubber | 36" | Heavy 3 | 4 | 0 | 1 | - |
| Hunter-killer missile | 48" | Heavy 1 | 8 | -2 | D6 | Each hunter-killer missile can only be fired once per battle. |
| Storm bolter | 24" | Rapid Fire 2 | 4 | 0 | 1 | - |

| WARGEAR OPTIONS | |
|---|---|
| | • This model may replace its heavy bolter with a heavy flamer.<br>• This model may take a heavy stubber or storm bolter.<br>• This model may take a hunter-killer missile. |

**ABILITIES**

**Explodes:** If this model is reduced to 0 wounds, roll a D6 before removing it from the battlefield. On a 6 it explodes, and each unit within 6" suffers D6 mortal wounds.

**Smoke Launchers:** Once per game, instead of shooting any weapons in the Shooting phase, this model can use its smoke launchers; until your next Shooting phase your opponent must subtract 1 from all hit rolls for ranged weapons that target this vehicle.

**The Hour is Nigh:** The Deathstrike missile cannot be fired normally in the Shooting phase or during Overwatch. In a friendly Shooting phase, if you wish to fire the Deathstrike missile, roll a D6 and add the battle round number. If the result is 8 or more, you can fire the Deathstrike missile during this Shooting phase. For example, in the third battle round, a roll of 5+ would be needed to fire the Deathstrike missile.

| FACTION KEYWORDS | IMPERIUM, ASTRA MILITARUM, <REGIMENT> |
|---|---|
| KEYWORDS | VEHICLE, DEATHSTRIKE |

Primed for launch, Deathstrikes are the Astra Militarum's most devastating and indiscriminate ordnance.

# LEMAN RUSS BATTLE TANKS

| NAME | M | WS | BS | S | T | W | A | Ld | Sv |
|---|---|---|---|---|---|---|---|---|---|
| Leman Russ Battle Tank | * | 6+ | * | 7 | 8 | 12 | * | 7 | 3+ |

**DAMAGE**

Some of this model's characteristics change as it suffers damage, as shown below:

| REMAINING W | M | BS | A |
|---|---|---|---|
| 7-12+ | 10" | 4+ | 3 |
| 4-6 | 7" | 5+ | D3 |
| 1-3 | 4" | 6+ | 1 |

This unit contains 1 Leman Russ Battle Tank. It can include 1 additional Leman Russ Battle Tank (**Power Rating +11**) or 2 additional Leman Russ Battle Tanks (**Power Rating +22**). Each model is equipped with a battle cannon and a heavy bolter.

| WEAPON | RANGE | TYPE | S | AP | D | ABILITIES |
|---|---|---|---|---|---|---|
| Battle cannon | 72" | Heavy D6 | 8 | -2 | D3 | - |
| Eradicator nova cannon | 36" | Heavy D6 | 6 | -2 | D3 | Units attacked by this weapon do not gain any bonus to their saving throws for being in cover. |
| Exterminator autocannon | 48" | Heavy 4 | 7 | -1 | 2 | - |
| Heavy bolter | 36" | Heavy 3 | 5 | -1 | 1 | - |
| Heavy flamer | 8" | Heavy D6 | 5 | -1 | 1 | This weapon automatically hits its target. |
| Heavy stubber | 36" | Heavy 3 | 4 | 0 | 1 | - |
| Hunter-killer missile | 48" | Heavy 1 | 8 | -2 | D6 | Each hunter-killer missile can only be fired once per battle. |
| Lascannon | 48" | Heavy 1 | 9 | -3 | D6 | - |
| Multi-melta | 24" | Heavy 1 | 8 | -4 | D6 | If the target is within half range of this weapon, roll two dice when inflicting damage with it and discard the lowest result. |
| Plasma cannon | When attacking with this weapon, choose one of the profiles below. | | | | | |
| - Standard | 36" | Heavy D3 | 7 | -3 | 1 | - |
| - Supercharge | 36" | Heavy D3 | 8 | -3 | 2 | On a hit roll of 1, the bearer is slain after all of this weapon's shots have been resolved. |
| Storm bolter | 24" | Rapid Fire 2 | 4 | 0 | 1 | - |
| Vanquisher battle cannon | 72" | Heavy 1 | 8 | -3 | D6 | Roll two dice when inflicting damage with this weapon and discard the lowest result. |

| WARGEAR OPTIONS | |
|---|---|
| | • Any model may replace its battle cannon with an eradicator nova cannon, exterminator autocannon or a vanquisher battle cannon.<br>• Any model may replace its heavy bolter with a heavy flamer or a lascannon.<br>• Any model may take two heavy bolters, two heavy flamers, two multi-meltas or two plasma cannons.<br>• Any model may take a heavy stubber or a storm bolter.<br>• Any model may take a hunter-killer missile. |

| ABILITIES | |
|---|---|
| | **Vehicle Squadron:** The first time this unit is set up, all models in this unit must be placed within 6" of each other. From that point onwards, each operates independently and is treated as a separate unit for all rules purposes.<br><br>**Grinding Advance:** This model does not suffer the penalty to turret weapon hit rolls for shooting a Heavy weapon on a turn in which it has moved. The following weapons are turret weapons: battle cannon, eradicator nova cannon, exterminator autocannon and vanquisher battle cannon.<br><br>**Explodes:** If this model is reduced to 0 wounds, roll a D6 before removing it from the battlefield. On a 6 it explodes, and each unit within 6" suffers D3 mortal wounds.<br><br>**Smoke Launchers:** Once per game, instead of shooting any weapons in the Shooting phase, this model can use its smoke launchers; until your next Shooting phase your opponent must subtract 1 from all hit rolls for ranged weapons that target this vehicle.<br><br>**Emergency Plasma Vents:** If this model fires a supercharged plasma cannon, and you roll one or more hit rolls of 1, it is not automatically destroyed. Instead, it suffers 6 mortal wounds and cannot fire any plasma cannons for the rest of the battle. |

| FACTION KEYWORDS | IMPERIUM, ASTRA MILITARUM, <REGIMENT> |
|---|---|
| KEYWORDS | VEHICLE, LEMAN RUSS, LEMAN RUSS BATTLE TANK |

# LEMAN RUSS DEMOLISHERS

| NAME | M | WS | BS | S | T | W | A | Ld | Sv |
|------|---|----|----|---|---|---|---|----|----|
| Leman Russ Demolisher | * | 6+ | * | 7 | 8 | 12 | * | 7 | 3+ |

This unit contains 1 Leman Russ Demolisher. It can include 1 additional Leman Russ Demolisher (**Power Rating +12**) or 2 additional Leman Russ Demolishers (**Power Rating +24**). Each model is equipped with a demolisher cannon and a heavy bolter.

**DAMAGE**
Some of this model's characteristics change as it suffers damage, as shown below:

| REMAINING W | M | BS | A |
|-------------|---|----|----|
| 7-12+ | 10" | 4+ | 3 |
| 4-6 | 7" | 5+ | D3 |
| 1-3 | 4" | 6+ | 1 |

| WEAPON | RANGE | TYPE | S | AP | D | ABILITIES |
|--------|-------|------|---|----|----|-----------|
| Demolisher cannon | 24" | Heavy D3 | 10 | -3 | D6 | When attacking units with 5 or more models, change this weapon's Type to Heavy D6. |
| Executioner plasma cannon | | When attacking with this weapon, choose one of the profiles below. | | | | |
| - Standard | 36" | Heavy D6 | 7 | -3 | 1 | - |
| - Supercharge | 36" | Heavy D6 | 8 | -3 | 2 | If you make one or more hit rolls of 1, the bearer suffers D6 mortal wounds after all of this weapon's shots have been resolved. |
| Heavy bolter | 36" | Heavy 3 | 5 | -1 | 1 | - |
| Heavy flamer | 8" | Heavy D6 | 5 | -1 | 1 | This weapon automatically hits its target. |
| Heavy stubber | 36" | Heavy 3 | 4 | 0 | 1 | - |
| Hunter-killer missile | 48" | Heavy 1 | 8 | -2 | D6 | Each hunter-killer missile can only be fired once per battle. |
| Lascannon | 48" | Heavy 1 | 9 | -3 | D6 | - |
| Multi-melta | 24" | Heavy 1 | 8 | -4 | D6 | If the target is within half range of this weapon, roll two dice when inflicting damage with it and discard the lowest result. |
| Plasma cannon | | When attacking with this weapon, choose one of the profiles below. | | | | |
| - Standard | 36" | Heavy D3 | 7 | -3 | 1 | - |
| - Supercharge | 36" | Heavy D3 | 8 | -3 | 2 | On a hit roll of 1, the bearer is slain after all of this weapon's shots have been resolved. |
| Punisher gatling cannon | 24" | Heavy 20 | 5 | 0 | 1 | - |
| Storm bolter | 24" | Rapid Fire 2 | 4 | 0 | 1 | - |

| WARGEAR OPTIONS | • Any model may replace its demolisher cannon with an executioner plasma cannon or punisher gatling cannon.<br>• Any model may replace its heavy bolter with a heavy flamer or lascannon.<br>• Any model may take two heavy bolters, two heavy flamers, two multi-meltas or two plasma cannons.<br>• Any model may take a heavy stubber or storm bolter.<br>• Any model may take a hunter-killer missile. |
|---|---|
| ABILITIES | **Vehicle Squadron:** The first time this unit is set up, all models in this unit must be placed within 6" of each other. From that point onwards, each operates independently and is treated as a separate unit for all rules purposes.<br><br>**Grinding Advance:** This model does not suffer the penalty to turret weapon hit rolls for shooting a Heavy weapon on a turn in which it has moved. The following weapons are turret weapons: demolisher cannon, executioner plasma cannon and punisher gatling cannon.<br><br>**Explodes:** If this model is reduced to 0 wounds, roll a D6 before removing it from the battlefield. On a 6 it explodes, and each unit within 6" suffers D3 mortal wounds.<br><br>**Smoke Launchers:** Once per game, instead of shooting any weapons in the Shooting phase, this model can use its smoke launchers; until your next Shooting phase your opponent must subtract 1 from all hit rolls for ranged weapons that target this vehicle.<br><br>**Emergency Plasma Vents:** If this model fires a supercharged plasma cannon, and you roll one or more hit rolls of 1, it is not automatically destroyed. Instead, it suffers 6 mortal wounds and cannot fire any plasma cannons for the rest of the battle (executioner plasma cannons are not affected). |
| FACTION KEYWORDS | IMPERIUM, ASTRA MILITARUM, <REGIMENT> |
| KEYWORDS | VEHICLE, LEMAN RUSS, DEMOLISHER |

# BANEBLADE

**30 POWER**

| NAME | M | WS | BS | S | T | W | A | Ld | Sv |
|---|---|---|---|---|---|---|---|---|---|
| Baneblade | * | 5+ | * | 9 | 8 | 26 | * | 8 | 3+ |

A Baneblade is a single model equipped with an autocannon, a Baneblade cannon, a demolisher cannon, a twin heavy bolter and adamantium tracks.

### DAMAGE
Some of this model's characteristics change as it suffers damage, as shown below:

| REMAINING W | M | BS | A |
|---|---|---|---|
| 14-26+ | 10" | 4+ | 9 |
| 7-13 | 7" | 5+ | 6 |
| 1-6 | 4" | 6+ | 3 |

| WEAPON | RANGE | TYPE | S | AP | D | ABILITIES |
|---|---|---|---|---|---|---|
| Autocannon | 48" | Heavy 2 | 7 | -1 | 2 | - |
| Baneblade cannon | 72" | Heavy 2D6 | 9 | -3 | 3 | - |
| Demolisher cannon | 24" | Heavy D3 | 10 | -3 | D6 | When attacking units with 5 or more models, change this weapon's Type to Heavy D6. |
| Heavy stubber | 36" | Heavy 3 | 4 | 0 | 1 | - |
| Hunter-killer missile | 48" | Heavy 1 | 8 | -2 | D6 | Each hunter-killer missile can only be fired once per battle. |
| Lascannon | 48" | Heavy 1 | 9 | -3 | D6 | - |
| Storm bolter | 24" | Rapid Fire 2 | 4 | 0 | 1 | - |
| Twin heavy bolter | 36" | Heavy 6 | 5 | -1 | 1 | - |
| Twin heavy flamer | 8" | Heavy 2D6 | 5 | -1 | 1 | This weapon automatically hits its target. |
| Adamantium tracks | Melee | Melee | User | -2 | D3 | - |

**WARGEAR OPTIONS**
- This model may take a hunter-killer missile.
- This model may take a storm bolter or a heavy stubber.
- This model may take either two sponsons, or four sponsons; each sponson is equipped with a lascannon and either a twin heavy bolter or twin heavy flamer.

**ABILITIES**

**Explodes:** If this model is reduced to 0 wounds, roll a D6 before removing it from the battlefield. On a 6 it explodes, and each unit within 2D6" suffers D6 mortal wounds.

**Smoke Launchers:** Once per game, instead of shooting any weapons in the Shooting phase, this model can use its smoke launchers; until your next Shooting phase your opponent must subtract 1 from all hit rolls for ranged weapons that target this vehicle.

**Steel Behemoth:** This model can Fall Back in the Movement phase and still shoot and/or charge during its turn. It can also still fire its weapons if enemy units are within 1" of it (but only its twin heavy bolter or twin heavy flamer can target units that are within 1" of it – its other guns must target other units). In addition this model only gains a bonus to its save in cover if at least half of the model is obscured from the firer.

**FACTION KEYWORDS** — IMPERIUM, ASTRA MILITARUM, \<REGIMENT\>

**KEYWORDS** — VEHICLE, TITANIC, BANEBLADE

Each Baneblade is a mobile fortress bristling with armaments, able to withstand the most punishing fire from the enemy.

# 26 POWER | BANEHAMMER

| NAME | M | WS | BS | S | T | W | A | Ld | Sv |
|------|---|----|----|---|---|---|---|----|----|
| Banehammer | * | 5+ | * | 9 | 8 | 26 | * | 8 | 3+ |

A Banehammer is a single model equipped with a tremor cannon, a twin heavy bolter and adamantium tracks.

### DAMAGE
Some of this model's characteristics change as it suffers damage, as shown below:

| REMAINING W | M | BS | A |
|-------------|---|----|---|
| 14-26+ | 10" | 4+ | 9 |
| 7-13 | 7" | 5+ | 6 |
| 1-6 | 4" | 6+ | 3 |

| WEAPON | RANGE | TYPE | S | AP | D | ABILITIES |
|--------|-------|------|---|----|----|-----------|
| Heavy stubber | 36" | Heavy 3 | 4 | 0 | 1 | - |
| Hunter-killer missile | 48" | Heavy 1 | 8 | -2 | D6 | Each hunter-killer missile can only be fired once per battle. |
| Lascannon | 48" | Heavy 1 | 9 | -3 | D6 | - |
| Storm bolter | 24" | Rapid Fire 2 | 4 | 0 | 1 | - |
| Tremor cannon | 60" | Heavy 2D6 | 8 | -2 | 3 | If a unit is hit by this weapon, in their following Movement phase they must halve their Move characteristic and cannot Advance. |
| Twin heavy bolter | 36" | Heavy 6 | 5 | -1 | 1 | - |
| Twin heavy flamer | 8" | Heavy 2D6 | 5 | -1 | 1 | This weapon automatically hits its target. |
| Adamantium tracks | Melee | Melee | User | -2 | D3 | - |

| WARGEAR OPTIONS | • This model may take a hunter-killer missile.<br>• This model may take a storm bolter or a heavy stubber.<br>• This model may take either two sponsons, or four sponsons; each sponson is equipped with a lascannon and either a twin heavy bolter or twin heavy flamer. |
|-----------------|---|
| ABILITIES | **Explodes:** If this model is reduced to 0 wounds, roll a D6 before removing it from the battlefield and before any embarked models disembark. On a 6 it explodes, and each unit within 2D6" suffers D6 mortal wounds.<br><br>**Firing Deck:** Up to 10 models being transported by a Banehammer can shoot in their Shooting phase, measuring and drawing line of sight from any point on the vehicle. Units that shoot in this manner count as having moved if they or the Banehammer moved in the preceding Movement phase.<br><br>**Smoke Launchers:** Once per game, instead of shooting any weapons in the Shooting phase, this model can use its smoke launchers; until your next Shooting phase your opponent must subtract 1 from all hit rolls for ranged weapons that target this vehicle.<br><br>**Steel Behemoth:** This model can Fall Back in the Movement phase and still shoot and/or charge during its turn. It can also still fire its weapons if enemy units are within 1" of it (but only its twin heavy bolter or twin heavy flamer can target units that are within 1" of it – its other guns must target other units). In addition this model only gains a bonus to its save in cover if at least half of the model is obscured from the firer. |
| TRANSPORT | This model can transport 25 **ASTRA MILITARUM INFANTRY** models. Each Heavy Weapons Team or Veteran Heavy Weapons Team takes the space of two other models and each **OGRYN** takes the space of three other models. |
| FACTION KEYWORDS | **IMPERIUM, ASTRA MILITARUM, <REGIMENT>** |
| KEYWORDS | **VEHICLE, TITANIC, TRANSPORT, BANEHAMMER** |

The shells of a Banehammer's tremor cannon explode underground, tearing apart the battlefield and those who stand upon it.

# BANESWORD

**25** POWER

| NAME | M | WS | BS | S | T | W | A | Ld | Sv |
|------|---|----|----|---|---|---|---|-----|-----|
| Banesword | * | 5+ | * | 9 | 8 | 26 | * | 8 | 3+ |

A Banesword is a single model equipped with a quake cannon, a twin heavy bolter and adamantium tracks.

## DAMAGE
Some of this model's characteristics change as it suffers damage, as shown below:

| REMAINING W | M | BS | A |
|-------------|---|----|----|
| 14-26+ | 10" | 4+ | 9 |
| 7-13 | 7" | 5+ | 6 |
| 1-6 | 4" | 6+ | 3 |

| WEAPON | RANGE | TYPE | S | AP | D | ABILITIES |
|--------|-------|------|---|----|----|-----------|
| Heavy stubber | 36" | Heavy 3 | 4 | 0 | 1 | - |
| Hunter-killer missile | 48" | Heavy 1 | 8 | -2 | D6 | Each hunter-killer missile can only be fired once per battle. |
| Lascannon | 48" | Heavy 1 | 9 | -3 | D6 | - |
| Quake cannon | 140" | Heavy D6 | 14 | -4 | D6 | When rolling for this weapon's damage, treat any rolls of 1 or 2 as 3 instead. |
| Storm bolter | 24" | Rapid Fire 2 | 4 | 0 | 1 | - |
| Twin heavy bolter | 36" | Heavy 6 | 5 | -1 | 1 | - |
| Twin heavy flamer | 8" | Heavy 2D6 | 5 | -1 | 1 | This weapon automatically hits its target. |
| Adamantium tracks | Melee | Melee | User | -2 | D3 | - |

| WARGEAR OPTIONS | |
|---|---|
| | • This model may take a hunter-killer missile. |
| | • This model may take a storm bolter or a heavy stubber. |
| | • This model may take either two sponsons, or four sponsons; each sponson is equipped with a lascannon and either a twin heavy bolter or twin heavy flamer. |

| ABILITIES | |
|---|---|
| | **Explodes:** If this model is reduced to 0 wounds, roll a D6 before removing it from the battlefield. On a 6 it explodes, and each unit within 2D6" suffers D6 mortal wounds.<br><br>**Smoke Launchers:** Once per game, instead of shooting any weapons in the Shooting phase, this model can use its smoke launchers; until your next Shooting phase your opponent must subtract 1 from all hit rolls for ranged weapons that target this vehicle. | **Steel Behemoth:** This model can Fall Back in the Movement phase and still shoot and/or charge during its turn. It can also still fire its weapons if enemy units are within 1" of it (but only its twin heavy bolter or twin heavy flamer can target units that are within 1" of it – its other guns must target other units). In addition this model only gains a bonus to its save in cover if at least half of the model is obscured from the firer. |

| FACTION KEYWORDS | IMPERIUM, ASTRA MILITARUM, <REGIMENT> |
|---|---|
| **KEYWORDS** | VEHICLE, TITANIC, BANESWORD |

# DOOMHAMMER

## DAMAGE
Some of this model's characteristics change as it suffers damage, as shown below:

| REMAINING W | M | BS | A |
| --- | --- | --- | --- |
| 14-26+ | 10" | 4+ | 9 |
| 7-13 | 7" | 5+ | 6 |
| 1-6 | 4" | 6+ | 3 |

| NAME | M | WS | BS | S | T | W | A | Ld | Sv |
| --- | --- | --- | --- | --- | --- | --- | --- | --- | --- |
| Doomhammer | * | 5+ | * | 9 | 8 | 26 | * | 8 | 3+ |

A Doomhammer is a single model equipped with a magma cannon, a twin heavy bolter and adamantium tracks.

| WEAPON | RANGE | TYPE | S | AP | D | ABILITIES |
| --- | --- | --- | --- | --- | --- | --- |
| Heavy stubber | 36" | Heavy 3 | 4 | 0 | 1 | - |
| Hunter-killer missile | 48" | Heavy 1 | 8 | -2 | D6 | Each hunter-killer missile can only be fired once per battle. |
| Lascannon | 48" | Heavy 1 | 9 | -3 | D6 | - |
| Magma cannon | 60" | Heavy D6 | 10 | -5 | D6 | Units attacked by this weapon do not gain any bonus to their saving throws for being in cover. In addition, if the target is within half range of this weapon, roll two dice when inflicting damage with it and discard the lowest result. |
| Storm bolter | 24" | Rapid Fire 2 | 4 | 0 | 1 | - |
| Twin heavy bolter | 36" | Heavy 6 | 5 | -1 | 1 | - |
| Twin heavy flamer | 8" | Heavy 2D6 | 5 | -1 | 1 | This weapon automatically hits its target. |
| Adamantium tracks | Melee | Melee | User | -2 | D3 | - |

| WARGEAR OPTIONS | • This model may take a hunter-killer missile.<br>• This model may take a storm bolter or a heavy stubber.<br>• This model may take either two sponsons, or four sponsons; each sponson is equipped with a lascannon and either a twin heavy bolter or twin heavy flamer. |
| --- | --- |
| ABILITIES | **Explodes:** If this model is reduced to 0 wounds, roll a D6 before removing it from the battlefield and before any embarked models disembark. On a 6 it explodes, and each unit within 2D6" suffers D6 mortal wounds.<br><br>**Firing Deck:** Up to 10 models being transported by a Doomhammer can shoot in their Shooting phase, measuring and drawing line of sight from any point on the vehicle. Units that shoot in this manner count as having moved if they or the Doomhammer moved in the preceding Movement phase.<br><br>**Smoke Launchers:** Once per game, instead of shooting any weapons in the Shooting phase, this model can use its smoke launchers; until your next Shooting phase your opponent must subtract 1 from all hit rolls for ranged weapons that target this vehicle.<br><br>**Steel Behemoth:** This model can Fall Back in the Movement phase and still shoot and/or charge during its turn. It can also still fire its weapons if enemy units are within 1" of it (but only its twin heavy bolter or twin heavy flamer can target units that are within 1" of it – its other guns must target other units). In addition this model only gains a bonus to its save in cover if at least half of the model is obscured from the firer. |
| TRANSPORT | This model can transport 25 **ASTRA MILITARUM INFANTRY** models. Each Heavy Weapons Team or Veteran Heavy Weapons Team takes the space of two other models and each **OGRYN** takes the space of three other models. |
| FACTION KEYWORDS | **IMPERIUM, ASTRA MILITARUM, <REGIMENT>** |
| KEYWORDS | **VEHICLE, TITANIC, TRANSPORT, DOOMHAMMER** |

## 31 POWER · HELLHAMMER

| NAME | M | WS | BS | S | T | W | A | Ld | Sv |
|---|---|---|---|---|---|---|---|---|---|
| Hellhammer | * | 5+ | * | 9 | 8 | 26 | * | 8 | 3+ |

A Hellhammer is a single model equipped with an autocannon, a demolisher cannon, a Hellhammer cannon, a twin heavy bolter, a lasgun and adamantium tracks.

**DAMAGE**
Some of this model's characteristics change as it suffers damage, as shown below:

| REMAINING W | M | BS | A |
|---|---|---|---|
| 14-26+ | 10" | 4+ | 9 |
| 7-13 | 7" | 5+ | 6 |
| 1-6 | 4" | 6+ | 3 |

| WEAPON | RANGE | TYPE | S | AP | D | ABILITIES |
|---|---|---|---|---|---|---|
| Autocannon | 48" | Heavy 2 | 7 | -1 | 2 | - |
| Demolisher cannon | 24" | Heavy D3 | 10 | -3 | D6 | When attacking units with 5 or more models, change this weapon's Type to Heavy D6. |
| Heavy stubber | 36" | Heavy 3 | 4 | 0 | 1 | - |
| Hellhammer cannon | 36" | Heavy 2D6 | 10 | -4 | 3 | Units attacked by this weapon do not gain any bonus to their saving throws for being in cover. |
| Hunter-killer missile | 48" | Heavy 1 | 8 | -2 | D6 | Each hunter-killer missile can only be fired once per battle. |
| Lascannon | 48" | Heavy 1 | 9 | -3 | D6 | - |
| Lasgun | 24" | Rapid Fire 1 | 3 | 0 | 1 | - |
| Storm bolter | 24" | Rapid Fire 2 | 4 | 0 | 1 | - |
| Twin heavy bolter | 36" | Heavy 6 | 5 | -1 | 1 | - |
| Twin heavy flamer | 8" | Heavy 2D6 | 5 | -1 | 1 | This weapon automatically hits its target. |
| Adamantium tracks | Melee | Melee | User | -2 | D3 | - |

| WARGEAR OPTIONS | |
|---|---|
| | • This model may take a hunter-killer missile. |
| | • This model may take a storm bolter or a heavy stubber. |
| | • This model may take either two sponsons, or four sponsons; each sponson is equipped with a lascannon and either a twin heavy bolter or twin heavy flamer. |

**ABILITIES**

**Explodes:** If this model is reduced to 0 wounds, roll a D6 before removing it from the battlefield. On a 6 it explodes, and each unit within 2D6" suffers D6 mortal wounds.

**Smoke Launchers:** Once per game, instead of shooting any weapons in the Shooting phase, this model can use its smoke launchers; until your next Shooting phase your opponent must subtract 1 from all hit rolls for ranged weapons that target this vehicle.

**Steel Behemoth:** This model can Fall Back in the Movement phase and still shoot and/or charge during its turn. It can also still fire its weapons if enemy units are within 1" of it (but only its twin heavy bolter or twin heavy flamer can target units that are within 1" of it – its other guns must target other units). In addition this model only gains a bonus to its save in cover if at least half of the model is obscured from the firer.

| FACTION KEYWORDS | IMPERIUM, ASTRA MILITARUM, <REGIMENT> |
|---|---|
| KEYWORDS | VEHICLE, TITANIC, HELLHAMMER |

34

## 27 POWER

# SHADOWSWORD

**DAMAGE**
Some of this model's characteristics change as it suffers damage, as shown below:

| REMAINING W | M | BS | A |
|---|---|---|---|
| 14-26+ | 10" | 4+ | 9 |
| 7-13 | 7" | 5+ | 6 |
| 1-6 | 4" | 6+ | 3 |

| NAME | M | WS | BS | S | T | W | A | Ld | Sv |
|---|---|---|---|---|---|---|---|---|---|
| Shadowsword | * | 5+ | * | 9 | 8 | 26 | * | 8 | 3+ |

A Shadowsword is a single model equipped with a volcano cannon, a twin heavy bolter and adamantium tracks.

| WEAPON | RANGE | TYPE | S | AP | D | ABILITIES |
|---|---|---|---|---|---|---|
| Heavy stubber | 36" | Heavy 3 | 4 | 0 | 1 | - |
| Hunter-killer missile | 48" | Heavy 1 | 8 | -2 | D6 | Each hunter-killer missile can only be fired once per battle. |
| Lascannon | 48" | Heavy 1 | 9 | -3 | D6 | - |
| Storm bolter | 24" | Rapid Fire 2 | 4 | 0 | 1 | - |
| Twin heavy bolter | 36" | Heavy 6 | 5 | -1 | 1 | - |
| Twin heavy flamer | 8" | Heavy 2D6 | 5 | -1 | 1 | This weapon automatically hits its target. |
| Volcano cannon | 120" | Heavy D6 | 16 | -5 | 2D6 | You can re-roll failed wound rolls when targeting **TITANIC** units with this weapon. |
| Adamantium tracks | Melee | Melee | User | -2 | D3 | - |

| WARGEAR OPTIONS | |
|---|---|
| | • This model may take a hunter-killer missile. |
| | • This model may take a storm bolter or a heavy stubber. |
| | • This model may take either two sponsons, or four sponsons; each sponson is equipped with a lascannon and either a twin heavy bolter or twin heavy flamer. |

| ABILITIES | |
|---|---|
| | **Explodes:** If this model is reduced to 0 wounds, roll a D6 before removing it from the battlefield. On a 6 it explodes, and each unit within 2D6" suffers D6 mortal wounds. |
| | **Smoke Launchers:** Once per game, instead of shooting any weapons in the Shooting phase, this model can use its smoke launchers; until your next Shooting phase your opponent must subtract 1 from all hit rolls for ranged weapons that target this vehicle. |
| | **Steel Behemoth:** This model can Fall Back in the Movement phase and still shoot and/or charge during its turn. It can also still fire its weapons if enemy units are within 1" of it (but only its twin heavy bolter or twin heavy flamer can target units that are within 1" of it – its other guns must target other units). In addition this model only gains a bonus to its save in cover if at least half of the model is obscured from the firer. |
| | **Shadowsword Targeters:** Add 1 to any hit rolls you make for this model for attacks that target **TITANIC** units. |

| FACTION KEYWORDS | IMPERIUM, ASTRA MILITARUM, <REGIMENT> |
|---|---|
| KEYWORDS | VEHICLE, TITANIC, SHADOWSWORD |

Each Shadowsword is mounted with a mighty volcano cannon – one of the most powerful primary weapons in the Imperial arsenal.

## STORMLORD

**27 POWER**

| NAME | M | WS | BS | S | T | W | A | Ld | Sv |
|------|---|----|----|----|----|----|----|----|----|
| Stormlord | * | 5+ | * | 9 | 8 | 26 | * | 8 | 3+ |

A Stormlord is a single model equipped with two heavy stubbers, a twin heavy bolter, a vulcan mega-bolter and adamantium tracks.

### DAMAGE
Some of this model's characteristics change as it suffers damage, as shown below:

| REMAINING W | M | BS | A |
|-------------|---|----|----|
| 14-26+ | 10" | 4+ | 9 |
| 7-13 | 7" | 5+ | 6 |
| 1-6 | 4" | 6+ | 3 |

| WEAPON | RANGE | TYPE | S | AP | D | ABILITIES |
|--------|-------|------|---|----|----|-----------|
| Heavy stubber | 36" | Heavy 3 | 4 | 0 | 1 | - |
| Hunter-killer missile | 48" | Heavy 1 | 8 | -2 | D6 | Each hunter-killer missile can only be fired once per battle. |
| Lascannon | 48" | Heavy 1 | 9 | -3 | D6 | - |
| Storm bolter | 24" | Rapid Fire 2 | 4 | 0 | 1 | - |
| Twin heavy bolter | 36" | Heavy 6 | 5 | -1 | 1 | - |
| Twin heavy flamer | 8" | Heavy 2D6 | 5 | -1 | 1 | This weapon automatically hits its target. |
| Vulcan mega-bolter | 60" | Heavy 20 | 6 | -2 | 2 | - |
| Adamantium tracks | Melee | Melee | User | -2 | D3 | - |

**WARGEAR OPTIONS**
- This model may take a hunter-killer missile.
- This model may take a storm bolter or an additional heavy stubber.
- This model may take either two sponsons, or four sponsons; each sponson is equipped with a lascannon and either a twin heavy bolter or twin heavy flamer.

**ABILITIES**

**Explodes:** If this model is reduced to 0 wounds, roll a D6 before removing it from the battlefield and before any embarked models disembark. On a 6 it explodes, and each unit within 2D6" suffers D6 mortal wounds.

**Extended Firing Deck:** Up to 20 models being transported by a Stormlord can shoot in their Shooting phase, measuring and drawing line of sight from any point on the vehicle. Units that shoot in this manner count as having moved if they or the Stormlord moved in the preceding Movement phase.

**Smoke Launchers:** Once per game, instead of shooting any weapons in the Shooting phase, this model can use its smoke launchers; until your next Shooting phase your opponent must subtract 1 from all hit rolls for ranged weapons that target this vehicle.

**Steel Behemoth:** This model can Fall Back in the Movement phase and still shoot and/or charge during its turn. It can also still fire its weapons if enemy units are within 1" of it (but only its twin heavy bolter or twin heavy flamer can target units that are within 1" of it – its other guns must target other units). In addition this model only gains a bonus to its save in cover if at least half of the model is obscured from the firer.

**TRANSPORT**
This model can transport 40 **ASTRA MILITARUM INFANTRY** models. Each Heavy Weapons Team or Veteran Heavy Weapons Team takes the space of two other models and each **OGRYN** takes the space of three other models.

**FACTION KEYWORDS**
**IMPERIUM, ASTRA MILITARUM, <REGIMENT>**

**KEYWORDS**
**VEHICLE, TITANIC, TRANSPORT, STORMLORD**

With its vulcan mega-bolter and massive transport capacity, the Stormlord is the ultimate close support tank.

# STORMSWORD

**25 POWER**

## DAMAGE
Some of this model's characteristics change as it suffers damage, as shown below:

| REMAINING W | M | BS | A |
|---|---|---|---|
| 14-26+ | 10" | 4+ | 9 |
| 7-13 | 7" | 5+ | 6 |
| 1-6 | 4" | 6+ | 3 |

| NAME | M | WS | BS | S | T | W | A | Ld | Sv |
|---|---|---|---|---|---|---|---|---|---|
| Stormsword | * | 5+ | * | 9 | 8 | 26 | * | 8 | 3+ |

A Stormsword is a single model equipped with a Stormsword siege cannon, a twin heavy bolter and adamantium tracks.

| WEAPON | RANGE | TYPE | S | AP | D | ABILITIES |
|---|---|---|---|---|---|---|
| Heavy stubber | 36" | Heavy 3 | 4 | 0 | 1 | - |
| Hunter-killer missile | 48" | Heavy 1 | 8 | -2 | D6 | Each hunter-killer missile can only be fired once per battle. |
| Lascannon | 48" | Heavy 1 | 9 | -3 | D6 | - |
| Storm bolter | 24" | Rapid Fire 2 | 4 | 0 | 1 | - |
| Stormsword siege cannon | 36" | Heavy D6 | 10 | -4 | D6 | Roll two dice for the number of attacks when firing this weapon and discard the lowest result. Units attacked by this weapon do not gain any bonus to their saving throws for being in cover. Re-roll damage rolls of 1 for this weapon. |
| Twin heavy bolter | 36" | Heavy 6 | 5 | -1 | 1 | - |
| Twin heavy flamer | 8" | Heavy 2D6 | 5 | -1 | 1 | This weapon automatically hits its target. |
| Adamantium tracks | Melee | Melee | User | -2 | D3 | - |

| WARGEAR OPTIONS | • This model may take a hunter-killer missile.<br>• This model may take a storm bolter or a heavy stubber.<br>• This model may take either two sponsons, or four sponsons; each sponson is equipped with a lascannon and either a twin heavy bolter or twin heavy flamer. |
|---|---|
| ABILITIES | **Explodes:** If this model is reduced to 0 wounds, roll a D6 before removing it from the battlefield. On a 6 it explodes, and each unit within 2D6" suffers D6 mortal wounds.<br><br>**Smoke Launchers:** Once per game, instead of shooting any weapons in the Shooting phase, this model can use its smoke launchers; until your next Shooting phase your opponent must subtract 1 from all hit rolls for ranged weapons that target this vehicle.<br><br>**Steel Behemoth:** This model can Fall Back in the Movement phase and still shoot and/or charge during its turn. It can also still fire its weapons if enemy units are within 1" of it (but only its twin heavy bolter or twin heavy flamer can target units that are within 1" of it – its other guns must target other units). In addition this model only gains a bonus to its save in cover if at least half of the model is obscured from the firer. |
| FACTION KEYWORDS | IMPERIUM, ASTRA MILITARUM, <REGIMENT> |
| KEYWORDS | VEHICLE, TITANIC, STORMSWORD |

# CADIAN SHOCK TROOPS

The Cadians are the benchmark against which all other Astra Militarum soldiers are measured, the inspirational figures that appear on propaganda slates and vid-reels across the Imperium. Small wonder they are held in such high esteem, for the Cadians are expert marksmen and stalwart castellans, holding the line against the horrors of Chaos for time immemorial.

A single Cadian regiment is said to be the equal of ten such formations of lesser men. So consistent and reliable are they that they are called upon not only to fight on the front line, but to inspire their fellow Imperial Guardsmen behind it. It is the staunch men and women of Cadia that teach lesser regiments how to truly excel in the ways of war. A single Cadian, it is said, can turn a rag-tag bunch of backwater militiamen into a stern and capable fighting force in the space of a week. A whole regiment can transform a vulnerable world into a fortress, ready to hurl back whatever baleful forces might try to wrest it from the Imperium's fold.

Hailing from the fortress world of Cadia, these indomitable soldiers have had more than their share of formidable threats to deal with. Their embattled home world stood sentinel over the Eye of Terror for ten thousand years. As the only stable route out of that colossal warp storm, it bore the brunt of countless Chaos incursions. Each time, the Cadians proved themselves equal to the task, driving hordes of traitor forces away from their gates. But even these tenacious warriors could only hold out for so long against so determined a foe. As the Imperium grew ever darker and more dangerous, Abaddon the Despoiler descended upon the planet with the full force of his Thirteenth Black Crusade. The Cadian Shock Troops defended their home world to the last, but ultimately, even they could not protect it from utter devastation. Now the surviving Cadians are scattered throughout the Imperium, forced to flee their home but never abandoning their cause.

The Cadian people, through necessity, are tough of mind and body, trained from an early age in the ways of the gun and the knife. It is said that on Cadia the birth rate and recruitment rate were synonymous, and that by the age of six all Cadians can field-strip a lasgun and identify the mainstay war engines of the Imperium's enemies. By their coming of age rituals at the age of sixteen, all Cadians are adept in endurance training, weapons handling, hand-to-hand combat, and vehicular and chemical warfare drills. Cadian recruits, known as Whiteshields, are recognisable by the thick white stripe upon their helms. It is said they fight as fiercely as any other Cadian in the heat of battle, but that only half of them will survive to make it to the ranks as a fully fledged member of the Imperial Guard.

The competency of the Cadians can be seen as a curse as well as a blessing. The Departmento Munitorum knows well of their reputation and the miracles of war they can perform, and hence they are deployed on the front line with unstinting frequency. Although this makes for a harsh, unforgiving and often prematurely ended life, their constant exposure to front-line warfare only serves to further hone the Cadians' skill. Those that survive this constant state of war are unrivalled experts in their field, rising through the ranks to become battle-seasoned leaders. As such, many Cadian officers prefer to lead from the front, often eschewing the safety of command posts to join their soldiers on the battlefield. There are a great many grizzled veterans and battle-tempered officers who will just as readily get the job done in person as they will hang back to give commands to their troops.

Inured to the horrors of war, the Cadians are known for their discipline and honourable conduct, though every one of them has a gallows humour beneath their professional mien. Led to war by veritable heroes of the Imperium, such as Knight Commander Pask – a stoic tank ace with more vehicle kills to his name than any other Astra Militarum officer alive – and Lord Castellan Ursarkar E. Creed – who personally led the defenders of Cadia in the planet's final war – these warriors have earned the respect and gratitude of the entire Imperium.

## LORD CASTELLAN CREED

**4** POWER

| NAME | M | WS | BS | S | T | W | A | Ld | Sv |
|---|---|---|---|---|---|---|---|---|---|
| Lord Castellan Creed | 6" | 3+ | 3+ | 3 | 3 | 4 | 3 | 9 | 4+ |

Lord Castellan Creed is a single model armed with two hot-shot laspistols and a power sword. Only one of this model may be included in your army.

| WEAPON | RANGE | TYPE | S | AP | D | ABILITIES |
|---|---|---|---|---|---|---|
| Hot-shot laspistol | 6" | Pistol 1 | 3 | -2 | 1 | - |
| Power sword | Melee | Melee | User | -3 | 1 | - |

| ABILITIES | **Voice of Command** (pg 10)<br><br>**Refractor Field:** Lord Castellan Creed has a 5+ invulnerable save.<br><br>**Tactical Genius:** If your army is Battle-forged, you receive an additional 2 Command Points if Lord Castellan Creed is your Warlord. | **Supreme Commander:** Lord Castellan Creed may use the Voice of Command ability three times in each of your turns. Resolve the effects of the first order before issuing the second order, and so on. |
|---|---|---|
| **FACTION KEYWORDS** | IMPERIUM, ASTRA MILITARUM, CADIAN | |
| **KEYWORDS** | CHARACTER, INFANTRY, OFFICER, LORD CASTELLAN CREED | |

## COLOUR SERGEANT KELL

**3** POWER

| NAME | M | WS | BS | S | T | W | A | Ld | Sv |
|---|---|---|---|---|---|---|---|---|---|
| Colour Sergeant Kell | 6" | 3+ | 3+ | 3 | 3 | 4 | 3 | 7 | 4+ |

Colour Sergeant Kell is a single model armed with a laspistol, power fist and power sword. Only one of this model may be included in your army.

| WEAPON | RANGE | TYPE | S | AP | D | ABILITIES |
|---|---|---|---|---|---|---|
| Laspistol | 12" | Pistol 1 | 3 | 0 | 1 | - |
| Power fist | Melee | Melee | x2 | -3 | D3 | When attacking with this weapon, you must subtract 1 from the hit roll. |
| Power sword | Melee | Melee | User | -3 | 1 | - |

| ABILITIES | **Colours of the Cadian 8th:** All CADIAN units within 6" of Colour Sergeant Kell may re-roll failed Morale tests.<br><br>**Listen Up, Maggots!:** You can make one additional order with a single friendly ASTRA MILITARUM OFFICER within 6" of Colour Sergeant Kell in each of your turns.<br><br>**Sworn Protector:** Roll a D6 each time Lord Castellan Creed loses a wound whilst he is within 3" of Colour Sergeant Kell; on a 2+ Lord Castellan Creed does not lose a wound but Colour Sergeant Kell suffers a mortal wound. |
|---|---|
| **FACTION KEYWORDS** | IMPERIUM, ASTRA MILITARUM, CADIAN |
| **KEYWORDS** | CHARACTER, INFANTRY, COLOUR SERGEANT KELL |

# KNIGHT COMMANDER PASK

| NAME | M | WS | BS | S | T | W | A | Ld | Sv |
|------|---|----|----|---|---|---|---|----|----|
| Knight Commander Pask | ✱ | 6+ | ✱ | 7 | 8 | 12 | ✱ | 8 | 3+ |

**DAMAGE**
Some of this model's characteristics change as it suffers damage, as shown below:

| REMAINING W | M | BS | A |
|-------------|---|----|----|
| 7-12+ | 10" | 2+ | 3 |
| 4-6 | 7" | 3+ | D3 |
| 1-3 | 4" | 4+ | 1 |

Knight Commander Pask is a single model. He rides to battle in the cupola of his trusty Leman Russ battle tank, *Hand of Steel*, which is equipped with a battle cannon and a heavy bolter. Only one of this model may be included in your army.

| WEAPON | RANGE | TYPE | S | AP | D | ABILITIES |
|--------|-------|------|---|----|----|-----------|
| Battle cannon | 72" | Heavy D6 | 8 | -2 | D3 | - |
| Demolisher cannon | 24" | Heavy D3 | 10 | -3 | D6 | When attacking units with 5 or more models, change this weapon's Type to Heavy D6. |
| Eradicator nova cannon | 36" | Heavy D6 | 6 | -2 | D3 | Units attacked by this weapon do not gain any bonus to their saving throws for being in cover. |
| Executioner plasma cannon | When attacking with this weapon, choose one of the profiles below. | | | | | |
| - Standard | 36" | Heavy D6 | 7 | -3 | 1 | - |
| - Supercharge | 36" | Heavy D6 | 8 | -3 | 2 | If you make one or more hit rolls of 1, the bearer suffers D6 mortal wounds after all of this weapon's shots have been resolved. |
| Exterminator autocannon | 48" | Heavy 4 | 7 | -1 | 2 | - |
| Heavy bolter | 36" | Heavy 3 | 5 | -1 | 1 | - |
| Heavy flamer | 8" | Heavy D6 | 5 | -1 | 1 | This weapon automatically hits its target. |
| Heavy stubber | 36" | Heavy 3 | 4 | 0 | 1 | - |
| Lascannon | 48" | Heavy 1 | 9 | -3 | D6 | - |
| Multi-melta | 24" | Heavy 1 | 8 | -4 | D6 | If the target is within half range of this weapon, roll two dice when inflicting damage with it and discard the lowest result. |
| Plasma cannon | When attacking with this weapon, choose one of the profiles below. | | | | | |
| - Standard | 36" | Heavy D3 | 7 | -3 | 1 | - |
| - Supercharge | 36" | Heavy D3 | 8 | -3 | 2 | On a hit roll of 1, the bearer is slain after all of this weapon's shots have been resolved. |
| Punisher gatling cannon | 24" | Heavy 20 | 5 | 0 | 1 | - |
| Storm bolter | 24" | Rapid Fire 2 | 4 | 0 | 1 | - |
| Vanquisher battle cannon | 72" | Heavy 1 | 8 | -3 | D6 | Roll two dice when inflicting damage with this weapon and discard the lowest result. |

| WARGEAR OPTIONS | • *Hand of Steel*'s battle cannon may be replaced with an exterminator autocannon, vanquisher battle cannon, eradicator nova cannon, demolisher cannon, punisher gatling cannon or executioner plasma cannon.<br>• *Hand of Steel*'s heavy bolter may be replaced with a heavy flamer or a lascannon.<br>• *Hand of Steel* may take two heavy bolters, two heavy flamers, two multi-meltas or two plasma cannons.<br>• *Hand of Steel* may take a heavy stubber or storm bolter. |
|---|---|

| ABILITIES | **Grinding Advance:** Knight Commander Pask does not suffer the penalty to turret weapon hit rolls for shooting a Heavy weapon on a turn in which it has moved. The following weapons are turret weapons: battle cannon, eradicator nova cannon, exterminator autocannon, vanquisher battle cannon, demolisher cannon, executioner plasma cannon and punisher gatling cannon.<br><br>**Smoke Launchers:** Once per game, instead of shooting any weapons in the Shooting phase, Knight Commander Pask can launch *Hand of Steel*'s smoke launchers; if he does so, until your next Shooting phase your opponent must subtract 1 from any hit rolls that target it.<br><br>**Tank Orders:** Knight Commander Pask can issue orders to a friendly **CADIAN LEMAN RUSS** at the start of your Shooting phase. To issue a Tank Order, pick a target **LEMAN RUSS** within 6" of Knight Commander Pask and choose which order you wish to issue from the table to the right. Each **LEMAN RUSS** can only be given a single order each turn.<br><br>**Knight Commander:** Knight Commander Pask may use the Tank Orders ability twice in each of your turns. Resolve the effects of the first order before issuing the second order. Note that Knight Commander Pask can issue orders to other **CADIAN LEMAN RUSS CHARACTERS**.<br><br>**Emergency Plasma Vents:** If this model fires a supercharged plasma cannon, and you roll one or more hit rolls of 1, it is not automatically destroyed. Instead, it suffers 6 mortal wounds and cannot fire any plasma cannons for the rest of the battle. | **Explodes:** If this model is reduced to 0 wounds, roll a D6 before removing it from the battlefield. On a 6 it explodes, and each unit within 6" suffers D3 mortal wounds.<br><br>**TANK ORDERS**<br><br>**ORDER**<br><br>**Full Throttle!** Instead of shooting this phase the ordered model immediately moves as if it were the Movement phase. It must Advance as part of this move, and cannot declare a charge during this turn.<br><br>**Gunners, Kill on Sight!** Re-roll hit rolls of 1 for the ordered model until the end of the phase.<br><br>**Strike and Shroud!** This order can only be issued to a model that has not yet used its smoke launchers during the battle. The ordered model can shoot its weapons and launch its smoke launchers during this phase. |
|---|---|---|

| FACTION KEYWORDS | IMPERIUM, ASTRA MILITARUM, CADIAN |
|---|---|
| KEYWORDS | CHARACTER, VEHICLE, LEMAN RUSS, TANK COMMANDER, KNIGHT COMMANDER PASK |

# CATACHAN JUNGLE FIGHTERS

**Uncouth and hard-headed, the jungle fighters of Catachan appear as muscle-bound louts next to the professional soldiery of the Cadians. Under their coarse exterior, however, dwells a core of iron – those heroic enough to survive upon the death world of Catachan make for truly formidable infantrymen, no matter the horrors of war in which they fight.**

Catachans are tough, hard-bitten warriors that hail from one of the most lethal worlds in the Imperium. The jungle planet of Catachan, classified as a Primaris-grade death world, is replete with poisonous, toxic and carnivorous plant life. Its fauna is even worse. The swamp leeches alone can drain a man of blood in an hour, and the Catachan Devil – a segmented monstrosity capable of ripping off a bunker door – is hunted by some Catachans for sport. For an outsider to survive even a day upon this planet is a significant achievement. The Catachans themselves have grown up there, and become inured to their ecosystem's endless attempts to kill them. Those that reach adulthood become almost fond of the hell-hole they call home, and will wistfully recall ordeals that normal men would do their level best to forget.

Needless to say, soldiers of such calibre make excellent recruits for the Imperial Guard. So inured are they to the dangers of their home planet that they are uniquely equipped, physically and mentally, to face the terrors of the galaxy at large. The people of Catachan send a vast tithe of warriors to the Departmento Munitorum in exchange for medical and military supplies; this arrangement has stood for thousands of years, and will likely remain until the Imperium itself gutters out. Born survivors, these warriors can thrive in any war zone, for hardship is meat and drink to them.

Catachans have a particular look to them that is all but unmistakeable. Their weather-beaten skin is hard as cured leather and frequently adorned with tattoos that show their regimental affiliation, and they wear red bandanas that symbolise the blood oath they swore upon joining their regiment. Each carries a sharp steel knife which acts as a symbol of status, a tool of survival and a weapon of war all at once. Almost all are uncannily strong – the infamous Sergeant 'Stonetooth' Harker is known for carrying his back-breakingly large heavy bolter 'Payback' much as normal man might carry a stub gun.

Catachans tend to be as headstrong as they are hardy, and they do not take kindly to outsiders telling them what to do. The respect of a Catachan must be earned the hard way. It is for this reason that tyrannical Commissars sometimes meet with unfortunate accidents when assigned to Catachan regiments. Their own officers get the best out of their men by leading from the front – Colonel 'Iron Hand' Straken is a prime example, a man whose heroics have won many a war, but seen him take so many grievous wounds that he is as much cybernetic as he is flesh. The inner strength of the Catachan people shines through in every officer, their crude banter and competitive machismo concealing a steely respect that binds these brothers in arms closer than any rank, number or protocol ever could.

## COLONEL 'IRON HAND' STRAKEN

**5 POWER**

| NAME | M | WS | BS | S | T | W | A | Ld | Sv |
|------|---|----|----|---|---|---|---|----|----|
| Colonel 'Iron Hand' Straken | 6" | 2+ | 3+ | 6 | 4 | 5 | 4 | 9 | 3+ |

Colonel 'Iron Hand' Straken is a single model armed with a plasma pistol, shotgun, krak grenades and a bionic arm with devil's claw. Only one of this model may be included in your army.

| WEAPON | RANGE | TYPE | S | AP | D | ABILITIES |
|--------|-------|------|---|----|----|-----------|
| Plasma pistol | When attacking with this weapon, choose one of the profiles below. | | | | | |
| - Standard | 12" | Pistol 1 | 7 | -3 | 1 | - |
| - Supercharge | 12" | Pistol 1 | 8 | -3 | 2 | On a hit roll of 1, the bearer is slain. |
| Shotgun | 12" | Assault 2 | 3 | 0 | 1 | If the target is within half range, add 1 to this weapon's Strength. |
| Bionic arm with devil's claw | Melee | Melee | User | -1 | 2 | - |
| Krak grenade | 6" | Grenade 1 | 6 | -1 | D3 | - |

| ABILITIES | **Voice of Command** (pg 10) | **Cold Steel and Courage:** All models in friendly CATACHAN units within 6" of Colonel 'Iron Hand' Straken at the start of the Fight phase can make 1 additional attack each time they fight during that phase. |
|-----------|------------------------------|-----------|
| | **Been There, Seen It, Killed It:** You can re-roll failed wound rolls made for Colonel 'Iron Hand' Straken in the Fight phase when targeting enemy MONSTERS. | |
| | **Refractor Field:** Colonel 'Iron Hand' Straken has a 5+ invulnerable save. | **Senior Officer:** Colonel 'Iron Hand' Straken may use the Voice of Command ability twice in each of your turns. Resolve the effects of the first order before issuing the second order. |

| FACTION KEYWORDS | IMPERIUM, ASTRA MILITARUM, CATACHAN |
|------------------|--------------------------------------|
| KEYWORDS | CHARACTER, INFANTRY, OFFICER, COLONEL 'IRON HAND' STRAKEN |

---

## SERGEANT HARKER

**3 POWER**

| NAME | M | WS | BS | S | T | W | A | Ld | Sv |
|------|---|----|----|---|---|---|---|----|----|
| Sergeant Harker | 6" | 3+ | 3+ | 4 | 3 | 3 | 4 | 7 | 5+ |

Sergeant Harker is a single model armed with Payback, frag grenades and krak grenades. Only one of this model may be included in your army.

| WEAPON | RANGE | TYPE | S | AP | D | ABILITIES |
|--------|-------|------|---|----|----|-----------|
| Payback | 36" | Assault 3 | 5 | -2 | 1 | - |
| Frag grenades | 6" | Grenade D6 | 3 | 0 | 1 | - |
| Krak grenades | 6" | Grenade 1 | 6 | -1 | D3 | - |

| ABILITIES | **Harker's Hellraisers:** You can re-roll hit rolls of 1 in the Shooting phase for friendly CATACHAN units within 6" of Sergeant Harker. |
|-----------|-----------|

| FACTION KEYWORDS | IMPERIUM, ASTRA MILITARUM, CATACHAN |
|------------------|--------------------------------------|
| KEYWORDS | CHARACTER, INFANTRY, SERGEANT HARKER |

# OFFICIO PREFECTUS

Stern and unyielding, the Commissars of the Officio Prefectus are iconic figures across the domains of Mankind. They form the rigid backbone of the Astra Militarum, lending strength and conviction to the regiments under their watchful eye. It is a duty they fulfil as often with the barrel of a bolt pistol as with their roared commands.

Most of the Imperium's citizens are familiar with the image of a Commissar standing bolt upright on the field of battle, greatcoat billowing and the aquila on his peaked cap shining bright even as the shadow of war swathes all around him. These warriors exhort the infantry of their assigned Astra Militarum regiments to ever greater acts of heroism, and their conviction and faith in the supremacy of Mankind is infectious. These are leaders of the most stern and unyielding sort, feared throughout the rank and file of every Imperial Guard army, and they do not suffer fools gladly. The taste of a Commissar's boot leather is well known to scurrilous recidivists across the ranks of the Imperial Guard.

The Officio Prefectus is a subset organisation that takes its recruits from the Schola Progenium. There, the war orphans of the Imperium are raised to adulthood under an oppressive regime that either sees them thrive – becoming agents of the Imperium ready to serve in the elite echelons of the Astra Militarum – or die with nobody to mourn them. Those who have the innate force of character and merciless conviction needed to rise through the ranks of these adolescent warriors might be chosen to join the Officio Prefectus, where their training begins anew. No small proportion are broken in the process, but the others go on to become the lynch-pins that hold the galaxy-spanning edifice of the Astra Militarum together.

## LORDS AMONGST MEN

The rank of Commissar comes with much authority and privilege – though most eschew the luxuries they are entitled to in favour of fighting alongside the rank and file. Some of these iron-willed disciplinarians are so skilled in the arts of leadership they are elevated to the rank of Lord Commissar. Though these figures make for terrifying authoritarians, their battlefield rhetoric is extremely inspiring. With a Lord Commissar to motivate it, a platoon of exhausted and battle-scarred warriors will charge screaming at the enemy with fire in their bellies and a joyous war-cry on their lips.

Those Guardsmen that are found wanting are used as another kind of inspiration. The sight of a terrified comrade having the wide muzzle of a Commissar's bolt pistol pressed into his head – or rather the gore-splattering detonation that follows – is so profound and unforgettable it has spurred men to fight on against the most insane odds. Even veteran Guardsmen talk about the Commissars with reverence and awe; most would rather a potentially violent death at the hands of the enemy than the ice-cold certainty and shame of the Commissar's summary justice.

# LORD COMMISSAR

**4 POWER**

| NAME | M | WS | BS | S | T | W | A | Ld | Sv |
|------|---|----|----|---|---|---|---|----|----|
| Lord Commissar | 6" | 2+ | 2+ | 3 | 3 | 4 | 3 | 9 | 4+ |

A Lord Commissar is a single model armed with a bolt pistol and power sword.

| WEAPON | RANGE | TYPE | S | AP | D | ABILITIES |
|--------|-------|------|---|----|----|-----------|
| Bolt pistol | 12" | Pistol 1 | 4 | 0 | 1 | - |
| Power sword | Melee | Melee | User | -3 | 0 | - |

| WARGEAR OPTIONS | • This model may replace its power sword with up to two items from the *Astra Militarum Melee Weapons* list.<br>• This model may replace its bolt pistol with one item from the *Astra Militarum Ranged Weapons* list. |
|-----------------|---|

| ABILITIES | **Aura of Discipline:** All friendly **Astra Militarum** units within 6" of a **Commissar** can use the Commissar's Leadership instead of their own.<br><br>**Refractor Field:** This model has a 5+ invulnerable save. | **Summary Execution:** Friendly **Astra Militarum** units within 6" of a **Commissar** can never lose more than one model as the result of any single failed Morale test. |
|-----------|---|---|

| FACTION KEYWORDS | **Imperium, Astra Militarum, Officio Prefectus** |
|------------------|---|
| KEYWORDS | **Character, Infantry, Commissar, Lord Commissar** |

# COMMISSAR

**2 POWER**

| NAME | M | WS | BS | S | T | W | A | Ld | Sv |
|------|---|----|----|---|---|---|---|----|----|
| Commissar | 6" | 3+ | 3+ | 3 | 3 | 3 | 3 | 8 | 5+ |

A Commissar is a single model armed with a bolt pistol.

| WEAPON | RANGE | TYPE | S | AP | D | ABILITIES |
|--------|-------|------|---|----|----|-----------|
| Bolt pistol | 12" | Pistol 1 | 4 | 0 | 1 | - |

| WARGEAR OPTIONS | • The Commissar may take up to two items from the *Astra Militarum Melee Weapons* list.<br>• The Commissar may replace their bolt pistol with an item from the *Astra Militarum Ranged Weapons* list. |
|-----------------|---|

| ABILITIES | **Aura of Discipline:** All friendly **Astra Militarum** units within 6" of a **Commissar** can use the Commissar's Leadership instead of their own.<br><br>**Summary Execution:** Friendly **Astra Militarum** units within 6" of a **Commissar** can never lose more than one model as the result of any single failed Morale test. |
|-----------|---|

| FACTION KEYWORDS | **Imperium, Astra Militarum, Officio Prefectus** |
|------------------|---|
| KEYWORDS | **Character, Infantry, Commissar** |

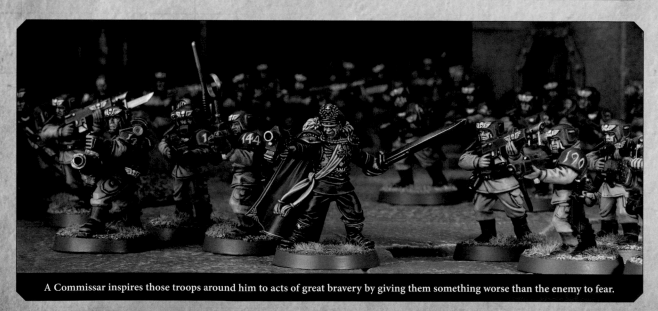

A Commissar inspires those troops around him to acts of great bravery by giving them something worse than the enemy to fear.

# COMMISSAR YARRICK

**7** POWER

| NAME | M | WS | BS | S | T | W | A | Ld | Sv |
|------|---|----|----|---|---|---|---|----|----|
| Commissar Yarrick | 6" | 2+ | 2+ | 3 | 4 | 4 | 3 | 9 | 4+ |

Commissar Yarrick is a single model armed with a bolt pistol, storm bolter, power klaw and the Bale Eye. Only one of this model may be included in your army.

| WEAPON | RANGE | TYPE | S | AP | D | ABILITIES |
|--------|-------|------|---|----|----|-----------|
| Bale Eye | 6" | Pistol 1 | 3 | -2 | 1 | - |
| Bolt pistol | 12" | Pistol 1 | 4 | 0 | 1 | - |
| Storm bolter | 24" | Rapid Fire 2 | 4 | 0 | 1 | - |
| Power klaw | Melee | Melee | x2 | -3 | D3 | When attacking with this weapon, you must subtract 1 from the hit roll. |

| ABILITIES | |
|-----------|--|
| | **Aura of Discipline:** All friendly **Astra Militarum** units within 6" of a **Commissar** can use the Commissar's Leadership instead of their own. | **Hero of Hades Hive:** You can re-roll hit rolls of 1 made for friendly **Astra Militarum** units within 6" of Commissar Yarrick. You may re-roll any failed hit rolls for friendly **Astra Militarum** units within 6" of Commissar Yarrick when attacking **Ork** units. |

**Iron Will:** Roll a D6 each time Commissar Yarrick loses his final wound; on a roll of 3+ that wound is not lost.

**Power Field:** Commissar Yarrick has a 4+ invulnerable save.

**Summary Execution:** Friendly **Astra Militarum** units within 6" of a **Commissar** can never lose more than one model as the result of any single failed Morale test.

| FACTION KEYWORDS | **Imperium, Astra Militarum, Officio Prefectus** |
|------------------|--------------------------------------------------|
| **KEYWORDS** | **Character, Infantry, Commissar, Yarrick** |

# MILITARUM TEMPESTUS

**The Militarum Tempestus are shock assault specialists with near inhuman skill and discipline. They are the best equipped and most extensively trained of all the assets that the Imperial Guard can bring to bear. Descending from the skies upon lightweight grav-chutes, they strike at the heart of the enemy army with hot-shot lasguns and devastating special weapons.**

The Schola Progenium is a training institution that recruits the orphaned offspring of highborn Imperial citizens. These protégés are immersed from infancy in the most rigorous and gruelling regime, trained to serve the Emperor above all else. Some have the faith and iron will necessary to become Commissars, later seconded to the Officio Prefectus. Others scale the heights of physical excellence, becoming Tempestus Scions, warriors extensively trained in the arts of death. It is these most deadly of operatives that make up the ranks of the Militarum Tempestus.

## TOOLS OF THE MERCILESS

The Tempestus Scions have the best personal wargear the Imperial Guard can provide. They are each clad in the hard plate of carapace armour over a flexible undersuit, a formidable combination that can turn aside even a bolter round. On their forearms they wear readout displays, known as slate monitrons, that illuminate their vital functions and pass their bio-signs on to nearby leaders and, in extremis, medics. These devices are the cause of many a guarded jibe that the Scions have no hearts inside their chests, but instead wear them upon their sleeves, locked in an iron box. The basic armament of the Militarum Tempestus is the hot-shot lasgun – also known as hellguns, these weapons have hyper-yield arrays worn as backpack rigs. Hot-shot weapons have such penetrative power that each eye-searing beam can punch through the thick ceramite of a Heretic Astartes warrior. Needless to say, this extensive and advanced suite of wargear is the envy of the rank and file Imperial Guardsmen. The common soldiery look upon the Militarum Tempestus with a mixture of hatred and awe, calling them Storm Troopers, glory boys or worse, and fondly imagining that but for a twist of fate, their roles would be reversed. They are dead wrong, for should a line trooper of the Imperial Guard be called upon to face the mind-shattering horrors that Militarum Tempestus platoons have to deal with on every battlefield they visit, his sanity would soon be forfeit.

The Militarum Tempestus do not rely on heavy, mass-produced transports as do the Imperial Guard, but instead utilise faster and more nimble machineries of war. The Taurox Prime APC is just such machine. A robust infantry assault vehicle, it is relatively small next to the motorised juggernauts of the Astra Militarum armoured companies. Yet its compact size lends it speed; it is able to traverse the most hostile terrain at an impressive pace, and boasts a variety of weapons, from scaled-down battle cannons to roof-mounted missile launchers. When heavier weaponry is called for, the Storm Troopers will make use of plasma guns and meltas to destroy elite infantry, rampaging alien behemoths or earth-grinding tanks. Should their duty require them to engage a horde of enemies, they will use flamers and overlapping fields of hot-shot volley gun fire to destroy dozens of targets at a time. On those occasions when the Militarum Tempestus take to the battlefield alongside the Astra Militarum, they fight as discrete strike forces given the most hazardous of missions; it is common enough for them to operate behind enemy lines, be assigned to the destruction of enemy super-heavy assets, or even take down the command structure of their adversaries with a pinpoint strike. So impressive and efficient are these troops they are sometimes requisitioned as personal bodyguards for the agents of the Emperor's Holy Inquisition – a high accolade indeed, given that such individuals carry the death of worlds upon their shoulders.

## 55TH KAPPIC EAGLES

The Kappic Eagles have a long and storied history, and none more so than the 55th. They have played a pivotal role in countless campaigns, including the destruction of the Ork scrapship *Scarfist* and the crippling of a Crimson Slaughter strike force upon the Ybrekian Ice Worlds. Perhaps their most notable operation was the retrieval of a stolen Ordo Tempestus relic known as the Barbed Gauntlets of Avitus, taken by the Aeldari of Craftworld Altansar. The 55th's retribution was swift and unremittingly brutal. The regiment went on to even greater glory fighting alongside Saint Celestine and the puritanical Inquisitor Greyfax against the horrors of Abaddon's Thirteenth Black Crusade.

# TEMPESTOR PRIME

**2 POWER**

| NAME | M | WS | BS | S | T | W | A | Ld | Sv |
|------|---|----|----|---|---|---|---|----|----|
| Tempestor Prime | 6" | 3+ | 3+ | 3 | 3 | 4 | 3 | 8 | 4+ |

A Tempestor Prime is a single model armed with a hot-shot laspistol, frag grenades and krak grenades.

| WEAPON | RANGE | TYPE | S | AP | D | ABILITIES |
|--------|-------|------|---|----|----|-----------|
| Bolt pistol | 12" | Pistol 1 | 4 | 0 | 1 | - |
| Hot-shot laspistol | 6" | Pistol 1 | 3 | -2 | 1 | - |
| Plasma pistol | When attacking with this weapon, choose one of the profiles below. | | | | | |
| - Standard | 12" | Pistol 1 | 7 | -3 | 1 | - |
| - Supercharge | 12" | Pistol 1 | 8 | -3 | 2 | On a hit roll of 1, the bearer is slain. |
| Chainsword | Melee | Melee | User | 0 | 1 | Each time the bearer fights, it can make 1 additional attack with this weapon. |
| Frag grenade | 6" | Grenade D6 | 3 | 0 | 1 | - |
| Krak grenade | 6" | Grenade 1 | 6 | -1 | D3 | - |

| WARGEAR OPTIONS | • This model may take a chainsword or one item from the *Astra Militarum Melee Weapons* list.<br>• This model may replace its hot-shot laspistol with a Tempestus command rod, a bolt pistol or a plasma pistol. |
|---|---|

| ABILITIES | **Voice of Command** (pg 10)<br><br>**Tempestus Command Rod:** A model with a Tempestus command rod may use the Voice of Command ability twice in each of your turns. Resolve the effects of the first order before issuing the second order. | **Aerial Drop:** During deployment, you can set up this model in a high-altitude transport, ready to deploy via grav-chute, instead of placing it on the battlefield. At the end of any of your Movement phases the model can make an aerial drop – set it up anywhere on the battlefield that is more than 9" away from any enemy models. |
|---|---|---|

| FACTION KEYWORDS | **IMPERIUM, ASTRA MILITARUM, MILITARUM TEMPESTUS** |
|---|---|
| KEYWORDS | **CHARACTER, INFANTRY, OFFICER, TEMPESTOR PRIME** |

A Militarum Tempestus Command Squad disembarks from its Taurox transport to bring cleansing fire to the enemies of the Imperium.

# MILITARUM TEMPESTUS COMMAND SQUAD

| NAME | M | WS | BS | S | T | W | A | Ld | Sv |
|------|---|----|----|----|---|---|---|----|----|
| Tempestus Scion | 6" | 4+ | 3+ | 3 | 3 | 1 | 1 | 6 | 4+ |

This unit contains 4 Tempestus Scions. Each model is armed with a hot-shot lasgun, frag grenades and krak grenades.

| WEAPON | RANGE | TYPE | S | AP | D | ABILITIES |
|--------|-------|------|---|----|----|-----------|
| Flamer | 8" | Assault D6 | 4 | 0 | 1 | This weapon automatically hits its target. |
| Grenade launcher | When attacking with this weapon, choose one of the profiles below. | | | | | |
| - Frag grenade | 24" | Assault D6 | 3 | 0 | 1 | - |
| - Krak grenade | 24" | Assault 1 | 6 | -1 | D3 | - |
| Hot-shot lasgun | 18" | Rapid Fire 1 | 3 | -2 | 1 | - |
| Hot-shot laspistol | 6" | Pistol 1 | 3 | -2 | 1 | - |
| Hot-shot volley gun | 24" | Heavy 4 | 4 | -2 | 1 | - |
| Meltagun | 12" | Assault 1 | 8 | -4 | D6 | If the target is within half range of this weapon, roll two dice when inflicting damage with it and discard the lowest result. |
| Plasma gun | When attacking with this weapon, choose one of the profiles below. | | | | | |
| - Standard | 24" | Rapid Fire 1 | 7 | -3 | 1 | |
| - Supercharge | 24" | Rapid Fire 1 | 8 | -3 | 2 | On a hit roll of 1, the bearer is slain after all of this weapon's shots have been resolved. |
| Frag grenade | 6" | Grenade D6 | 3 | 0 | 1 | - |
| Krak grenade | 6" | Grenade 1 | 6 | -1 | D3 | - |

**WARGEAR OPTIONS**
- One model may replace its hot-shot lasgun with a hot-shot laspistol and a vox-caster.
- One other model may replace its hot-shot lasgun with a hot-shot laspistol and a medi-pack.
- One other model may take a platoon standard.
- Up to four other models may replace their hot-shot lasgun with a flamer, meltagun, plasma gun, grenade launcher or hot-shot volley gun.

**ABILITIES**

**Aerial Drop:** During deployment, you can set up this unit in a high-altitude transport, ready to deploy via grav-chute, instead of placing it on the battlefield. At the end of any of your Movement phases the unit can make an aerial drop – set it up anywhere on the battlefield that is more than 9" away from any enemy models.

**Platoon Standard:** All friendly MILITARUM TEMPESTUS units within 6" of any units with a platoon standard may add 1 to their Leadership when taking Morale tests.

**Medi-pack:** At the end of any of your Movement phases, a model with a medi-pack can attempt to heal a single model. Select a friendly ASTRA MILITARUM INFANTRY unit within 3" and roll a D6. On a roll of 4+, one model in the unit recovers a wound it lost earlier in the battle (if the unit has a Wounds characteristic of 1, one model slain earlier in the battle is returned to the unit instead). A unit can only be the target of this ability once in each turn.

**Vox-caster:** If a friendly OFFICER is within 3" of a unit with a vox-caster when using their Voice of Command ability, you may extend the range of the order to 18" if the target unit also contains a vox-caster.

| **FACTION KEYWORDS** | IMPERIUM, ASTRA MILITARUM, MILITARUM TEMPESTUS |
|------|------|
| **KEYWORDS** | INFANTRY, TEMPESTUS COMMAND SQUAD |

# MILITARUM TEMPESTUS SCIONS

**3 POWER**

| NAME | M | WS | BS | S | T | W | A | Ld | Sv |
|------|---|----|----|---|---|---|---|----|----|
| Tempestus Scion | 6" | 4+ | 3+ | 3 | 3 | 1 | 1 | 6 | 4+ |
| Tempestor | 6" | 3+ | 3+ | 3 | 3 | 1 | 2 | 7 | 4+ |

This unit contains 1 Tempestor and 4 Tempestus Scions. It can include up to 5 additional Tempestus Scions (**Power Rating +3**).
• Each Tempestus Scion is armed with a hot-shot lasgun, frag grenades and krak grenades.
• The Tempestor is armed with a hot-shot laspistol, chainsword, frag grenades and krak grenades.

| WEAPON | RANGE | TYPE | S | AP | D | ABILITIES |
|--------|-------|------|---|----|----|-----------|
| Bolt pistol | 12" | Pistol 1 | 4 | 0 | 1 | - |
| Flamer | 8" | Assault D6 | 4 | 0 | 1 | This weapon automatically hits its target. |
| Grenade launcher | When attacking with this weapon, choose one of the profiles below. | | | | | |
| - Frag grenade | 24" | Assault D6 | 3 | 0 | 1 | - |
| - Krak grenade | 24" | Assault 1 | 6 | -1 | D3 | - |
| Hot-shot lasgun | 18" | Rapid Fire 1 | 3 | -2 | 1 | - |
| Hot-shot laspistol | 6" | Pistol 1 | 3 | -2 | 1 | - |
| Hot-shot volley gun | 24" | Heavy 4 | 4 | -2 | 1 | - |
| Meltagun | 12" | Assault 1 | 8 | -4 | D6 | If the target is within half range of this weapon, roll two dice when inflicting damage with it and discard the lowest result. |
| Plasma pistol | When attacking with this weapon, choose one of the profiles below. | | | | | |
| - Standard | 12" | Pistol 1 | 7 | -3 | 1 | - |
| - Supercharge | 12" | Pistol 1 | 8 | -3 | 2 | On a hit roll of 1, the bearer is slain. |
| Plasma gun | When attacking with this weapon, choose one of the profiles below. | | | | | |
| - Standard | 24" | Rapid Fire 1 | 7 | -3 | 1 | - |
| - Supercharge | 24" | Rapid Fire 1 | 8 | -3 | 2 | On a hit roll of 1, the bearer is slain after all of this weapon's shots have been resolved. |
| Chainsword | Melee | Melee | User | 0 | 1 | Each time the bearer fights, it can make 1 additional attack with this weapon. |
| Frag grenade | 6" | Grenade D6 | 3 | 0 | 1 | - |
| Krak grenade | 6" | Grenade 1 | 6 | -1 | D3 | - |

| WARGEAR OPTIONS | |
|-----------------|---|
| | • One Tempestus Scion may replace their hot-shot lasgun with a hot-shot laspistol and take a vox-caster. |
| | • For every five models in the unit, up to two other Tempestus Scions may replace their hot-shot lasgun with a flamer, meltagun, plasma gun, grenade launcher or hot-shot volley gun. |
| | • The Tempestor may replace their chainsword with an item from the *Astra Militarum Melee Weapons* list. |
| | • The Tempestor may replace their hot-shot laspistol with a bolt pistol or plasma pistol. |

| ABILITIES | |
|-----------|---|
| | **Aerial Drop:** During deployment, you can set up this unit in a high-altitude transport, ready to deploy via grav-chute, instead of placing it on the battlefield. At the end of any of your Movement phases the unit can make an aerial drop – set it up anywhere on the battlefield that is more than 9" away from any enemy models. |
| | **Vox-caster:** If a friendly **OFFICER** is within 3" of a unit with a vox-caster when using their Voice of Command ability, you may extend the range of the order to 18" if the target unit also contains a vox-caster. |

| FACTION KEYWORDS | **IMPERIUM, ASTRA MILITARUM, MILITARUM TEMPESTUS** |
|-----------------|---|
| **KEYWORDS** | **INFANTRY, TEMPESTUS SCIONS** |

# TAUROX PRIME

| REMAINING W | M | BS | A |
|---|---|---|---|
| 6-10+ | 14" | 3+ | 3 |
| 3-5 | 10" | 4+ | D3 |
| 1-2 | 6" | 5+ | 1 |

| NAME | M | WS | BS | S | T | W | A | Ld | Sv |
|---|---|---|---|---|---|---|---|---|---|
| Taurox Prime | * | 6+ | * | 6 | 6 | 10 | * | 7 | 3+ |

A Taurox Prime is a single model equipped with a Taurox battle cannon and two hot-shot volley guns.

| WEAPON | RANGE | TYPE | S | AP | D | ABILITIES |
|---|---|---|---|---|---|---|
| Autocannon | 48" | Heavy 2 | 7 | -1 | 2 | - |
| Heavy stubber | 36" | Heavy 3 | 4 | 0 | 1 | - |
| Hot-shot volley gun | 24" | Heavy 4 | 4 | -2 | 1 | - |
| Storm bolter | 24" | Rapid Fire 2 | 4 | 0 | 1 | - |
| Taurox battle cannon | 48" | Heavy D6 | 7 | -1 | D3 | - |
| Taurox gatling cannon | 24" | Heavy 20 | 4 | 0 | 1 | - |
| Taurox missile launcher | When attacking with this weapon, choose one of the profiles below. | | | | | |
| - Frag missile | 48" | Heavy 2D6 | 4 | 0 | 1 | - |
| - Krak missile | 48" | Heavy 2 | 8 | -2 | D6 | - |

| WARGEAR OPTIONS | • This model may replace its Taurox battle cannon with a Taurox gatling cannon or a Taurox missile launcher.<br>• This model may replace its two hot-shot volley guns with two autocannons.<br>• This model may take a storm bolter or a heavy stubber. |
|---|---|
| ABILITIES | **Explodes:** If this model is reduced to 0 wounds, roll a D6 before removing it from the battlefield and before any embarked models disembark. On a 6 it explodes, and each unit within 6" suffers D3 mortal wounds. |
| TRANSPORT | This model can transport 10 **MILITARUM TEMPESTUS** or **OFFICIO PREFECTUS INFANTRY** models. |
| FACTION KEYWORDS | **IMPERIUM, ASTRA MILITARUM, MILITARUM TEMPESTUS** |
| KEYWORDS | **VEHICLE, TRANSPORT, TAUROX PRIME** |

The redoubtable Taurox Prime is the perfect infantry support vehicle, with a large transport capacity and an array of deadly weapons.

# MILITARUM AUXILLA

**Humanity has spread so widely that it has evolved an endless variety of genetic strains and offshoots. Some of these are nigh unrecognisable as humans, though they still hail from the bloodlines of the Imperium. As such, these abhumans serve in the Emperor's armies, their regiments seconded to the Astra Militarum wherever their specialist skills are needed most.**

The most common bloodlines of abhuman are the Ogryns, hulking brutes almost ten feet in height, and the diminutive Ratlings, famous for their resourceful cunning and sharp eyes. There are many other officially ratified types of abhuman in the Militarum Auxilla, from the spindle-limbed Longshanks and the stocky, capable Squats to the amphibious Pelagers and the persecuted

Beastmen. These sub-species are rarely seen on the battlefield and some are restricted to their home planets. The Ogryn and Ratling strains, however, have become so stable and widespread over the millennia they are a relatively common sight in the battle groups of the Astra Militarum. Nevertheless, it would be untrue to say that these auxiliaries are trusted by the rest of the Astra Militarum, for mutants of any kind are treated with suspicion.

## OGRYNS

Ogryns hail from worlds with unusually high gravity, and have evolved to compensate for the adverse conditions of their homes. Regardless of origin, each Ogryn is immensely muscular and heavy-set, weighing the best part of a ton and with the strength of a grox in its brawny frame. However, for all its might, it has very little in the way of wits. Ogryns must be carefully mentored in their faith and duty, directed in the true path of the Imperial servant lest they follow their stomachs instead of the commands of their officers. They are simple in their behaviour, having to be goaded into the confines of transports should they believe it to be too dark in their cavernous hulls. The effort it takes to shepherd the Ogryns to the front line pays off in great measure when these mighty warriors charge in to the fray. They are armed with extremely robust weaponry – of which the ripper gun is the most famous – and are liable to improvise a highly effective club out of anything that comes to hand. They absolutely devastate the line infantry of the foe, crushing them, bowling them over and even ripping them bodily apart.

Some are true primitives, such as the Krourk Ogryn Auxilla deployed on Armageddon, who would use their ripper guns to bludgeon their foes to death. Canny commanders learned quickly how effective the Krourk were when deployed extremely close to the front lines. Others Ogryns have been known to learn a semblance of professionalism and responsibility from the humans they spend time with. The heavily-armed Bullgryns use grenadier gauntlets and slabshields to storm enemy positions whilst their smaller comrades march in their wake. Nork Deddog, long-serving veteran of the Imperial Guard, is so loyal and strong he is counted amongst the best bodyguards an Astra Militarum officer could hope to employ, and can even be trusted to do up his uniform correctly and aim his gun without instruction.

## RATLINGS

Stocky, hairy, and rarely over four feet tall, Ratlings are sneered at by many a Guardsman in the Emperor's armies. To underestimate them is a dangerous folly, however. Ratlings are naturally excellent snipers, and have a low cunning that keeps them one step ahead of those that would cause them harm. Most Ratlings come from worlds with extremely dangerous fauna; unable to overcome their food sources at close quarters, they have adapted to hide and hunt from afar, using stealth, marksmanship and nimble-footed agility instead of bravery and brute force.

A Ratling can shoot an Ork in the eye socket from two hundred yards and have redeployed to another vantage point before the slain xenos' comrades even think to return fire. They go to war barefoot, preferring to feel the lay of the land through the thick skin of their soles, and are very partial to comestibles of all kinds – a Ratling Auxilla detachment has more than once been likened to a plague of vermin by angered quartermasters, for this breed of abhuman is notoriously light-fingered. They make excellent cooks, having a taste for the finer things in life, and form the core of an ad-hoc black market within the Imperial Guard. Any who decide to pick on them due to their small size do so at their own peril; in the heat of battle they may find their ammunition supplies have been replaced with empty clips, their tank is suddenly out of fuel in the middle of open ground, or their aircraft's engine starts gouting poisonous smoke as soon as they take off. Provided this lethal ingenuity is kept pointed at the enemy, Ratlings make for a potent asset in the Astra Militarum's wider forces.

## OGRYNS

**4 POWER**

| NAME | M | WS | BS | S | T | W | A | Ld | Sv |
|------|---|-----|-----|---|---|---|---|-----|-----|
| Ogryn | 6" | 3+ | 4+ | 5 | 5 | 3 | 3 | 7 | 5+ |
| Ogryn Bone 'ead | 6" | 3+ | 4+ | 5 | 5 | 3 | 4 | 8 | 5+ |

This unit contains 1 Ogryn Bone 'ead and 2 Ogryns. It may contain up to 3 additional Ogryns (**Power Rating +4**) or up to 6 additional Ogryns (**Power Rating +8**). Each model is armed with a ripper gun and frag bombs.

| WEAPON | RANGE | TYPE | S | AP | D | ABILITIES |
|--------|-------|------|---|-----|---|-----------|
| Ripper gun | 12" | Assault 3 | 5 | 0 | 1 | - |
| Frag bomb | 6" | Grenade D6 | 4 | 0 | 1 | - |

| ABILITIES | **Avalanche of Muscle:** On a turn in which this unit made a successful charge, models in this unit can make one additional attack in the Fight phase the first time they fight. |
|-----------|------------------|

| FACTION KEYWORDS | **IMPERIUM, ASTRA MILITARUM, MILITARUM AUXILLA** |
|------------------|----------------|

| KEYWORDS | **INFANTRY, OGRYN** |
|----------|---------------|

## BULLGRYNS

**7 POWER**

| NAME | M | WS | BS | S | T | W | A | Ld | Sv |
|------|---|-----|-----|---|---|---|---|-----|-----|
| Bullgryn | 6" | 3+ | 4+ | 5 | 5 | 3 | 3 | 7 | 4+ |
| Bullgryn Bone 'ead | 6" | 3+ | 4+ | 5 | 5 | 3 | 4 | 8 | 4+ |

This unit contains 1 Bullgryn Bone 'ead and 2 Bullgryns. It may contain up to 3 additional Bullgryns (**Power Rating +7**) or up to 6 additional Bullgryns (**Power Rating +14**). Each model is armed with a grenadier gauntlet and frag bombs and equipped with a slabshield.

| WEAPON | RANGE | TYPE | S | AP | D | ABILITIES |
|--------|-------|------|---|-----|---|-----------|
| Grenadier gauntlet | 12" | Assault D6 | 4 | 0 | 1 | - |
| Bullgryn maul | Melee | Melee | +2 | -1 | 2 | - |
| Frag bomb | 6" | Grenade D6 | 4 | 0 | 1 | - |

| WARGEAR OPTIONS | • Any model may replace its grenadier gauntlet with a Bullgryn maul.<br>• Any model may replace its slabshield with a brute shield. |
|-----------------|----------------|

| ABILITIES | **Bruteshield:** Models equipped with a brute shield have a 4+ invulnerable save.<br><br>**Slabshield:** Models equipped with slabshields have a Save characteristic of 2+. | **Avalanche of Muscle:** On a turn in which this unit made a successful charge, models in this unit can make one additional attack in the Fight phase the first time they fight. |
|-----------|------------------|------------------|

| FACTION KEYWORDS | **IMPERIUM, ASTRA MILITARUM, MILITARUM AUXILLA** |
|------------------|----------------|

| KEYWORDS | **INFANTRY, OGRYN, BULLGRYNS** |
|----------|---------------|

Massive, lumbering and absurdly resilient, Ogryns make up for a lack of wits with prodigious strength and utter loyalty.

## RATLINGS

**POWER 2**

| NAME | M | WS | BS | S | T | W | A | Ld | Sv |
|------|---|----|----|---|---|---|---|----|----|
| Ratling | 6" | 5+ | 3+ | 2 | 2 | 1 | 1 | 5 | 6+ |

This unit contains 5 Ratlings. It may contain up to 5 additional Ratlings (**Power Rating +2**). Each model is armed with a sniper rifle.

| WEAPON | RANGE | TYPE | S | AP | D | ABILITIES |
|--------|-------|------|---|----|----|-----------|
| Sniper rifle | 36" | Heavy 1 | 4 | 0 | 1 | A model firing a sniper weapon can target an enemy **CHARACTER** even if they are not the closest enemy unit. If you roll a wound roll of 6+ for this weapon, it inflicts a mortal wound in addition to its normal damage. |

| ABILITIES | |
|-----------|--|
| | **Find the Best Spot:** Instead of deploying normally, this unit may wait until both armies are fully deployed and then be placed anywhere on the board that is more than 18" from any enemy models. |
| | **Shoot Sharp and Scarper:** Immediately after making a Shooting attack, this unit can move as if it were the Movement phase (though it cannot Advance as part of this move). |
| | **Naturally Stealthy:** Models in this unit receive a +2 bonus to their saving throw when they receive the benefits of cover instead of only +1. |

| FACTION KEYWORDS | **IMPERIUM, ASTRA MILITARUM, MILITARUM AUXILLA** |
|------------------|--------------------------------------------------|
| **KEYWORDS** | **INFANTRY, RATLINGS** |

## NORK DEDDOG

**POWER 4**

| NAME | M | WS | BS | S | T | W | A | Ld | Sv |
|------|---|----|----|---|---|---|---|----|----|
| Nork Deddog | 6" | 3+ | 4+ | 5 | 5 | 6 | 4 | 8 | 4+ |

Nork Deddog is a single model armed with a ripper gun, a huge knife and frag bombs. He can also deliver a thunderous headbutt in melee combat. Only one of this model may be included in your army.

| WEAPON | RANGE | TYPE | S | AP | D | ABILITIES |
|--------|-------|------|---|----|----|-----------|
| Ripper gun | 12" | Assault 3 | 5 | 0 | 1 | - |
| Huge knife | Melee | Melee | User | -1 | 2 | - |
| Thunderous headbutt | Melee | Melee | +3 | -2 | D3 | Nork can only make a single thunderous headbutt attack each time he fights. |
| Frag bomb | 6" | Grenade D6 | 4 | 0 | 1 | - |

| ABILITIES | | |
|-----------|--|--|
| | **Avalanche of Muscle:** On a turn in which he makes a successful charge, you can make one additional attack in the Fight phase with Nork Deddog the first time he fights. | **Loyal to the End:** Roll a D6 each time a friendly **ASTRA MILITARUM CHARACTER** loses a wound whilst he is within 3" of Nork Deddog; on a 2+ the Astra Militarum Character does not lose a wound but Nork Deddog suffers a mortal wound. |
| | **Heroic Sacrifice:** If Nork Deddog is slain in the Fight phase, you can immediately fight with him before removing his model as a casualty, even if he has already been chosen to fight during that phase. | |

| FACTION KEYWORDS | **IMPERIUM, ASTRA MILITARUM, MILITARUM AUXILLA** |
|------------------|--------------------------------------------------|
| **KEYWORDS** | **CHARACTER, INFANTRY, OGRYN, NORK DEDDOG** |

# AERONAUTICA IMPERIALIS

**Fighting in support of the Astra Militarum's endless columns of infantry and smoke-belching vehicles, the pilots of the Aeronautica Imperialis are a vital part of the Imperial war machine. Without them, the Imperial Guard would not have a hope of controlling the skies above; with them, they rule the heavens as well as the earth.**

The Imperial Navy is an institution of galaxy-spanning size, so immense that none can possibly comprehend the vastness of its armadas or the sector-crushing power it can bring to bear. Though its most iconic warships are those that ply the sea of stars, navigating realspace and the dangers of the warp in order to bring war to the enemies of the Imperium, the more conventional aircraft of the Aeronautica Imperialis are equally valuable to the Imperial war effort. The atmospheric craft deployed by the Navy can help the Astra Militarum conquer a world without utterly annihilating it, providing pinpoint firepower from above to support the advance of troops on the ground.

Valkyries are primarily transport craft, though they are of impressive pedigree. Massive of hull and thick of armour plates, the Valkyrie can sustain a tremendous amount of punishment as it soars through the flak-churned skies, shrugging off the explosive rounds of anti-aircraft artillery. This craft has wing-mounted jet thrusters that allow it to perform vertical take-off and landing manoeuvres – it is adept at navigating in close confines and can hover on the spot. The Valkyrie carries a full squad of Astra Militarum troops, usually veterans or other high-value personnel. When the target is in sight, the passengers will grav-chute, rappel or otherwise bail out of the aircraft as it bellies in low.

The Militarum Tempestus make great use of Valkyrie Squadrons to launch their assaults from above, as their air cavalry tactics make them exceptional shock troops. Debarking from their aircraft mid-flight, they descend on grav-chutes, the searing beams of their hot-shot lasguns stabbing down from the inky skies to slay priority targets before the enemy even realises it is under attack.

Some regiments – the Harakoni Warhawks and Elysian Drop Troops foremost amongst them – maintain such close ties with the Aeronautica Imperialis they go to war entirely airborne. Few are the enemies that can withstand the air-to-ground assaults of these drop specialists; the skies are criss-crossed with laser fire as the pilots and gunners of their myriad aircraft squadrons take their toll, and moments later, squads of drop troops descend with guns blazing, filling the skies with a sudden hailstorm of death when they had been clear and untroubled mere moments before.

The Valkyrie can be fitted with a versatile load-out of weaponry, from multi-lasers and lascannons to side-mounted heavy bolters and devastating hellstrike missiles, making it suitable for a wide variety of battlefield roles. After dropping off its passengers, a squadron of Valkyries can remain low to the ground, weaving and jinking around tall mountains, sky-scraping buildings and any other perilous obstacle that might bar its path as it provides covering fire for its disembarked troops; or it can climb high above the battlefield, letting loose its guns to clear the skies of enemy aircraft. A squadron will never stray far from its ground troops, the pilots ever ready to return to the thick of battle to rapidly extract their squad from the hot zone.

Not all the Aeronautica Imperialis assets used by the Imperial Guard are airborne. The most privileged of command squads will be assigned an Officer of the Fleet, a proven veteran of the Imperial Navy. Though lightly armed and armoured, this advisor often holds the key to victory in the air and on the ground. He has the authority to call down an air strike, formations of heavy bombers unleashing a precise, devastating bombardment to obliterate the designated target. He can also provide strafing coordinates to the flight wings under his command, ensuring every shot will meet its mark.

## OFFICER OF THE FLEET

**2** POWER

| NAME | M | WS | BS | S | T | W | A | Ld | Sv |
|---|---|---|---|---|---|---|---|---|---|
| Officer of the Fleet | 6" | 4+ | 3+ | 3 | 3 | 3 | 2 | 6 | 5+ |

An Officer of the Fleet is a single model armed with a laspistol.

| WEAPON | RANGE | TYPE | S | AP | D | ABILITIES |
|---|---|---|---|---|---|---|
| Laspistol | 12" | Pistol 1 | 3 | 0 | 1 | - |

| ABILITIES | |
|---|---|
| | **Air Raid Requested:** Once per battle, in your Shooting phase, you can pick an enemy unit, other than a **CHARACTER**, which is visible to this model anywhere on the battlefield, and then roll a D6. On a roll of 1-3, nothing happens. On a roll of 4-5 the target unit suffers D3 mortal wounds. On a roll of 6, the target unit suffers 3 mortal wounds. You may only call in one air raid per turn, regardless of the number of Officers of the Fleet.

**Strafing Coordinates:** At the start of the Shooting phase, pick an enemy unit, other than one which can **FLY**, within 18" of this model. For the duration of the phase, you can re-roll hit rolls of 1 for any friendly **AERONAUTICA IMPERIALIS** units that target the unit you picked. |

| FACTION KEYWORDS | **IMPERIUM, ASTRA MILITARUM, AERONAUTICA IMPERIALIS** |
|---|---|
| KEYWORDS | **CHARACTER, INFANTRY, OFFICER OF THE FLEET** |

Roaring into battle at supersonic speed, Valkyries unleash a devastating salvo before deploying their human cargo into the fray.

# VALKYRIES

## DAMAGE
Some of this model's characteristics change as it suffers damage, as shown below:

| REMAINING W | M | BS |
|---|---|---|
| 8-14+ | 20-45" | 4+ |
| 4-7 | 20-30" | 5+ |
| 1-3 | 20" | 6+ |

| NAME | M | WS | BS | S | T | W | A | Ld | Sv |
|---|---|---|---|---|---|---|---|---|---|
| Valkyrie | * | 6+ | * | 7 | 7 | 14 | 3 | 7 | 3+ |

This unit contains 1 Valkyrie. It can include 1 additional Valkyrie (**Power Rating +10**) or 2 additional Valkyries (**Power Rating +20**). Each model is equipped with a multi-laser and hellstrike missiles.

| WEAPON | RANGE | TYPE | S | AP | D | ABILITIES |
|---|---|---|---|---|---|---|
| Heavy bolter | 36" | Heavy 3 | 5 | -1 | 1 | - |
| Hellstrike missiles | 72" | Heavy 1 | 8 | -2 | D6 | Roll two dice when inflicting damage with this weapon and discard the lowest result. |
| Lascannon | 48" | Heavy 1 | 9 | -3 | D6 | - |
| Multi-laser | 36" | Heavy 3 | 6 | 0 | 1 | - |
| Multiple rocket pod | 36" | Heavy D6 | 5 | -1 | 1 | - |

**WARGEAR OPTIONS**
- Any model may replace its multi-laser with a lascannon.
- Any model may replace its hellstrike missiles with two multiple rocket pods.
- Any model may take two heavy bolters.

**ABILITIES**

**Vehicle Squadron:** The first time this unit is set up, all models in this unit must be placed within 6" of each other. From that point onwards, each operates independently and is treated as a separate unit for all rules purposes.

**Grav-chute Insertion:** Models may disembark from this vehicle at any point during its move, but if the Valkyrie moves more than 20", you must roll a D6 for each model disembarking. On a 1, that model is slain. Models that disembark in this manner must be set up more than 9" from any enemy models.

**Hover Jet:** Before this model moves in your Movement phase, you can declare it will hover. Its Move characteristic becomes 20" until the end of the phase, and it loses the Airborne, Hard to Hit and Supersonic abilities until the beginning of your next Movement phase.

**Airborne:** This model cannot charge, can only be charged by units that can **FLY**, and can only attack or be attacked in the Fight phase by units that can **FLY**.

**Hard to Hit:** Your opponent must subtract 1 from hit rolls for attacks that target this model in the Shooting phase.

**Supersonic:** Each time this model moves, first pivot it on the spot up to 90° (this does not contribute to how far the model moves), and then move the model straight forwards. Note that it cannot pivot again after the initial pivot. When this model Advances, increase its Move characteristic by 20" until the end of the phase – do not roll a dice.

**Crash and Burn:** If this model is reduced to 0 wounds, roll a D6 before removing it from the battlefield and before any embarked models disembark. On a 6 it crashes in a fiery explosion and each unit within 6" suffers D3 mortal wounds.

**TRANSPORT** | This model can transport 12 **ASTRA MILITARUM INFANTRY** models. Each Heavy Weapons Team or Veteran Heavy Weapons Team takes the space of two other models and each **OGRYN** takes the space of three other models.

**FACTION KEYWORDS** | IMPERIUM, ASTRA MILITARUM, AERONAUTICA IMPERIALIS

**KEYWORDS** | VEHICLE, TRANSPORT, FLY, VALKYRIES

# ADEPTUS MECHANICUS

**The Adeptus Mechanicus is an ancient and powerful institution that traces its roots to the very founding of the Imperium. Acquisitive and ambitious, the Tech-Priests of Mars are obsessed with the idea that knowledge is power – though whether they put that knowledge to good use is another matter.**

The priesthood of the Adeptus Mechanicus acknowledges the Emperor as Master of Mankind, but does not recognise the authority of the official Imperial Cult or the Ecclesiarchy. Instead, the Adeptus Mechanicus follows its own dark and mysterious strictures. According to the Cult Mechanicus, knowledge is the supreme expression of divinity, and all creatures and artefacts that embody knowledge are holy because of it. The Emperor is the ultimate object of worship because he comprehends so much; he is the Omnissiah, the earthly manifestation of the Machine God and harbinger of the Motive Force that drives the physical realm. Machines which preserve knowledge from ancient times are also considered holy, and blessed robots are seen as no less divine than saints of flesh and blood. A man's worth is only the sum of his knowledge – his body is simply an organic machine capable of preserving intellect.

The Cult Mechanicus has a virtual monopoly on the Imperium's technology. Its own tenets and beliefs permeate through their obsessively maintained rituals into the common superstition of Imperial citizens. The Tech-Priests rule over a thousand forge worlds and more, each a hub of military and industrial power that anchors the worlds around it and provides them with the tools of war they need to survive in a hostile galaxy.

Each forge world owned by the Adeptus Mechanicus is in part a vast factory. As well as constructing endless streams of tanks, guns and ammunition, they create marvels of military science such as super-heavy tanks, Imperial Knights, and even the colossal land-battleships known as Titans, worshipped as god-machines by the faithful flock. A forge world is far more than a place of creation, however, it is also a treasure trove of carefully accumulated knowledge. Each world's immense libraries and databanks of information are highly eclectic and disorganised – one is as likely to find a crystal storage device containing information of bioengineering as a scroll covered with designs for steam locomotives. The Tech-Priests of each forge world jealously

guard their independence, and it is a rash or brave soul that dares interfere with their interests. Such incautious men usually disappear without trace, and are rarely mourned, for the Cult Mechanicus is vital to the continued survival of the Imperium.

The Tech-Priests of the Adeptus Mechanicus form a holy order that has a dizzying and byzantine logic. Each branch forms a separate hierarchy that worships the Machine God and the intimate knowledge of technology he holds. The lowest ranks of Tech-Priest have mainly maintenance and construction duties, but as Tech-Adepts progress and acquire greater knowledge, they are relieved from mundane duties and given free rein to study the most profound of mysteries and techniques. Their hard-won gains are rarely shared for the betterment of Humanity, but instead jealously hoarded and pored over with the avarice of a miser secretly counting his gold. By maintaining its stranglehold on the technology of the Imperium, the Adeptus Mechanicus keeps its position of knowledge and authority throughout the millennia. A Tech-Priest who feels this is threatened will go to any lengths to protect his power, including murder, extortion, sabotage, and the declaration of outright war.

## THE QUEST FOR KNOWLEDGE

The Adeptus Mechanicus is driven by its compulsion to amass all knowledge and technology and return it to their holdings, there to be studied and archived in heavily protected data-vaults. To achieve this imperative, Tech-Priests explore the galaxy, prepared to wage war with any force that prevents them from obtaining some valuable device or schematic. Their ultimate quest is the search for Standard Template Constructs. Otherwise known as STCs, these repositories of knowledge were created during the high point of Mankind's scientific achievements, devised to facilitate the conquest of the stars. They allow the user to manufacture certain key machineries from a variety of raw materials, each design so robust that it can be put to good use in the vast majority of environments.

From the STCs of ages past come the lasgun and the bolter, the Rhino and the Chimera, the Bastion and the Fortress of Redemption. Though the vast majority of these sacred blueprints have been lost over the countless years since their inception, they remain scattered across the stars – should the Cult Mechanicus uncover a hitherto uncatalogued portion of a core STC, it is returned to Mars amidst great rejoicing. The recovery of a complete STC system would be a turning point for Humanity, the holy grail of the Cult Mechanicus that would see it rise to utmost prominence and rule the stars as it has always intended. So it is that the Adeptus Mechanicus is always at war on several fronts at once, both to defend the knowledge it has already torn from the galaxy, and prosecuting its wars of avarice with every weapon and tactic it can muster.

# ADEPTUS MECHANICUS ARMY LIST

This section contains all of the datasheets that you will need in order to fight battles with your Adeptus Mechanicus miniatures. Each datasheet includes the characteristics profiles of the unit it describes, as well as any wargear and abilities it may have. Some rules are common to several units, and are described on these pages and referenced on the datasheets.

## KEYWORDS

Throughout this section you will come across a keyword that is within angular brackets, specifically <FORGE WORLD>. This is shorthand for a keyword of your own choosing, as described below.

## <FORGE WORLD>

The forces of the Adeptus Mechanicus all belong to a forge world. When you include an Adeptus Mechanicus unit in your army, you must nominate which forge world that unit is from. There are many different forge worlds to choose from; you can use any of the forge worlds described in our books, or make up your own forge world if you prefer. You then simply replace the <FORGE WORLD> keyword in every instance on that unit's datasheet with the name of your chosen forge world.

For example, if you were to include a Tech-Priest Dominus in your army, and you decided they were from Mars, then their <FORGE WORLD> keyword is changed to MARS, and their 'Lord of the Machine Cult' ability would say 'You can re-roll hit rolls of 1 in the Shooting phase for friendly MARS units within 6".'

## ABILITIES

The following ability is common to several Adeptus Mechanicus units:

### CANTICLES OF THE OMNISSIAH

All units with this ability gain a bonus during the battle depending on the Canticle of the Omnissiah currently being canted.

At the start of each battle round, pick which Canticle of the Omnissiah from the table below is in effect for the duration of the battle round. The same Canticle may not be picked twice during the same battle.

Alternatively, you can randomly determine which Canticle of the Omnissiah is in effect by rolling a D6 and consulting the table below. Note that if you randomly determine a Canticle, it takes effect even if the same Canticle has been in effect earlier in the battle.

If you have a Battle-forged army, units only receive the bonus if every model in their Detachment has this ability.

## WARGEAR

Many of the units you will find on the following pages reference one or more of the wargear lists below. When this is the case, the unit may take any item from the appropriate list. The profiles for the items in these lists can be found in the appendix (pg 150-151).

### SPECIAL WEAPONS
- Arc rifle
- Plasma caliver
- Transuranic arquebus

### PISTOL WEAPONS
- Arc pistol
- Phosphor blast pistol
- Radium pistol

### MELEE WEAPONS
- Arc maul
- Power sword
- Taser goad

## CANTICLES OF THE OMNISSIAH TABLE

| D6 | CANTICLE |
|---|---|
| 1 | **Incantation of the Iron Soul** <br> You can re-roll failed Morale tests for affected units. |
| 2 | **Litany of the Electromancer** <br> Roll a D6 for each enemy unit that is within 1" of any affected units; on a roll of 6, the unit being rolled for suffers D3 mortal wounds. |
| 3 | **Chant of the Remorseless Fist** <br> You can re-roll any failed hit rolls of 1 for affected units in the Fight phase. |
| 4 | **Shroudpsalm** <br> Affected units gain the bonus to their armour saving throws as if they were in cover. Units already in cover are unaffected. |
| 5 | **Invocation of Machine Might** <br> Affected units have +1 Strength. |
| 6 | **Benediction of the Omnissiah** <br> You can re-roll failed hit rolls of 1 for affected units in the Shooting phase. |

# CULT MECHANICUS

**The cybernetic convocations of the Adeptus Mechanicus are both magnificent and terrible. Every warrior and priest is extensively modified with bionics and augmetics that they see as holy artefacts powered by the essence of the Machine God. Though disparate of form, they share a unifying purpose – the acquisition of power and knowledge unbound.**

The Cult Mechanicus is the inner core of the forge world empire. Together they form an endless procession of crusaders as lethal as they are bizarre, each priest and magos so cybernetically enhanced they have put simple humanity long behind them. Theirs is an unquenchable thirst for knowledge; they will not be content until they have amassed every last screed of information there is to know about every life form, phenomenon and location in the galaxy. The fact this will likely result in the demise or potential destruction of that which they study is an entirely secondary concern – for the Cult Mechanicus, knowledge is an end unto itself.

Only when the greatest of treasures have been located does the Cult Mechanicus bring its full might to bear. Some conquests are so important that they cannot be left solely to the Skitarii legions, and are attended to in person by the Tech-Priests Dominus. These many-limbed lords of the forge worlds are armed with the finest of man-portable weapons, as are their cybernetic retinues. Other members of the Machine God's clergy march alongside these scavenger kings. Electro-Priests chant and crackle with potential energy as they run towards the foe. The Fulgurites are eager to steal the life energy from their victims with their electroleech staves; conversely, the Corpuscarii are just as intent upon unleashing it with their electrostatic gauntlets so that the Motive Force might flow at maximum voltage through the unbelievers.

The Datasmiths of the Legio Cybernetica are another breed of Tech-Priest entirely. It is they who tend to the mighty hosts of automata known as Kastelan Robot Maniples. Each metallic golem is a towering, iron-bodied hulk whose guns spit phosphorescent death and whose mighty limbs can crush an enemy warrior's bones with a single pulverising blow. By switching out the bio-slivers known as doctrina wafers from their charges' bodies, the Datasmiths can switch their robots from walking ballistics platforms to rampaging monsters that bellow praise to the Machine God in a static-laced monotone. Last but most numerous amongst the military assets that form the Tech-Priests' honour guards are Kataphron battle servitors, hulking ex-criminals whose punishment was to be reborn as half-human, half-robotic gun platforms that trundle to war on broad track units. Much as their Skitarii brethren can be controlled from afar, the constructs and war servitors of the Cult Mechanicus can be driven to truly superhuman feats of heroism by chansons, hymns and canticles laced with binary imperatives. When knowledge itself is at stake, the Tech-Priests of Mars will use every tool at their disposal and willingly expend every iota of power they have marshalled in order to glean the vital information they crave – if that causes the death of entire populations in the process, then so be it.

## MARS

The planet Mars has changed enormously since Man first set foot upon its barren and arid surface. In the early days of Mankind's expansion into the stars it was terraformed extensively, given life-supporting atmosphere, oceans made from melted Terran ice and fertile soil where deserts had formerly swathed the lands. However, the true bounty of the planet was mineral, and it was not long before that world was heavily industrialised. It was Mars that became the first human hive world, a centre for scientific endeavours and manufactorums of all kinds. As its name became synonymous with technological advancement, it became the hub for further space exploration – Mars still bears extensive docks around its circumference that harbour hundreds of thousands of ships each year. Yet the rampant industry of the planet has taken a horrible toll over the millennia. Ravaged by extensive pollution, Mars has become an irradiated wasteland of terracotta sands and howling electrical storms. A journey through its internal travel tubes now takes a person from the extremes of new construction to ancient industrial wastes, from shining ziggurats to chasms and deserts haunted by decommissioned servitors and stalker-machines that flit like hungry ghosts through the twilight.

The Adeptus Mechanicus controls the entire governmental, industrial and religious affairs of Mars. In its broadest terms, the population is divided into two parts. The greater mass of the Martian populace are worker-slaves called Servitors. Servitors are not really fully human, but half-machine creatures whose minds have been partially programmed to perform specific duties. The remainder of the populace are the faithful Skitarii, and the strange hierarchy of the Tech-Priests that control them. For all its hostility and corruption as a domain of men, Mars is still an incredibly powerful society, holding its position as the lynchpin of the Imperium's industrial powerbase. It is the father of all forge worlds, the red heart of an empire within an empire, and its influence will span the stars forever.

'Evaluation report ceta nine-gamma, decimus thirty-three. Subtle alterations to the Kastelans' assault protocols produced unsatisfactory results, including an anomalous tendency for prolonged mutilation at the expense of efficiency. I shall continue my experimentation.'

- Magos Xygrus Octelans

## BELISARIUS CAWL

**13** POWER

| NAME | M | WS | BS | S | T | W | A | Ld | Sv |
|---|---|---|---|---|---|---|---|---|---|
| Belisarius Cawl | 6" | 2+ | 2+ | 5 | 6 | 8 | 4 | 9 | 2+ |

Belisarius Cawl is a single model armed with an arc scourge, an Omnissian axe, a solar atomiser and a mechadendrite hive. Only one of this model may be included in your army.

| WEAPON | RANGE | TYPE | S | AP | D | ABILITIES |
|---|---|---|---|---|---|---|
| Solar atomiser | 12" | Assault D3 | 10 | -4 | D3 | If the target is within half range of this weapon, it has a Damage of D6. |
| Arc scourge | Melee | Melee | x2 | -1 | 1 | When attacking a **VEHICLE**, this weapon has a Damage of D3. |
| Mechadendrite hive | Melee | Melee | User | 0 | 1 | Each time Belisarius Cawl fights, he can make 2D6 additional attacks with this weapon. |
| Omnissian axe | Melee | Melee | +1 | -2 | 2 | - |

| ABILITIES | |
|---|---|
| **Canticles of the Omnissiah** (pg 63)<br><br>**Archmagos:** Whilst Belisarius Cawl is on the battlefield, you can add or subtract 1 when rolling on the Canticles of the Omnissiah table (pg 63).<br><br>**Refractor Field:** Belisarius Cawl has a 5+ invulnerable save.<br><br>**Artificer Self-repair Mechanisms:** At the beginning of each of your turns, Belisarius Cawl heals D3 wounds. | **Master of Machines:** At the end of your Movement phase Belisarius Cawl can repair a single friendly **ADEPTUS MECHANICUS** model within 3" (but not himself). That model regains D3 lost wounds. A model may not be the target of the Master of Machines ability more than once per turn, regardless of the source.<br><br>**Lord of Mars:** You can re-roll any hit rolls in the Shooting phase for friendly **MARS** units within 6". |

| FACTION KEYWORDS | **IMPERIUM, ADEPTUS MECHANICUS, CULT MECHANICUS, MARS** |
|---|---|
| KEYWORDS | **CHARACTER, INFANTRY, TECH-PRIEST, BELISARIUS CAWL** |

Archmagos Belisarius Cawl leads the armies of Mars to war, in search of lost knowledge and forgotten secrets.

## TECH-PRIEST DOMINUS

**7 POWER**

| NAME | M | WS | BS | S | T | W | A | Ld | Sv |
|------|---|----|----|---|---|---|---|----|----|
| Tech-Priest Dominus | 6" | 3+ | 2+ | 4 | 4 | 5 | 3 | 8 | 2+ |

A Tech-Priest Dominus is a single model armed with an Omnissian axe, a volkite blaster and a macrostubber.

| WEAPON | RANGE | TYPE | S | AP | D | ABILITIES |
|--------|-------|------|---|----|----|-----------|
| Eradication ray | 24" | Heavy D3 | 6 | -2 | 1 | Attacks from this weapon that target enemies at 8" or less are resolved with an AP of -4 and a Damage of D3. |
| Macrostubber | 12" | Pistol 5 | 4 | 0 | 1 | - |
| Volkite blaster | 24" | Heavy 3 | 6 | 0 | 1 | Each time you make a wound roll of 6+ for this weapon, the target suffers a mortal wound in addition to any other damage. |
| Omnissian axe | Melee | Melee | +1 | -2 | 2 | - |
| Phosphor serpenta | 18" | Assault 1 | 5 | -1 | 1 | Units attacked by this weapon do not gain any bonus to their saving throws for being in cover. |

| WARGEAR OPTIONS | • This model may replace its volkite blaster with an eradication ray.<br>• This model may replace its macrostubber with a phosphor serpenta. |
|-----------------|---|

**ABILITIES**

Canticles of the Omnissiah (pg 63)

Refractor Field: This model has a 5+ invulnerable save.

Master of Machines: At the end of your Movement phase this model can repair a single friendly ADEPTUS MECHANICUS model within 3" (but not itself). That model regains D3 lost wounds. A model may not be the target of the Master of Machines ability more than once per turn, regardless of the source.

Masterwork Bionics: At the beginning of each of your turns, remove up to D3 wounds that this model has suffered earlier in the battle.

Lord of the Machine Cult: You can re-roll hit rolls of 1 in the Shooting phase for friendly <FORGE WORLD> units within 6".

| FACTION KEYWORDS | IMPERIUM, ADEPTUS MECHANICUS, CULT MECHANICUS, <FORGE WORLD> |
|------------------|---|
| KEYWORDS | CHARACTER, INFANTRY, TECH-PRIEST, DOMINUS |

## TECH-PRIEST ENGINSEER

**3 POWER**

| NAME | M | WS | BS | S | T | W | A | Ld | Sv |
|------|---|----|----|---|---|---|---|----|----|
| Tech-Priest Enginseer | 6" | 4+ | 4+ | 4 | 4 | 4 | 2 | 8 | 3+ |

A Tech-Priest Enginseer is a single model armed with an Omnissian axe, a laspistol and a servo-arm.

| WEAPON | RANGE | TYPE | S | AP | D | ABILITIES |
|--------|-------|------|---|----|----|-----------|
| Laspistol | 12" | Pistol 1 | 3 | 0 | 1 | - |
| Omnissian axe | Melee | Melee | +1 | -2 | 2 | - |
| Servo-arm | Melee | Melee | x2 | -2 | 3 | Each servo-arm can only be used to make one attack each time this model fights. When a model attacks with this weapon, you must subtract 1 from the hit roll. |

**ABILITIES**

Canticles of the Omnissiah (pg 63)

Bionics: This model has a 6+ invulnerable save.

Master of Machines: At the end of your Movement phase this model can repair a single friendly <FORGE WORLD> or ASTRA MILITARUM VEHICLE within 3". That model regains D3 lost wounds. A model may not be the target of the Master of Machines ability more than once per turn, regardless of the source.

| FACTION KEYWORDS | IMPERIUM, ASTRA MILITARUM, ADEPTUS MECHANICUS, CULT MECHANICUS, <FORGE WORLD> |
|------------------|---|
| KEYWORDS | CHARACTER, INFANTRY, TECH-PRIEST, ENGINSEER |

# ⏵ ⑨ KATAPHRON BREACHERS

| NAME | M | WS | BS | S | T | W | A | Ld | Sv |
|------|---|----|----|---|---|---|---|----|----|
| Kataphron Breacher | 5" | 4+ | 4+ | 5 | 5 | 3 | 2 | 7 | 3+ |

This unit contains 3 Kataphron Breachers. It may contain up to 3 additional Kataphron Breachers (**Power Rating +9**), up to 6 additional Kataphron Breachers (**Power Rating +18**) or up to 9 additional Kataphron Breachers (**Power Rating +27**). Each Kataphron Breacher is armed with a heavy arc rifle and an arc claw.

| WEAPON | RANGE | TYPE | S | AP | D | ABILITIES |
|--------|-------|------|---|----|----|-----------|
| Heavy arc rifle | 36" | Heavy 2 | 6 | -2 | D3 | When attacking a **Vehicle**, this weapon has a Damage of D6. |
| Torsion cannon | 24" | Heavy 1 | 8 | -4 | D6 | - |
| Arc claw | Melee | Melee | +1 | -1 | 1 | When attacking a **Vehicle**, this weapon has a Damage of D3. |
| Hydraulic claw | Melee | Melee | x2 | -1 | D3 | When attacking with this weapon, you must subtract 1 from the hit roll. |

| WARGEAR OPTIONS | • Any model may replace its heavy arc rifle with a torsion cannon.<br>• Any model may replace its arc claw with a hydraulic claw. |
|-----------------|---|
| ABILITIES | **Canticles of the Omnissiah** (pg 63)<br><br>**Bionics:** All models in this unit have a 6+ invulnerable save.<br><br>**Heavy Battle Servitor:** Models in this unit can only Advance D3", but do not suffer the penalty for firing a Heavy weapon after moving. |
| FACTION KEYWORDS | **Imperium, Adeptus Mechanicus, Cult Mechanicus, <Forge World>** |
| KEYWORDS | **Infantry, Kataphron Breachers** |

# ⏵ ⑩ KATAPHRON DESTROYERS

| NAME | M | WS | BS | S | T | W | A | Ld | Sv |
|------|---|----|----|---|---|---|---|----|----|
| Kataphron Destroyer | 5" | 4+ | 4+ | 5 | 5 | 3 | 1 | 7 | 4+ |

This unit contains 3 Kataphron Destroyers. It may contain up to 3 additional Kataphron Destroyers (**Power Rating +10**), up to 6 additional Kataphron Destroyers (**Power Rating +20**) or up to 9 additional Kataphron Destroyers (**Power Rating +30**). Each Kataphron Destroyer is armed with a plasma culverin and a phosphor blaster.

| WEAPON | RANGE | TYPE | S | AP | D | ABILITIES |
|--------|-------|------|---|----|----|-----------|
| Cognis flamer | 8" | Assault D6 | 4 | 0 | 1 | This weapon automatically hits its target. In addition, when firing Overwatch with this weapon, roll two dice when determining how many attacks it makes and discard the lowest result. |
| Heavy grav-cannon | 30" | Heavy 5 | 5 | -3 | 1 | If the target has a Save characteristic of 3+ or better, this weapon has a Damage characteristic of D3. |
| Phosphor blaster | 24" | Rapid Fire 1 | 5 | -1 | 1 | Units attacked by this weapon do not gain any bonus to their saving throws for being in cover. |
| Plasma culverin | When attacking with this weapon, choose one of the profiles below. | | | | | |
| - Standard | 36" | Heavy D6 | 7 | -3 | 1 | - |
| - Supercharge | 36" | Heavy D6 | 8 | -3 | 2 | On a hit roll of 1, the bearer is slain after all of this weapon's shots have been resolved. |

| WARGEAR OPTIONS | • Any model may replace its plasma culverin with a heavy grav-cannon.<br>• Any model may replace its phosphor blaster with a cognis flamer. |
|-----------------|---|
| ABILITIES | **Canticles of the Omnissiah** (pg 63)<br><br>**Bionics:** All models in this unit have a 6+ invulnerable save.<br><br>**Heavy Battle Servitor:** Models in this unit can only Advance D3", but do not suffer the penalty for firing a Heavy weapon after moving. |
| FACTION KEYWORDS | **Imperium, Adeptus Mechanicus, Cult Mechanicus, <Forge World>** |
| KEYWORDS | **Infantry, Kataphron Destroyers** |

# FULGURITE ELECTRO-PRIESTS

**4** POWER

| NAME | M | WS | BS | S | T | W | A | Ld | Sv |
|---|---|---|---|---|---|---|---|---|---|
| Fulgurite Electro-Priest | 6" | 3+ | 4+ | 3 | 3 | 1 | 2 | 8 | 6+ |

This unit contains 5 Fulgurite Electro-Priests. It can include up to 5 additional Fulgurite Electro-Priests (**Power Rating +4**), up to 10 additional Fulgurite Electro-Priests (**Power Rating +8**) or up to 15 additional Fulgurite Electro-Priests (**Power Rating +12**). Each Fulgurite Electro-Priest is armed with an electroleech stave.

| WEAPON | RANGE | TYPE | S | AP | D | ABILITIES |
|---|---|---|---|---|---|---|
| Electroleech stave | Melee | Melee | +2 | -2 | D3 | Each time you make a wound roll of 6+ with this weapon, the target suffers D3 mortal wounds instead of the normal damage. |

| ABILITIES | |
|---|---|
| | **Canticles of the Omnissiah** (pg 63) |
| | **Voltagheist Field:** All models in this unit have a 5+ invulnerable save. When this unit completes a charge move, pick one of the target units you charged and roll a D6 for each model in the charging unit. Any rolls of 6 inflict a mortal wound on the unit you picked. |
| | **Siphoned Vigour:** If this unit wipes out an enemy unit in the Fight phase, their invulnerable save is increased to 3+ for the rest of the battle. |
| | **Fanatical Devotion:** Each time a model in this unit loses a wound, roll a D6; on a roll of 5 or 6, the model does not lose that wound. |

| FACTION KEYWORDS | IMPERIUM, ADEPTUS MECHANICUS, CULT MECHANICUS, <FORGE WORLD> |
|---|---|
| KEYWORDS | INFANTRY, ELECTRO-PRIESTS, FULGURITE |

# CORPUSCARII ELECTRO-PRIESTS

**3** POWER

| NAME | M | WS | BS | S | T | W | A | Ld | Sv |
|---|---|---|---|---|---|---|---|---|---|
| Corpuscarii Electro-Priest | 6" | 4+ | 3+ | 3 | 3 | 1 | 2 | 8 | 6+ |

This unit contains 5 Corpuscarii Electro-Priests. It can include up to 5 additional Corpuscarii Electro-Priests (**Power Rating +3**), up to 10 additional Corpuscarii Electro-Priests (**Power Rating +6**) or up to 15 additional Corpuscarii Electro-Priests (**Power Rating +9**). Each Corpuscarii Electro-Priest is armed with electrostatic gauntlets.

| WEAPON | RANGE | TYPE | S | AP | D | ABILITIES |
|---|---|---|---|---|---|---|
| Electrostatic gauntlets (shooting) | 12" | Assault 3 | 5 | 0 | 1 | Each hit roll of 6+ with this weapon causes 3 hits rather than 1. |
| Electrostatic gauntlets (melee) | Melee | Melee | 5 | 0 | 1 | |

| ABILITIES | |
|---|---|
| | **Canticles of the Omnissiah** (pg 63) |
| | **Voltagheist Field:** All models in this unit have a 5+ invulnerable save. When this unit completes a charge move, pick one of the target units you charged and roll a D6 for each model in the charging unit. Any rolls of 6 inflict a mortal wound on the unit you picked. |
| | **Fanatical Devotion:** Each time a model in this unit loses a wound, roll a D6; on a roll of 5 or 6, the model does not lose that wound. |

| FACTION KEYWORDS | IMPERIUM, ADEPTUS MECHANICUS, CULT MECHANICUS, <FORGE WORLD> |
|---|---|
| KEYWORDS | INFANTRY, ELECTRO-PRIESTS, CORPUSCARII |

## KASTELAN ROBOTS

**12 POWER**

| NAME | M | WS | BS | S | T | W | A | Ld | Sv |
|------|---|----|----|----|---|---|---|----|----|
| Kastelan Robot | 8" | 4+ | 4+ | 6 | 7 | 6 | 3 | 10 | 3+ |

This unit contains 2 Kastelan Robots. It can include up to 2 additional Kastelan Robots (**Power Rating +12**) or up to 4 additional Kastelan Robots (**Power Rating +24**). Each Kastelan Robot is armed with Kastelan fists and an incendine combustor.

| WEAPON | RANGE | TYPE | S | AP | D | ABILITIES |
|--------|-------|------|---|----|----|-----------|
| Heavy phosphor blaster | 36" | Heavy 3 | 6 | -2 | 1 | Units attacked by this weapon do not gain any bonus to their saving throws for being in cover. |
| Incendine combustor | 12" | Heavy D6 | 5 | -1 | 1 | This weapon automatically hits its target. |
| Kastelan fists | Melee | Melee | +4 | -3 | 3 | - |

| WARGEAR OPTIONS | |
|---|---|
| | • Any model may replace its incendine combustor with a heavy phosphor blaster. |
| | • Any model may replace its Kastelan fists with two heavy phosphor blasters. |

| ABILITIES | |
|---|---|
| | **Canticles of the Omnissiah** (pg 63) |
| | **Repulsor Grid:** All models in this unit have a 5+ invulnerable save against shooting attacks. In addition, each time you roll a 6+ for a repulsor grid's invulnerable saving throw, the unit that made that attack suffers a mortal wound. |
| | **Battle Protocols:** When this unit is set up, the Aegis Protocol (see below) is in effect. You can attempt to change the unit's battle protocol at the start of each of your Movement phases if there is a friendly **<Forge World>** Cybernetica Datasmith within 6". To do so, roll a D6; on a 2+ the attempt is successful and you can select any one of the three battle protocols to take effect from the start of the next battle round. Otherwise, the attempt fails and the unit's current protocol remains in effect. |
| | • **Aegis Protocol:** Whilst this battle protocol is in effect, you can add 1 to any armour and invulnerable saving throws you make for models in the unit. |
| | • **Conqueror Protocol:** Whilst this battle protocol is in effect, this unit cannot shoot, but it can fight twice in each Fight phase instead of only once. |
| | • **Protector Protocol:** Whilst this battle protocol is in effect, this unit cannot move or charge, but it can shoot twice in each of your Shooting phases (and shoot twice when firing Overwatch). |
| | **Explodes:** If a model in this unit is reduced to 0 wounds, roll a D6 before removing the model from the battlefield; on a 6 it explodes, and each unit within 3" suffers D3 mortal wounds. |

| FACTION KEYWORDS | **Imperium, Adeptus Mechanicus, Cult Mechanicus, <Forge World>** |
|---|---|
| KEYWORDS | **Vehicle, Kastelan Robots** |

## CYBERNETICA DATASMITH

**3 POWER**

| NAME | M | WS | BS | S | T | W | A | Ld | Sv |
|------|---|----|----|----|---|---|---|----|----|
| Cybernetica Datasmith | 6" | 3+ | 3+ | 4 | 4 | 4 | 2 | 8 | 2+ |

A Cybernetica Datasmith is a single model armed with a power fist and gamma pistol.

| WEAPON | RANGE | TYPE | S | AP | D | ABILITIES |
|--------|-------|------|---|----|----|-----------|
| Gamma pistol | 12" | Pistol 1 | 6 | -3 | 2 | You can re-roll failed wound rolls for this weapon when attacking a **Vehicle**. |
| Power fist | Melee | Melee | x2 | -3 | D3 | When attacking with this weapon, you must subtract 1 from the hit roll. |

| ABILITIES | |
|---|---|
| | **Canticles of the Omnissiah** (pg 63) |
| | **Master of Machines:** At the end of your Movement phase this model can repair a single friendly Kastelan Robot within 3". That model regains D3 lost wounds. A model may not be the target of the Master of Machines ability more than once per turn, regardless of the source. |
| | **Refractor Field:** This model has a 5+ invulnerable save. |

| FACTION KEYWORDS | **Imperium, Adeptus Mechanicus, Cult Mechanicus, <Forge World>** |
|---|---|
| KEYWORDS | **Character, Infantry, Tech-Priest, Cybernetica Datasmith** |

# SERVITORS

| NAME | M | WS | BS | S | T | W | A | Ld | Sv |
|------|---|----|----|---|---|---|---|----|----|
| Servitor | 5" | 5+ | 5+ | 3 | 3 | 1 | 1 | 6 | 4+ |

This unit contains 4 Servitors. Each Servitor is armed with a servo-arm.

| WEAPON | RANGE | TYPE | S | AP | D | ABILITIES |
|--------|-------|------|---|----|----|-----------|
| Heavy bolter | 36" | Heavy 3 | 5 | -1 | 1 | - |
| Multi-melta | 24" | Heavy 1 | 8 | -4 | D6 | If the target is within half range of this weapon, roll two dice when inflicting damage with it and discard the lowest result. |
| Plasma cannon | When attacking with this weapon, choose one of the profiles below. | | | | | |
| - Standard | 36" | Heavy D3 | 7 | -3 | 1 | - |
| - Supercharge | 36" | Heavy D3 | 8 | -3 | 2 | On a hit roll of 1, the bearer is slain after all of this weapon's shots have been resolved. |
| Servo-arm | Melee | Melee | x2 | -2 | 3 | Each servo-arm can only be used to make one attack each time this model fights. When a model attacks with this weapon, you must subtract 1 from the hit roll. |

| WARGEAR OPTIONS | • Up to two models may replace their servo-arm with a heavy bolter, plasma cannon or multi-melta. |
|-----------------|---|
| ABILITIES | **Canticles of the Omnissiah** (pg 63)<br><br>**Mindlock:** Servitors improve both their Weapon Skill and Ballistic Skill to 4+, and their Leadership to 9, whilst they are within 6" of any friendly **TECH-PRIESTS**. |
| FACTION KEYWORDS | **IMPERIUM, ADEPTUS MECHANICUS, <FORGE WORLD>** |
| KEYWORDS | **INFANTRY, SERVITORS** |

Kastelan Robots enact their protector protocols, blasting anyone who approaches their Electro-Priest wards into smoking atoms.

# SKITARII

**Faithful soldiers of the Machine God, the Skitarii are metal-limbed cyborgs utterly devoted to the Adeptus Mechanicus. Armed and armoured with the ingenious wargear of the forge worlds, they stalk the battlefield in tireless formations before unleashing truly esoteric forms of death upon their enemies.**

The Skitarii are the true believers of the Machine Cult. Few amongst the Imperium's warrior brotherhoods have such unstinting faith in their patrons. This the Skitarii express not only in acts of selfless courage and fortitude upon the field of battle, but in their constant search for ways to be closer to the Omnissiah – principally involving surgery that renders them more metal than flesh.

The Skitarii can trace their origins to the first settlers of Mars, when early explorers walked their legs to bloody stumps in order to chart the red planet's endless deserts and hence make it their home. In homage to those early pioneers, the soldiery of each Skitarii regiment have their own lower legs replaced with metallic augmetics to this day. This is far from their only cybernetic modification; the Skitarii make use of a profusion of bionic optical arrays, rebreathers, waste-processing recyclers, intravenous elixirs and even auto-sanctified hearts. Should a soldier suffer a debilitating wound in battle, he will see it as a blessing as much as a curse – should he survive he will likely return to service with a new and interesting bionic that will bring him closer to the Machine God. Flesh is seen as weak and frail by comparison to the mighty gears and pistons of the engine; this philosophy even extends to the Skitarius' brain. Upon induction the devotees of the Skitarii are fitted with neural systems and plugs that allow them to become a part of a far greater machine – that of the army with whom they march to war.

The augmented neural systems of the Skitarii are the modus through which their masters control them on the field of battle. The Tech-Priests of the Cult Mechanicus do not risk life and limb without good reason; the vast majority of them prefer to wage their wars remotely. This is where the Skitarii legions find the most use. Their overseers use the noospheric links in each soldier's brain to download special behavioural programs known as doctrina imperatives – these override the human part of the Skitarius' brain and force him to act with machine-like precision and focus.

A Skitarii army is a force of specialist units, each equipped with esoteric weaponry designed for specific battlefield uses. The stalker-killers of the Sicarian Infiltrators are amongst the most sinister of infantry; these dome-headed stealth troops mow down those debilitated by their neurostatic aura with rapid bursts from their stubcarbines and flechette blasters. Their cousins in destruction are the Sicarian Ruststalkers; organised into swiftly skittering killclades, these mech-assassins strike with transonic blades and chordclaws that can render even heavy battle plate a mere inconvenience.

The greater Skitarii maniples make use of a veritable arsenal of weapons and war machines. The most common of these is the Ironstrider, a bipedal machine that is able to sustain a near perpetual motion. The Ballistarii and

Sydonian Dragoons that fight from atop these strange steeds lope at great speed across the most hostile terrain, blasting the enemy from their high vantage points before closing in to stamp the survivors into the dust. Another iconic war machine of the Skitarii hosts is the Onager Dunecrawler, a four-legged walker tank protected by a powerful emanatus force field. They mount very powerful weapons for their size, from Icarus arrays that spit missiles and solid-shot flak into the skies, to the deadly eradication beamers and neutron lasers that can utterly destroy an enemy war engine with a single blinding blast. When a squadron of Onager Dunecrawlers forms a gun line and opens fire, the sky is lit by the strobing, shattering power they release.

# SKITARII RANGERS

**4** POWER

| NAME | M | WS | BS | S | T | W | A | Ld | Sv |
|------|---|----|----|----|----|----|----|----|-----|
| Skitarii Ranger | 6" | 4+ | 3+ | 3 | 3 | 1 | 1 | 6 | 4+ |
| Ranger Alpha | 6" | 4+ | 3+ | 3 | 3 | 1 | 2 | 7 | 4+ |

This unit contains 1 Ranger Alpha and 4 Skitarii Rangers. It can include up to 5 additional Skitarii Rangers (**Power Level +4**). Each model is armed with a galvanic rifle.

| WEAPON | RANGE | TYPE | S | AP | D | ABILITIES |
|--------|-------|------|---|----|----|-----------|
| Galvanic rifle | 30" | Rapid Fire 1 | 4 | 0 | 1 | Each time you make a wound roll of 6+ for this weapon, that hit is resolved with an AP of -1. |

| WARGEAR OPTIONS | |
|---|---|
| | • Up to two Skitarii Rangers may replace their galvanic rifle with one item from the *Adeptus Mechanicus Special Weapons* list. |
| | • If the unit numbers ten models, one additional Skitarii Ranger may replace their galvanic rifle with one item from the *Adeptus Mechanicus Special Weapons* list. |
| | • One Skitarii Ranger may also have either an enhanced data-tether or an omnispex. |
| | • The Ranger Alpha may take one item from the *Adeptus Mechanicus Melee Weapons* list, and may replace their galvanic rifle with one item from the *Adeptus Mechanicus Pistols* list. |

| ABILITIES | |
|---|---|
| | **Canticles of the Omnissiah** (pg 63) |
| | **Bionics:** All models in this unit have a 6+ invulnerable save. |
| | **Omnispex:** Enemy units do not receive the benefit to their saving throws for being in cover against attacks made by a unit that includes a model with an omnispex. |
| | **Enhanced Data-tether:** You can re-roll failed Morale tests for a unit that includes a model with an enhanced data-tether. |

| FACTION KEYWORDS | IMPERIUM, ADEPTUS MECHANICUS, SKITARII, <FORGE WORLD> |
|---|---|
| **KEYWORDS** | INFANTRY, SKITARII RANGERS |

# SKITARII VANGUARD

| NAME | M | WS | BS | S | T | W | A | Ld | Sv |
|------|---|----|----|---|---|---|---|----|----|
| Skitarii Vanguard | 6" | 4+ | 3+ | 3 | 3 | 1 | 1 | 6 | 4+ |
| Vanguard Alpha | 6" | 4+ | 3+ | 3 | 3 | 1 | 2 | 7 | 4+ |

This unit contains 1 Vanguard Alpha and 4 Skitarii Vanguard. It can include up to 5 additional Skitarii Vanguard (**Power Level +4**). Each model is armed with a radium carbine.

| WEAPON | RANGE | TYPE | S | AP | D | ABILITIES |
|--------|-------|------|---|----|----|-----------|
| Radium carbine | 18" | Assault 3 | 3 | 0 | 1 | Each time you make a wound roll of 6+ for this weapon, that hit inflicts 2 damage instead of 1. |

| WARGEAR OPTIONS | |
|---|---|
| | • Up to two Skitarii Vanguard may replace their radium carbine with one item from the *Adeptus Mechanicus Special Weapons* list.<br>• If the unit numbers ten models, one additional Skitarii Vanguard may replace their radium carbine with one item from the *Adeptus Mechanicus Special Weapons* list.<br>• One Skitarii Vanguard may also have either an enhanced data-tether or an omnispex.<br>• The Vanguard Alpha may take one item from the *Adeptus Mechanicus Melee Weapons* list, and may replace their radium carbine with one item from the *Adeptus Mechanicus Pistols* list. |

| ABILITIES | |
|---|---|
| | **Canticles of the Omnissiah** (pg 63)<br><br>**Bionics:** All models in this unit have a 6+ invulnerable save.<br><br>**Rad-saturation:** Reduce the Toughness of enemy units (other than **Vehicles**) by 1 whilst they are within 1" of any Skitarii Vanguard units.<br><br>**Omnispex:** Enemy units do not receive the benefit to their saving throws for being in cover against attacks made by a unit that includes a model with an omnispex.<br><br>**Enhanced Data-tether:** You can re-roll failed Morale tests for a unit that includes a model with an enhanced data-tether. |

| FACTION KEYWORDS | IMPERIUM, ADEPTUS MECHANICUS, SKITARII, <FORGE WORLD> |
|---|---|
| KEYWORDS | INFANTRY, SKITARII VANGUARD |

Beams of flesh-melting energy and superheated ion blasts crackle through the air as a Skitarii maniple launches an assault upon a T'au position.

## SICARIAN INFILTRATORS

**6 POWER**

| NAME | M | WS | BS | S | T | W | A | Ld | Sv |
|---|---|---|---|---|---|---|---|---|---|
| Sicarian Infiltrator | 8" | 3+ | 3+ | 4 | 3 | 2 | 3 | 6 | 4+ |
| Infiltrator Princeps | 8" | 3+ | 3+ | 4 | 3 | 2 | 4 | 7 | 4+ |

This unit contains 1 Infiltrator Princeps and 4 Sicarian Infiltrators. It can include up to 5 additional Sicarian Infiltrators (**Power Level +6**). Each model is armed with a stubcarbine and power sword.

| WEAPON | RANGE | TYPE | S | AP | D | ABILITIES |
|---|---|---|---|---|---|---|
| Flechette blaster | 12" | Pistol 5 | 3 | 0 | 1 | - |
| Stubcarbine | 18" | Pistol 3 | 4 | 0 | 1 | - |
| Power sword | Melee | Melee | User | -3 | 1 | - |
| Taser goad | Melee | Melee | +2 | 0 | 1 | Each hit roll of 6+ with this weapon causes 3 hits rather than 1. |

| WARGEAR OPTIONS | • Any model may replace its stubcarbine and power sword with a flechette blaster and taser goad. |
|---|---|

| ABILITIES | **Canticles of the Omnissiah** (pg 63)<br><br>**Bionics:** All models in this unit have a 6+ invulnerable save.<br><br>**Infiltrators:** During deployment, you can set this unit up in concealment instead of placing it on the battlefield. At the end of any of your Movement phases, this unit can reveal its location – set it up anywhere on the battlefield that is more than 9" from any enemy model.<br><br>**Neurostatic Aura:** Enemy units within 3" of any Sicarian Infiltrators must subtract 1 from their Leadership. |
|---|---|

| FACTION KEYWORDS | **IMPERIUM, ADEPTUS MECHANICUS, SKITARII, <FORGE WORLD>** |
|---|---|
| KEYWORDS | **INFANTRY, SICARIAN INFILTRATORS** |

## SICARIAN RUSTSTALKERS

**5 POWER**

| NAME | M | WS | BS | S | T | W | A | Ld | Sv |
|---|---|---|---|---|---|---|---|---|---|
| Sicarian Ruststalker | 8" | 3+ | 3+ | 4 | 3 | 2 | 3 | 6 | 4+ |
| Ruststalker Princeps | 8" | 3+ | 3+ | 4 | 3 | 2 | 4 | 7 | 4+ |

This unit contains 1 Ruststalker Princeps and 4 Sicarian Ruststalkers. It can include up to 5 additional Sicarian Ruststalkers (**Power Level +5**). Each model is armed with a transonic razor and chordclaw.

| WEAPON | RANGE | TYPE | S | AP | D | ABILITIES |
|---|---|---|---|---|---|---|
| Chordclaw | Melee | Melee | User | 0 | D3 | A chordclaw can only be used to make one attack each time this model fights. Each time you make a wound roll of 6+ with this weapon, the target suffers D3 mortal wounds instead of the normal damage. |
| Transonic blades | Melee | Melee | +1 | 0 | 1 | Each time you make a wound roll of 6+ with this weapon, the target suffers a mortal wound instead of the normal damage. |
| Transonic razor | Melee | Melee | User | 0 | 1 | Each time you make a wound roll of 6+ with this weapon, the target suffers a mortal wound instead of the normal damage. |

| WARGEAR OPTIONS | • Any Sicarian Ruststalker may replace its transonic razor and chordclaw with transonic blades.<br>• The Ruststalker Princeps may replace its transonic razor with transonic blades. |
|---|---|

| ABILITIES | **Canticles of the Omnissiah** (pg 63)<br><br>**Bionics:** All models in this unit have a 6+ invulnerable save. |
|---|---|

| FACTION KEYWORDS | **IMPERIUM, ADEPTUS MECHANICUS, SKITARII, <FORGE WORLD>** |
|---|---|
| KEYWORDS | **INFANTRY, SICARIAN RUSTSTALKERS** |

# IRONSTRIDER BALLISTARII

**4 POWER**

| NAME | M | WS | BS | S | T | W | A | Ld | Sv |
|------|---|----|----|----|----|----|----|----|----|
| Ironstrider Ballistarius | 10" | 3+ | 3+ | 5 | 6 | 6 | 2 | 8 | 4+ |

This unit contains 1 Ironstrider Ballistarius. It can include up to 5 additional Ironstrider Ballistarii (**Power Level +4 per model**). Each model is equipped with a twin cognis autocannon and broad spectrum data-tether.

| WEAPON | RANGE | TYPE | S | AP | D | ABILITIES |
|--------|-------|------|---|----|----|-----------|
| Twin cognis autocannon | 48" | Heavy 4 | 7 | -1 | 2 | You may fire this weapon even if the firing model Advanced but you must subtract 2 from any hit rolls if you do so. |
| Twin cognis lascannon | 48" | Heavy 2 | 9 | -3 | D6 | You may fire this weapon even if the firing model Advanced but you must subtract 2 from any hit rolls if you do so. |

| WARGEAR OPTIONS | • Any model may replace its twin cognis autocannon with a twin cognis lascannon. |
|-----------------|---|

| ABILITIES | **Canticles of the Omnissiah** (pg 63)<br><br>**Bionics:** All models in this unit have a 6+ invulnerable save.<br><br>**Broad Spectrum Data-tether:** <Forge World> units within 3" of any friendly models equipped with a broad spectrum data-tether at the start of the Morale phase add 1 to their Leadership for the duration of the phase.<br><br>**Explodes:** If a model in this unit is reduced to 0 wounds, roll a D6 before removing the model from the battlefield; on a 6 it explodes, and each unit within 3" suffers 1 mortal wound. |
|-----------|---|

| FACTION KEYWORDS | **Imperium, Adeptus Mechanicus, Skitarii, <Forge World>** |
|-------------------|---|
| KEYWORDS | **Vehicle, Ironstrider Ballistarii** |

# SYDONIAN DRAGOONS

**3 POWER**

| NAME | M | WS | BS | S | T | W | A | Ld | Sv |
|------|---|----|----|----|----|----|----|----|----|
| Sydonian Dragoon | 10" | 3+ | 3+ | 5 | 6 | 6 | 3 | 8 | 4+ |

This unit contains 1 Sydonian Dragoon. It can include up to 5 additional Sydonian Dragoons (**Power Level +3 per model**). Each model is equipped with a taser lance and broad spectrum data-tether.

| WEAPON | RANGE | TYPE | S | AP | D | ABILITIES |
|--------|-------|------|---|----|----|-----------|
| Phosphor serpenta | 18" | Assault 1 | 5 | -1 | 1 | Units attacked by this weapon do not gain any bonus to their saving throws for being in cover. |
| Radium jezzail | 30" | Heavy 2 | 5 | 0 | 1 | This weapon may target a **Character** even if it is not the closest enemy unit. Each time you make a wound roll of 6+ for this weapon, it inflicts a mortal wound in addition to its normal damage. |
| Taser lance | Melee | Melee | +3 | 0 | 2 | Each hit roll of 6+ with this weapon causes 3 hits rather than 1. |

| WARGEAR OPTIONS | • Any model may replace its taser lance with a radium jezzail.<br>• Any model may take a phosphor serpenta. |
|-----------------|---|

| ABILITIES | **Canticles of the Omnissiah** (pg 63)<br><br>**Bionics:** All models in this unit have a 6+ invulnerable save.<br><br>**Broad Spectrum Data-tether:** <Forge World> units within 3" of any friendly models equipped with a broad spectrum data-tether at the start of the Morale phase add 1 to their Leadership for the duration of the phase. | **Explodes:** If a model in this unit is reduced to 0 wounds, roll a D6 before removing the model from the battlefield; on a 6 it explodes, and each unit within 3" suffers 1 mortal wound.<br><br>**Incense Cloud:** Your opponent must subtract 1 from all hit rolls for ranged weapons that target this unit. |
|-----------|---|---|

| FACTION KEYWORDS | **Imperium, Adeptus Mechanicus, Skitarii, <Forge World>** |
|-------------------|---|
| KEYWORDS | **Vehicle, Sydonian Dragoons** |

# ONAGER DUNECRAWLER

**6 POWER**

| NAME | M | WS | BS | S | T | W | A | Ld | Sv |
|---|---|---|---|---|---|---|---|---|---|
| Onager Dunecrawler | * | 5+ | * | 6 | 7 | 11 | * | 8 | 3+ |

An Onager Dunecrawler is a single model equipped with an eradication beamer.

**DAMAGE**
Some of an this model's characteristics change as it suffers damage in battle, as shown below:

| REMAINING W | M | BS | A |
|---|---|---|---|
| 7-11+ | 8" | 3+ | 3 |
| 3-5 | 6" | 4+ | D3 |
| 1-2 | 4" | 5+ | 1 |

| WEAPON | RANGE | TYPE | S | AP | D | ABILITIES |
|---|---|---|---|---|---|---|
| Cognis heavy stubber | 36" | Heavy 3 | 4 | 0 | 1 | You may fire this weapon even if the firing model Advanced but you must subtract 2 from any hit rolls if you do so. |
| Eradication beamer | 36" | Heavy D6 | 8 | -2 | D3 | When attacking units within 12", change this weapon's Type to Heavy D3, but resolve the shots with an AP of -4 and a Damage of D6. |
| Icarus array | When attacking with this weapon, you can fire all three of the profiles below. | | | | | |
| - Daedalus missile launcher | 48" | Heavy 1 | 7 | -3 | D6 | Add 1 to all hit rolls made for this weapon against targets that can **FLY**. Subtract 1 from hit rolls against all other targets. |
| - Gatling rocket launcher | 48" | Heavy 5 | 6 | -2 | 1 | |
| - Twin Icarus autocannon | 48" | Heavy 4 | 7 | -1 | 2 | |
| Neutron laser | 48" | Heavy D3 | 10 | -4 | D6 | Treat damage rolls of 1 or 2 made by this weapon as 3 instead. |
| Twin heavy phosphor blaster | 36" | Heavy 6 | 6 | -2 | 1 | Enemy units do not receive the benefit to their saving throws for being in cover against attacks made with this weapon. |

**WARGEAR OPTIONS**
- This model may replace its eradication beamer with either a neutron laser and cognis heavy stubber, a twin heavy phosphor blaster or an Icarus array.
- This model may take a cognis heavy stubber.
- This model may take either a broad spectrum data-tether or smoke launchers.

**ABILITIES**

**Canticles of the Omnissiah** (pg 63)

**Emanatus Force Field:** This model has a 5+ invulnerable save. You can re-roll invulnerable saving throws of 1 for any Onager Dunecrawler if it is within 6" of at least one other friendly <FORGE WORLD> Onager Dunecrawler.

**Smoke Launchers:** Once per game, a model equipped with smoke launchers can use them instead of shooting any weapons in the Shooting phase; until your next Shooting phase your opponent must subtract 1 from all hit rolls for ranged weapons that target this vehicle.

**Broad Spectrum Data-tether:** <FORGE WORLD> units within 3" of any friendly models equipped with a broad spectrum data-tether at the start of the Morale phase add 1 to their Leadership for the duration of the phase.

**Crawler:** This model can only Advance D3", but ignores the -1 penalty to its hit rolls for moving and firing a Heavy weapon.

**Explodes:** If this model is reduced to 0 wounds, roll a D6 before removing the model from the battlefield; on a 6 it explodes, and each unit within 6" suffers D3 mortal wounds.

**FACTION KEYWORDS**
IMPERIUM, ADEPTUS MECHANICUS, SKITARII, <FORGE WORLD>

**KEYWORDS**
VEHICLE, ONAGER DUNECRAWLER

An Onager Dunecrawler lays waste to the enemy ahead of a Skitarii advance, unleashing pinpoint blasts from its eradication beamer.

# QUESTOR IMPERIALIS

**To the sound of fanfare and ground-shaking footfalls, the mighty war engines of the Questor Imperialis – often called Imperial Knights – stride onto the battlefield. Enemy fire clangs harmlessly off armour, or flares brilliantly as protective ion shields repel incoming shots. When the Knights bring their blades and cannon to bear, even the bravest of foes quake in fear.**

The Knights have been defending their worlds since before the Emperor founded the Imperium. During the Age of Technology Mankind spread outwards from Terra, venturing deep into the galaxy in search of life-supporting planets. They paid a high price for their conquests; in addition to hostile flora and fauna, they found many alien races that begrudged Mankind's intrusion and saw them as a new kind of prey. To protect themselves the settlers used their Standard Template Constructs – miracles of technology that allowed them to produce objects without the need for skilled engineers. The most impressive of all defences were the Knights – enormous bipedal walkers crewed by a single pilot. Knight suits did more than just protect colonists. The Throne Mechanicum – the mechanism that allows warriors to bond with their suits – also implanted notions of honour, duty, and fealty within the psyches of those who piloted a Knight for any length of time. This nobility shaped their societies, and drove the Knights towards the glory and heroism of battle.

The expansion of Mankind was dealt a severe blow when a new era descended, the terrible period known now as the Long Night, or the Age of Strife. Worlds were left to fend for themselves and many were destroyed by an influx of warp storms and Daemons. However, a surprising number of Knight worlds, as they came to be called, clung to existence despite the odds. During the millennia of isolation the Knight defenders established lines of Nobles that ruled over feudal societies. Some five thousand years later, the Great Crusade, the Emperor's campaign to reclaim Mankind's long-lost colonies, spread across the galaxy and reconnected with those once-secluded worlds. Many factions of the newborn Imperium sought to assimilate the Knight worlds, particularly the Adeptus Mechanicus of Mars. Many Knight households – including the most powerful of their kind, the Great Houses – were brought into the Imperial fold during this time.

The Nobles on each Knight world owe allegiance to one of its knightly households, each a self-contained organisation ruled by a leader, often called a High King, but sometimes known by other titles such as Ritter or Patriarch. Those Knight worlds most closely aligned with the Adeptus Mechanicus typically use the title Princeps. It is this leader that calls for war, either in defence of their planet, or to aid the Imperium, or due to any reasons outlined in the Code Chivalric, such as besmirched honour. Directly beneath a High King in rank are the Barons, and a large Knightly house can have many of these. Each Baron commands a stronghold or vital territory and is a lord in his own right, ruling over knightly vassals that can be called to war at need. A High King will ask the most powerful of Barons, or Barons Prime, to join his Exalted Court.

Many Imperial Commanders have reservations when their troops are joined by members of the Questor Imperialis, for their archaic ways and officious ceremonies are, at best, inconvenient. Such complaints quickly dry up when they witness the Knights in action. A lone Knight can engage a tank squadron and emerge victorious, and a lance formation of Knights can reduce entire armies to ruin.

Each mark of Knight suit has its own specialties. Knights Paladin bear rapid-fire battle cannons for long-ranged fire support, but also carry reaper chainswords capable of tearing open reinforced plasteel bunkers. Knights Errant are ideally suited for closer quarters, fitting the more aggressive nature of their pilots. Foes not melted to slag by blasts from a Knight Errant's thermal cannon must then face the scything blows of its melee weapon. Against numerous foes the Knight Warden deploys its avenger gatling gun to mow down hordes at a time, its heavy flamer driving out any who seek cover. Foregoing any close combat weapon, a Knight Crusader mounts two enormous guns, an avenger gatling cannon in one hand, and in the other either a rapid-fire battle cannon or a thermal cannon. Conversely, a Knight Gallant is loaded out with a pair of close combat weapons, the better to unleash its fury. Equipped with reaper chainsword and thunderstrike gauntlet, even a Titan must fear closing with such a powerful opponent.

# QUESTOR IMPERIALIS ARMY LIST

This section contains all of the datasheets that you will need in order to fight battles with your Questor Imperialis miniatures. Each datasheet includes the characteristics profiles of the unit it describes, as well as any wargear and abilities it may have. Some rules are common to several units, and are described on these pages and referenced on the datasheets.

## KEYWORDS

Throughout this section you will come across a keyword that is within angular brackets, specifically <HOUSEHOLD>. This is shorthand for a keyword of your own choosing, as described below.

## <HOUSEHOLD>

With the exception of Freeblades, all Imperial Knights belong to a household – a noble house which owes its allegiance to the Imperium or to the Adeptus Mechanicus.

Imperial Knights datasheets have the <HOUSEHOLD> keyword. When you include such a unit in your army, you must nominate which household that unit is from. You then simply replace the <HOUSEHOLD> keyword in every instance on that unit's Datasheet with the name of your chosen household. You can use any of the households that you have read about, or make up your own.

For example, if you were to include a Knight Errant your army, and you decided it was from House Taranis, its <HOUSEHOLD> Faction keyword is changed to **HOUSE TARANIS**.

You can instead nominate any Imperial Knight to be a Freeblade. If you do so, replace the <HOUSEHOLD> keyword in every instance on that unit's Datasheet with the **FREEBLADE** keyword.

## WARGEAR

The units you will find on the following pages reference the following wargear list. These units may take any item from this list. The profiles for the items in this list can be found in the appendix (pg 153).

### CARAPACE WEAPONS

- Twin Icarus autocannon
- Stormspear rocket pod
- Ironstorm missile pod

# KNIGHT ERRANT

**23** POWER

| NAME | M | WS | BS | S | T | W | A | Ld | Sv |
|---|---|---|---|---|---|---|---|---|---|
| Knight Errant | ✱ | ✱ | ✱ | 8 | 8 | 24 | 4 | 9 | 3+ |

A Knight Errant is a single model equipped with a reaper chainsword, a thermal cannon, a heavy stubber and titanic feet.

**DAMAGE**
Some of this model's characteristics change as it suffers damage, as shown below:

| REMAINING W | M | WS | BS |
|---|---|---|---|
| 13-24+ | 12" | 3+ | 3+ |
| 7-12 | 9" | 4+ | 4+ |
| 1-6 | 6" | 5+ | 5+ |

| WEAPON | RANGE | TYPE | S | AP | D | ABILITIES |
|---|---|---|---|---|---|---|
| Heavy stubber | 36" | Heavy 3 | 4 | 0 | 1 | - |
| Meltagun | 12" | Assault 1 | 8 | -4 | D6 | If the target is within half range of this weapon, roll two dice when inflicting damage with it and discard the lowest result. |
| Thermal cannon | 36" | Heavy D3 | 9 | -4 | D6 | When targeting units with 5 or more models, change this weapon's Type to Heavy D6. If the target is within half range of this weapon, roll two dice when inflicting damage with it and discard the lowest result. |
| Reaper chainsword | Melee | Melee | +4 | -3 | 6 | - |
| Thunderstrike gauntlet | Melee | Melee | x2 | -4 | 6 | When attacking with this weapon, you must subtract 1 from the hit roll. If a **VEHICLE** or **MONSTER** is slain by this weapon, pick an enemy unit within 9" of the bearer and roll a D6. On a 4+ that unit suffers D3 mortal wounds. |
| Titanic feet | Melee | Melee | User | -2 | D3 | Make 3 hit rolls for each attack made with this weapon, instead of 1. |

| WARGEAR OPTIONS | |
|---|---|
| | • This model may take an item from the *Carapace Weapons* list. |
| | • This model may replace its reaper chainsword with a thunderstrike gauntlet. |
| | • This model may replace its heavy stubber with a meltagun. |

| ABILITIES | |
|---|---|
| | **Ion Shield:** This model has a 5+ invulnerable save against shooting attacks.<br><br>**Explodes:** If this model is reduced to 0 wounds, roll a D6 before removing it from the battlefield. On a 6 it explodes, and each unit within 2D6" suffers D6 mortal wounds. | **Super-heavy Walker:** This model can Fall Back in the Movement phase and still shoot and/or charge in the same turn. When this model Falls Back, it can move over enemy **INFANTRY** models, though it must end its move more than 1" from any enemy units. In addition, this model can move and fire Heavy weapons without suffering the penalty to its hit rolls. Finally, this model only gains a bonus to its save for being in cover if at least half of the model is obscured from the firer. |

| FACTION KEYWORDS | IMPERIUM, QUESTOR IMPERIALIS, <HOUSEHOLD> |
|---|---|
| **KEYWORDS** | TITANIC, VEHICLE, KNIGHT ERRANT |

## KNIGHT PALADIN

**24 POWER**

**DAMAGE**
Some of this model's characteristics change as it suffers damage, as shown below:

| REMAINING W | M | WS | BS |
|---|---|---|---|
| 13-24+ | 12" | 3+ | 3+ |
| 7-12 | 9" | 4+ | 4+ |
| 1-6 | 6" | 5+ | 5+ |

| NAME | M | WS | BS | S | T | W | A | Ld | Sv |
|---|---|---|---|---|---|---|---|---|---|
| Knight Paladin | * | * | * | 8 | 8 | 24 | 4 | 9 | 3+ |

A Knight Paladin is a single model equipped with a reaper chainsword, a rapid-fire battle cannon, two heavy stubbers and titanic feet.

| WEAPON | RANGE | TYPE | S | AP | D | ABILITIES |
|---|---|---|---|---|---|---|
| Heavy stubber | 36" | Heavy 3 | 4 | 0 | 1 | - |
| Meltagun | 12" | Assault 1 | 8 | -4 | D6 | If the target is within half range of this weapon, roll two dice when inflicting damage with it and discard the lowest result. |
| Rapid-fire battle cannon | 72" | Heavy 2D6 | 8 | -2 | D3 | - |
| Reaper chainsword | Melee | Melee | +4 | -3 | 6 | |
| Thunderstrike gauntlet | Melee | Melee | x2 | -4 | 6 | When attacking with this weapon, you must subtract 1 from the hit roll. If a VEHICLE or MONSTER is slain by this weapon, pick an enemy unit within 9" of the bearer and roll a D6. On a 4+ that unit suffers D3 mortal wounds. |
| Titanic feet | Melee | Melee | User | -2 | D3 | Make 3 hit rolls for each attack made with this weapon, instead of 1. |

| WARGEAR OPTIONS | |
|---|---|
| | • This model may take an item from the *Carapace Weapons* list.<br>• This model may replace its reaper chainsword with a thunderstrike gauntlet.<br>• This model may replace one heavy stubber with a meltagun. |

| ABILITIES | |
|---|---|
| | **Ion Shield:** This model has a 5+ invulnerable save against shooting attacks.<br><br>**Explodes:** If this model is reduced to 0 wounds, roll a D6 before removing it from the battlefield. On a 6 it explodes, and each unit within 2D6" suffers D6 mortal wounds. | **Super-heavy Walker:** This model can Fall Back in the Movement phase and still shoot and/or charge in the same turn. When this model Falls Back, it can move over enemy INFANTRY models, though it must end its move more than 1" from any enemy units. In addition, this model can move and fire Heavy weapons without suffering the penalty to its hit rolls. Finally, this model only gains a bonus to its save for being in cover if at least half of the model is obscured from the firer. |

| FACTION KEYWORDS | IMPERIUM, QUESTOR IMPERIALIS, <HOUSEHOLD> |
|---|---|
| KEYWORDS | TITANIC, VEHICLE, KNIGHT PALADIN |

A Knight Paladin's battle cannon is a terrifying long-range weapon, capable of mowing down scores of infantry and light vehicles.

# KNIGHT WARDEN

**25** POWER

| DAMAGE | | | |
|---|---|---|---|
| Some of this model's characteristics change as it suffers damage, as shown below: | | | |
| REMAINING W | M | WS | BS |
| 13-24+ | 12" | 3+ | 3+ |
| 7-12 | 9" | 4+ | 4+ |
| 1-6 | 6" | 5+ | 5+ |

| NAME | M | WS | BS | S | T | W | A | Ld | Sv |
|---|---|---|---|---|---|---|---|---|---|
| Knight Warden | * | * | * | 8 | 8 | 24 | 4 | 9 | 3+ |

A Knight Warden is a single model equipped with a reaper chainsword, an avenger gatling cannon, a heavy stubber, a heavy flamer and titanic feet.

| WEAPON | RANGE | TYPE | S | AP | D | ABILITIES |
|---|---|---|---|---|---|---|
| Avenger gatling cannon | 36" | Heavy 12 | 6 | -2 | 2 | - |
| Heavy flamer | 8" | Heavy D6 | 5 | -1 | 1 | This weapon automatically hits its target. |
| Heavy stubber | 36" | Heavy 3 | 4 | 0 | 1 | - |
| Meltagun | 12" | Assault 1 | 8 | -4 | D6 | If the target is within half range of this weapon, roll two dice when inflicting damage with it and discard the lowest result. |
| Reaper chainsword | Melee | Melee | +4 | -3 | 6 | - |
| Thunderstrike gauntlet | Melee | Melee | x2 | -4 | 6 | When attacking with this weapon, you must subtract 1 from the hit roll. If a **VEHICLE** or **MONSTER** is slain by this weapon, pick an enemy unit within 9" of the bearer and roll a D6. On a 4+ that unit suffers D3 mortal wounds. |
| Titanic feet | Melee | Melee | User | -2 | D3 | Make 3 hit rolls for each attack made with this weapon, instead of 1. |

| WARGEAR OPTIONS | |
|---|---|
| | • This model may take an item from the *Carapace Weapons* list.<br>• This model may replace its reaper chainsword with a thunderstrike gauntlet.<br>• This model may replace its heavy stubber with a meltagun. |

| ABILITIES | |
|---|---|
| | **Ion Shield:** This model has a 5+ invulnerable save against shooting attacks.<br><br>**Explodes:** If this model is reduced to 0 wounds, roll a D6 before removing it from the battlefield. On a 6 it explodes, and each unit within 2D6" suffers D6 mortal wounds. | **Super-heavy Walker:** This model can Fall Back in the Movement phase and still shoot and/or charge in the same turn. When this model Falls Back, it can move over enemy **INFANTRY** models, though it must end its move more than 1" from any enemy units. In addition, this model can move and fire Heavy weapons without suffering the penalty to its hit rolls. Finally, this model only gains a bonus to its save for being in cover if at least half of the model is obscured from the firer. |

| FACTION KEYWORDS | **IMPERIUM, QUESTOR IMPERIALIS, <HOUSEHOLD>** |
|---|---|
| KEYWORDS | **TITANIC, VEHICLE, KNIGHT WARDEN** |

Knights Warden excel at storming strongholds, flushing the enemy out with heavy flamers and storms of gatling cannon rounds.

# KNIGHT GALLANT

**DAMAGE**
Some of this model's characteristics change as it suffers damage, as shown below:

| REMAINING W | M | WS | BS |
|---|---|---|---|
| 13-24+ | 12" | 3+ | 3+ |
| 7-12 | 9" | 4+ | 4+ |
| 1-6 | 6" | 5+ | 5+ |

| NAME | M | WS | BS | S | T | W | A | Ld | Sv |
|---|---|---|---|---|---|---|---|---|---|
| Knight Gallant | * | * | * | 8 | 8 | 24 | 4 | 9 | 3+ |

A Knight Gallant is a single model equipped with a reaper chainsword, a thunderstrike gauntlet, a heavy stubber and titanic feet.

| WEAPON | RANGE | TYPE | S | AP | D | ABILITIES |
|---|---|---|---|---|---|---|
| Heavy stubber | 36" | Heavy 3 | 4 | 0 | 1 | - |
| Meltagun | 12" | Assault 1 | 8 | -4 | D6 | If the target is within half range of this weapon, roll two dice when inflicting damage with it and discard the lowest result. |
| Reaper chainsword | Melee | Melee | +4 | -3 | 6 | - |
| Thunderstrike gauntlet | Melee | Melee | x2 | -4 | 6 | When attacking with this weapon, you must subtract 1 from the hit roll. If a **VEHICLE** or **MONSTER** is slain by this weapon, pick an enemy unit within 9" of the bearer and roll a D6. On a 4+ that unit suffers D3 mortal wounds. |
| Titanic feet | Melee | Melee | User | -2 | D3 | Make 3 hit rolls for each attack made with this weapon, instead of 1. |

| WARGEAR OPTIONS | • This model may take an item from the *Carapace Weapons* list.<br>• This model may replace its heavy stubber with a meltagun. |
|---|---|

| ABILITIES | **Ion Shield:** This model has a 5+ invulnerable save against shooting attacks.<br><br>**Explodes:** If this model is reduced to 0 wounds, roll a D6 before removing it from the battlefield. On a 6 it explodes, and each unit within 2D6" suffers D6 mortal wounds. | **Super-heavy Walker:** This model can Fall Back in the Movement phase and still shoot and/or charge in the same turn. When this model Falls Back, it can move over enemy **INFANTRY** models, though it must end its move more than 1" from any enemy units. In addition, this model can move and fire Heavy weapons without suffering the penalty to its hit rolls. Finally, this model only gains a bonus to its save for being in cover if at least half of the model is obscured from the firer. |
|---|---|---|

| FACTION KEYWORDS | IMPERIUM, QUESTOR IMPERIALIS, <HOUSEHOLD> |
|---|---|
| KEYWORDS | TITANIC, VEHICLE, KNIGHT GALLANT |

Knights Gallant tear their foes apart with earth-shattering blows from their reaper chainswords and thunderstrike gauntlets.

**27** POWER

# KNIGHT CRUSADER

| NAME | M | WS | BS | S | T | W | A | Ld | Sv |
|---|---|---|---|---|---|---|---|---|---|
| Knight Crusader | * | * | * | 8 | 8 | 24 | 4 | 9 | 3+ |

| DAMAGE | | | |
|---|---|---|---|
| Some of this model's characteristics change as it suffers damage, as shown below: | | | |
| REMAINING W | M | WS | BS |
| 13-24+ | 12" | 3+ | 3+ |
| 7-12 | 9" | 4+ | 4+ |
| 1-6 | 6" | 5+ | 5+ |

A Knight Crusader is a single model equipped with an avenger gatling cannon, a thermal cannon, a heavy stubber, a heavy flamer and titanic feet.

| WEAPON | RANGE | TYPE | S | AP | D | ABILITIES |
|---|---|---|---|---|---|---|
| Avenger gatling cannon | 36" | Heavy 12 | 6 | -2 | 2 | - |
| Heavy flamer | 8" | Heavy D6 | 5 | -1 | 1 | This weapon automatically hits its target. |
| Heavy stubber | 36" | Heavy 3 | 4 | 0 | 1 | - |
| Meltagun | 12" | Assault 1 | 8 | -4 | D6 | If the target is within half range of this weapon, roll two dice when inflicting damage with it and discard the lowest result. |
| Rapid-fire battle cannon | 72" | Heavy 2D6 | 8 | -2 | D3 | - |
| Thermal cannon | 36" | Heavy D3 | 9 | -4 | D6 | When targeting units with 5 or more models, change this weapon's Type to Heavy D6. If the target is within half range of this weapon, roll two dice when inflicting damage with it and discard the lowest result. |
| Titanic feet | Melee | Melee | User | -2 | D3 | Make 3 hit rolls for each attack made with this weapon, instead of 1. |

| WARGEAR OPTIONS | |
|---|---|
| | • This model may take an item from the *Carapace Weapons* list. |
| | • This model may replace its thermal cannon with a rapid-fire battle cannon and a heavy stubber. |
| | • This model may replace one heavy stubber with a meltagun. |

| ABILITIES | |
|---|---|
| | **Ion Shield:** This model has a 5+ invulnerable save against shooting attacks. **Explodes:** If this model is reduced to 0 wounds, roll a D6 before removing it from the battlefield. On a 6 it explodes, and each unit within 2D6" suffers D6 mortal wounds. | **Super-heavy Walker:** This model can Fall Back in the Movement phase and still shoot and/or charge in the same turn. When this model Falls Back, it can move over enemy INFANTRY models, though it must end its move more than 1" from any enemy units. In addition, this model can move and fire Heavy weapons without suffering the penalty to its hit rolls. Finally, this model only gains a bonus to its save for being in cover if at least half of the model is obscured from the firer. |

| FACTION KEYWORDS | IMPERIUM, QUESTOR IMPERIALIS, <HOUSEHOLD> |
|---|---|
| KEYWORDS | TITANIC, VEHICLE, KNIGHT CRUSADER |

# ADEPTUS MINISTORUM

United by the fires of a single faith, the Emperor's forces find their conviction stoked to a blazing roar in the presence of the bombastic preachers of the Adeptus Ministorum, who inspire their flock with chanted war-hymns and smite the blasphemer wherever he lurks.

The Adeptus Ministorum is a galaxy-spanning organisation that leads Mankind in the worship of the God-Emperor. Through its preachers, confessors, missionaries and cardinals, the Ministorum – also known as the Ecclesiarchy – controls the veneration of the masses and gives their devotion to the Emperor an organised focus. The Imperial Creed practised by the Ecclesiarchy and its trillions of adherents is the only official religion of the Imperium, and it is violent and merciless in the persecution of its beliefs. Although the interpretation of the Ecclesiarchy's rites and dogma can vary, any deviance from its strictures is considered heresy and is usually punishable by death. With its myriad of faithful warriors, Adepta Sororitas allies and arcane machineries of war, it smashes the unbeliever and the heretic into the dust.

The Ecclesiarchy has guided the servants of the Emperor for nearly ten thousand years. Following the Master of Mankind's ultimate sacrifice at the end of the Horus Heresy and his interment into the Golden Throne, the Imperium was swept by a general upsurge in adoration and worship for their saviour. Visionaries and prophets rose to prominence on every world, and cults soon sprang up around these divinely inspired individuals. There was no central organisation, however – no system of control to unite those who worshipped the Emperor as a sun god with those who saw him as an avenging angel of death or a revered ancestor. Even on the same planet there could be hundreds of different denominations, each performing their role in a different manner, every one of them interpreting the Emperor's will in a slightly different way.

Only when the Temple of the Saviour Emperor rose upon Holy Terra to unite them was a semblance of unity imposed upon the disparate cults. With the backing of the Adeptus Terra, that holy body had integrated and merged so many cults that by the start of the 31st Millennium, almost two-thirds of the Imperium was united in the worship of the Emperor. The Temple was recognised as the official religion of the Imperium and renamed the Adeptus Ministorum. Scant centuries later, the head of the Ministorum, the Ecclesiarch Veneris II, became a High Lord of Terra. Three hundred years after that the Ecclesiarch's seat on the council of the High Lords was made permanent. It is still a position of great influence to this day.

The reach of the Adeptus Ministorum can be felt on every civilised world, and in the vast majority of the Imperium's military forces. Many regiments of the Astra Militarum have Ministorum Priests assigned to them, and with good reason. The soldiery of the Imperial Guard, superstitious even before their induction into the hidebound culture of the Astra Militarum, have their faith reinforced by the presence of these holy figures. Against the manifold perils of a hostile galaxy, faith alone can carry a soldier through no man's land to fight hellish monsters and alien creatures with nothing but a lasgun and a bayonet.

Ministorum Priests are fearsome combatants in their own right, so strong in their faith they are able to perform miracles of battle when the light of the Emperor shines through them. Those truly steeped in the favour of the Lord of Mankind, such as the fiery demagogue Uriah Jacobus, manifest otherworldly powers in order to smite the heretic and the fiend.

These holy men are far from the only assets the Ministorum can call upon in times of war, however. The Crusaders are veteran warriors that stand guard over the holy prosecutors of the Ministorum's will; armed with power swords and mighty shields, they hack down those who oppose their masters and give their lives willingly should the cause be threatened. Alongside less puritanical masters are found the Death Cults, those macabre offshoots of the Imperial Creed that venerate the Emperor as a morbid grave-god. More sinister still are the Arco-flagellants, base criminals who are punished by being cybernetically refashioned into whip-limbed killers driven from enforced passivity to crazed berserker rages by a simple code word. Such holy assassins are one with death, and gladly inflict it in the Master of Mankind's name. Storming past the Emperor's flock come the Penitent Engines, buzzsaw-wielding walkers piloted by hooded wrongdoers that are thrust into the heat of battle as punishment for their sins. For the militarised carnivalia of the Ecclesiarchy, to kill is to worship, and to die in the Emperor's name is the truest reward of all.

# ADEPTUS MINISTORUM ARMY LIST

This section contains all of the datasheets that you will need in order to fight battles with your Adeptus Ministorum miniatures. Each datasheet includes the characteristics profiles of the unit it describes, as well as any wargear and abilities it may have. Some rules are common to several Adeptus Ministorum units – these are described below and referenced on the datasheets.

## KEYWORDS

Throughout this section you will come across a keyword that is within angular brackets, specifically <ORDER>. This is shorthand for a keyword of your own choosing, as described below.

## <ORDER>

All members of the Adepta Sororitas belong to an Order and have the <ORDER> keyword. When you include such a unit in your army, you must nominate which Order that unit is from. You then simply replace the <ORDER> keyword in every instance on that unit's datasheet with the name of your chosen Order. You can use any of the Orders that you have read about, or make up your own.

For example, if you were to include a Canoness in your army, and you decided she was from the Order of Our Martyred Lady, her <ORDER> Faction keyword is changed to ORDER OF OUR MARTYRED LADY, and her Lead the Righteous ability would then say 'You can re-roll all hit rolls of 1 for friendly ORDER OF OUR MARTYRED LADY units within 6" of this model.'

## ABILITIES

The following abilities are common to several Adeptus Ministorum units:

## ACTS OF FAITH

Roll a D6 at the start of each of your turns. On a roll of 2+, one unit from your army with the Acts of Faith ability can perform an Act of Faith chosen from the following list. Some abilities may allow you to use more than one Act of Faith in the same turn; when this is the case, a different unit must be chosen to perform each Act of Faith.

**Hand of the Emperor:** The unit can immediately move as if it were the Movement phase.

**Divine Guidance:** The unit can immediately shoot as if it were the Shooting phase.

**The Passion:** The unit can, if it is within 1" of an enemy unit, immediately pile in and attack as if it were the Fight phase.

**Spirit of the Martyr:** One model in the unit recovers D3 lost wounds, or you can return a single slain model to the unit with 1 wound remaining.

## SHIELD OF FAITH

Models with the Shield of Faith ability have a 6+ invulnerable save. In addition, units with the Shield of Faith ability can attempt to deny one psychic power in each enemy Psychic phase in the same manner as a PSYKER. However, if they do so, instead of rolling 2D6, only roll a single D6; the psychic power is resisted if the roll is greater than the result of the Psychic test that manifested the power.

## ZEALOT

You can re-roll failed hit rolls for a unit with this ability in a turn in which it charged, made a heroic intervention, or was charged by an enemy unit.

## WARGEAR

Many of the units you will find on the following pages reference one or more of the following wargear lists (e.g. Ranged Weapons). When this is the case, the unit may take any item from the appropriate list below. The profiles for the weapons in these lists can be found in the appendix (pg 157-158).

### RANGED WEAPONS

- Boltgun
- Combi-flamer
- Combi-melta
- Combi-plasma
- Condemnor boltgun
- Storm bolter

### SPECIAL WEAPONS

- Storm bolter
- Flamer
- Meltagun

### PISTOLS

- Bolt pistol
- Plasma pistol
- Inferno pistol

### MELEE WEAPONS

- Chainsword
- Power axe
- Power maul
- Power sword

### HEAVY WEAPONS

- Heavy bolter
- Heavy flamer
- Multi-melta

# URIAH JACOBUS

**5 POWER**

| NAME | M | WS | BS | S | T | W | A | Ld | Sv |
|------|---|-----|-----|---|---|---|---|-----|-----|
| Uriah Jacobus | 6" | 3+ | 3+ | 3 | 3 | 5 | 4 | 8 | 6+ |

Uriah Jacobus is a single model armed with the Redeemer, a bolt pistol, a chainsword, frag grenades and krak grenades. Only one of this model may be included in your army.

| WEAPON | RANGE | TYPE | S | AP | D | ABILITIES |
|--------|-------|------|---|-----|---|-----------|
| Bolt pistol | 12" | Pistol 1 | 4 | 0 | 1 | - |
| The Redeemer | 24" | Assault 2 | 4 | -1 | 1 | Any attacks with a wound roll of 6+ for this weapon have a Damage characteristic of 2 instead of 1. |
| Chainsword | Melee | Melee | User | 0 | 1 | Each time the bearer fights, it can make 1 additional attack with this weapon. |
| Frag grenade | 6" | Grenade D6 | 3 | 0 | 1 | - |
| Krak grenade | 6" | Grenade 1 | 6 | -1 | D3 | - |

| ABILITIES | **Shield of Faith, Zealot** (pg 90)<br><br>**Banner of Sanctity:** Friendly **ADEPTUS MINISTORUM** and **ASTRA MILITARUM** units within 6" of Uriah Jacobus add 1 to their Leadership characteristic. | **War Hymns:** You can add 1 to the Attacks characteristic of all friendly **ADEPTUS MINISTORUM INFANTRY** and **ASTRA MILITARUM INFANTRY** units that are within 6" of any friendly **MINISTORUM PRIEST**.<br><br>**Rosarius:** Uriah Jacobus has a 4+ invulnerable save. |
|-----------|---|---|
| **FACTION KEYWORDS** | **IMPERIUM, ADEPTUS MINISTORUM, ASTRA MILITARUM** | |
| **KEYWORDS** | **CHARACTER, INFANTRY, MINISTORUM PRIEST, URIAH JACOBUS** | |

# MINISTORUM PRIEST

**3 POWER**

| NAME | M | WS | BS | S | T | W | A | Ld | Sv |
|------|---|-----|-----|---|---|---|---|-----|-----|
| Ministorum Priest | 6" | 4+ | 4+ | 3 | 3 | 4 | 3 | 7 | 6+ |

A Ministorum Priest is a single model armed with a laspistol, frag grenades and krak grenades.

| WEAPON | RANGE | TYPE | S | AP | D | ABILITIES |
|--------|-------|------|---|-----|---|-----------|
| Autogun | 24" | Rapid Fire 1 | 3 | 0 | 1 | - |
| Laspistol | 12" | Pistol 1 | 3 | 0 | 1 | - |
| Plasma gun | When attacking with this weapon, choose one of the profiles below. | | | | | |
| - Standard | 24" | Rapid Fire 1 | 7 | -3 | 1 | |
| - Supercharge | 24" | Rapid Fire 1 | 8 | -3 | 2 | On a hit roll of 1, the bearer is slain after all of this weapon's shots have been resolved. |
| Shotgun | 12" | Assault 2 | 3 | 0 | 1 | If the target is within half range, add 1 to this weapon's Strength. |
| Eviscerator | Melee | Melee | x2 | -4 | D3 | When attacking with this weapon, you must subtract 1 from the hit roll. |
| Frag grenade | 6" | Grenade D6 | 3 | 0 | 1 | - |
| Krak grenade | 6" | Grenade 1 | 6 | -1 | D3 | - |

| WARGEAR OPTIONS | • This model may replace its laspistol with an item from the *Pistols* list.<br>• This model may take an eviscerator, autogun, plasma gun, shotgun or an item from the *Melee Weapons* or *Ranged Weapons* list. | |
|-----------------|---|---|
| **ABILITIES** | **Zealot** (pg 90)<br><br>**Rosarius:** This model has a 4+ invulnerable save. | **War Hymns:** You can add 1 to the Attacks characteristic of all models in **ADEPTUS MINISTORUM INFANTRY** and **ASTRA MILITARUM INFANTRY** units that are within 6" of any friendly **MINISTORUM PRIESTS**. |
| **FACTION KEYWORDS** | **IMPERIUM, ADEPTUS MINISTORUM, ASTRA MILITARUM** | |
| **KEYWORDS** | **CHARACTER, INFANTRY, MINISTORUM PRIEST** | |

## CRUSADERS

**1 POWER**

| NAME | M | WS | BS | S | T | W | A | Ld | Sv |
|---|---|---|---|---|---|---|---|---|---|
| Crusader | 6" | 3+ | 4+ | 3 | 3 | 1 | 2 | 7 | 4+ |

This unit contains 2 Crusaders. It may contain up to 2 additional Crusaders (**Power Rating +1**), up to 4 additional Crusaders (**Power Rating +2**), up to 6 additional Crusaders (**Power Rating +3**) or up to 8 additional Crusaders (**Power Rating +4**). Each Crusader is armed with a power sword.

| WEAPON | RANGE | TYPE | S | AP | D | ABILITIES |
|---|---|---|---|---|---|---|
| Power sword | Melee | Melee | User | -3 | 1 | - |

| ABILITIES | **Acts of Faith, Shield of Faith, Zealot** (pg 90)<br><br>**Storm Shield:** This model has a 3+ invulnerable save. |
|---|---|
| **FACTION KEYWORDS** | **IMPERIUM, ADEPTUS MINISTORUM** |
| **KEYWORDS** | **INFANTRY, CRUSADERS** |

## DEATH CULT ASSASSINS

**1 POWER**

| NAME | M | WS | BS | S | T | W | A | Ld | Sv |
|---|---|---|---|---|---|---|---|---|---|
| Death Cult Assassin | 7" | 3+ | 4+ | 4 | 3 | 1 | 4 | 7 | 5+ |

This unit contains 2 Death Cult Assassins. It may contain up to 2 additional Death Cult Assassins (**Power Rating +1**), up to 4 additional Death Cult Assassins (**Power Rating +2**), up to 6 additional Death Cult Assassins (**Power Rating +3**) or up to 8 additional Death Cult Assassins (**Power Rating +4**). Each Death Cult Assassin is armed with Death Cult power blades.

| WEAPON | RANGE | TYPE | S | AP | D | ABILITIES |
|---|---|---|---|---|---|---|
| Death Cult power blades | Melee | Melee | User | -2 | 1 | - |

| ABILITIES | **Zealot** (pg 90)<br><br>**Uncanny Reflexes:** Models in this unit have a 5+ invulnerable save. |
|---|---|
| **FACTION KEYWORDS** | **IMPERIUM, ADEPTUS MINISTORUM** |
| **KEYWORDS** | **INFANTRY, DEATH CULT ASSASSINS** |

Fanatically devoted to the Imperial Creed, Death Cult Assassins fall upon their foes in a whirling frenzy of flesh-tearing blades.

## ARCO-FLAGELLANTS

**2 POWER**

| NAME | M | WS | BS | S | T | W | A | Ld | Sv |
|------|---|----|----|---|---|---|---|----|----|
| Arco-flagellant | 7" | 3+ | 6+ | 4 | 3 | 2 | 2 | 7 | 7+ |

This unit contains 3 Arco-flagellants. It may contain up to 3 additional Arco-flagellants (**Power Rating +2**) or up to 6 additional Arco-flagellants (**Power Rating +4**). Each Arco-flagellant is armed with arco-flails.

| WEAPON | RANGE | TYPE | S | AP | D | ABILITIES |
|--------|-------|------|---|----|---|-----------|
| Arco-flails | Melee | Melee | +1 | 0 | 1 | When you make an attack with this weapon, roll D3 dice instead of 1. |

| ABILITIES | **Zealot** (pg 90)<br><br>**Berserk Killing Machines:** Models in this unit have a 5+ invulnerable save. |
|-----------|------|
| **FACTION KEYWORDS** | **IMPERIUM, ADEPTUS MINISTORUM** |
| **KEYWORDS** | **INFANTRY, ARCO-FLAGELLANTS** |

## PENITENT ENGINES

**6 POWER**

| NAME | M | WS | BS | S | T | W | A | Ld | Sv |
|------|---|----|----|---|---|---|---|----|----|
| Penitent Engine | 7" | 3+ | 5+ | 5 | 6 | 7 | 4 | 8 | 4+ |

This unit contains 1 Penitent Engine. It can include 1 additional Penitent Engine (**Power Rating +6**) or 2 additional Penitent Engines (**Power Rating +12**). Each Penitent Engine is equipped with penitent buzz-blades and two heavy flamers.

| WEAPON | RANGE | TYPE | S | AP | D | ABILITIES |
|--------|-------|------|---|----|---|-----------|
| Heavy flamer | 8" | Heavy D6 | 5 | -1 | 1 | This weapon automatically hits its target. |
| Penitent buzz-blades | Melee | Melee | x2 | -3 | 3 | - |

| ABILITIES | **Zealot** (pg 90)<br><br>**Desperate for Redemption:** Roll a D6 after completing the first set of attacks for a unit of Penitent Engines in each Fight phase. On roll of 4+, the unit can immediately pile in and attack for a second time. |
|-----------|------|
| **FACTION KEYWORDS** | **IMPERIUM, ADEPTUS MINISTORUM** |
| **KEYWORDS** | **VEHICLE, PENITENT ENGINES** |

A Penitent Engine is piloted by a repentant sinner who can only earn absolution by spilling the blood of heretics and traitors.

# ADEPTA SORORITAS

**Stalwart, determined, iron-sure in their faith, the Sisters of Battle are the military incarnation of the Emperor's creed. They are the fiery torch that burns away heresy, the shining blade that cuts the corruption of lesser souls from the greater body of the Imperium. With the holy weaponry of their orders they bring death to the enemies of Mankind.**

The orders of the Adepta Sororitas are vast and sprawling organisations unto themselves. They can trace their origins to a time of great upheaval in the history of the Imperium. In M36 the Ecclesiarchy had been led astray by a succession of dubiously qualified leaders, but when the corrupt High Lord Goge Vandire extended his control from the Administratum to the Adeptus Ministorum, the organisation plumbed new depths in the name of faith.

Goge Vandire was insane, a demagogue whose merciless desire for supremacy saw him secure a position at the pinnacle of the Ecclesiarchy's hierarchy after a bloody coup. The Age of Apostasy, as the time of his ascendancy was known, affected the entire Imperium, and the Reign of Blood that followed was a time of crushing tyranny when Vandire held supreme power.

A small cult of holy women that the Adeptus Ministorum had located on the agri world of San Leor, known as the Daughters of the Emperor, came to Vandire's notice. They practised the clearing of the mind from worldly concerns, and the perfection of the arts of battle. He arranged to meet this cult in person and, through the forging of a miracle, tricked them into becoming his retinue. Renamed the Brides of the Emperor, they were trained by veterans of the Imperial Guard to become his constant guardians and silent executioners. When the Holy Synod arranged to have Vandire assassinated out of fear, the Brides of the Emperor successfully defended their master and took his rivals' heads instead.

It was the true faith of Sebastian Thor that brought the darkness of Vandire's rule to an end. The ascendant preacher had dared to challenge the Reign of Blood, and with the Imperium's citizenry pushed too far, he had no shortage of followers to aid him – his allies numbered even the legions of the Adeptus Mechanicus and several Chapters of Space Marines. Yet even they could not overcome the Brides of the Emperor, who by this time numbered ten thousand and more. It was a member of the Adeptus Custodes who, by laying down his arms and delivering an impassioned treaty, led five of the Brides to the throne room of the Emperor himself. There, amongst the golden light of the Sanctum Imperialis, they were granted a vision that saw the folly of their allegiance to Vandire revealed. Reborn in truth, they returned to the man they once called lord, and beheaded him where he stood.

With the Ecclesiarchy's dominance proving so disastrous, the organisation was reforged as an organ of religious rather than governmental power. The Decree Passive forbade the Adeptus Ministorum from raising men under arms, intending to rob it of military power. Yet those who had once been the Daughters of the Emperor did not technically fall under this prohibition. With the Imperium all but bereft of law and guidance after Vandire's reign, none questioned the newly formed Ecclesiarchy's exploitation of this semantic glitch too loudly. So it was that the Sisters of Battle were recruited by the million, their orders rising from the flames of a cataclysm that saw the Imperium all but devour itself.

To this day, the Sisters of Battle are the most ardent of faith in the Imperium's manifold armies. Guided by the information harvesters of the Orders Dialogus and bolstered by the medics of the Orders Hospitaller, the warriors of the Adepta Sororitas form a terrifyingly effective force – they wear revered suits of battle plate and fight with the sacred weapons of bolter, flamer and melta much like their brothers in the Adeptus Astartes, but in numerical strength the Chapter Masters can only dream of. Together they bring the vengeance of the Emperor to the unbeliever, the heretic and the abomination, ridding the realm of Mankind of that which would harm it from without or from within.

*'Heretics crave the cleansing fire of absolution. They need not fear, for we shall deliver it to them.'*

*- Canoness Josmane, Order of the Sacred Rose*

# CELESTINE

**8 POWER**

| NAME | M | WS | BS | S | T | W | A | Ld | Sv |
|------|---|----|----|---|---|---|---|----|----|
| Celestine | 12" | 2+ | 2+ | 3 | 3 | 7 | 6 | 9 | 2+ |
| Geminae Superia | 12" | 3+ | 3+ | 3 | 3 | 2 | 3 | 9 | 2+ |

Celestine is a single model armed with the Ardent Blade. Her unit can also include 1 Geminae Superia (**Power Rating +3**) or 2 Geminae Superia (**Power Rating +6**), each armed with a bolt pistol, power sword, frag grenades and krak grenades.

| WEAPON | RANGE | TYPE | S | AP | D | ABILITIES |
|--------|-------|------|---|----|----|-----------|
| The Ardent Blade (shooting) | 8" | Assault D6 | 5 | -1 | 1 | This weapon automatically hits its target. |
| Bolt pistol | 12" | Pistol 1 | 4 | 0 | 1 | - |
| The Ardent Blade (melee) | Melee | Melee | +4 | -3 | 2 | - |
| Power sword | Melee | Melee | User | -3 | 1 | - |
| Frag grenades | 6" | Grenade D6 | 3 | 0 | 1 | - |
| Krak grenades | 6" | Grenade 1 | 6 | -1 | D3 | - |

| ABILITIES | |
|-----------|---|

**Acts of Faith, Shield of Faith** (pg 90)

**Beacon of Faith:** All friendly **ADEPTA SORORITAS** units within 6" of Celestine add 1 to their Shield of Faith invulnerable saves. All friendly **ADEPTUS MINISTORUM** and **ASTRA MILITARUM** units that are within 6" of Celestine gain a 6+ invulnerable save.

**The Armour of Saint Katherine:** Celestine has a 4+ invulnerable save. Furthermore, any Geminae Superia in her unit also have a 4+ invulnerable save thanks to her divine protection.

**Saintly Blessings:** At the start of any of your turns, you can pick a friendly **ADEPTA SORORITAS** unit within 6" of Celestine and perform an Act of Faith with it. This is in addition to the Act of Faith you are normally allowed to perform in a turn.

**Healing Tears:** At the start of each of your Movement phases, you can set up a single slain Geminae Superia with all her wounds restored within 2" of Celestine and more than 1" away from any enemy models.

**Miraculous Intervention:** Once per game, if Celestine loses her last wound, roll a D6. On a roll of 2+ she is not removed, but is instead resurrected with all her wounds restored; set up Celestine's model within 2" of a Geminae Superia. If it is impossible to do so – because, for example, no Geminae Superia remain in play – you can instead place Celestine anywhere on the battlefield that is more than 9" from any enemy models. On a roll of 1 Celestine is needed elsewhere; remove any remaining Geminae Superia, and count Celestine and her bodyguard as having been slain for the purposes of any mission rules or victory conditions.

| FACTION KEYWORDS | IMPERIUM, ADEPTUS MINISTORUM, ADEPTA SORORITAS |
|------------------|------------------------------------------------|
| KEYWORDS | CHARACTER, INFANTRY, JUMP PACK, FLY, CELESTINE |

# CANONESS

**4** POWER

| NAME | M | WS | BS | S | T | W | A | Ld | Sv |
|------|---|----|----|---|---|---|---|----|----|
| Canoness | 6" | 2+ | 2+ | 3 | 3 | 5 | 4 | 9 | 3+ |

A Canoness is a single model armed with a bolt pistol, chainsword, frag grenades and krak grenades.

| WEAPON | RANGE | TYPE | S | AP | D | ABILITIES |
|--------|-------|------|---|----|----|-----------|
| Bolt pistol | 12" | Pistol 1 | 4 | 0 | 1 | - |
| Boltgun | 24" | Rapid Fire 1 | 4 | 0 | 1 | - |
| Chainsword | Melee | Melee | User | 0 | 1 | Each time the bearer fights, it can make 1 additional attack with this weapon. |
| Eviscerator | Melee | Melee | x2 | -4 | D3 | When attacking with this weapon, you must subtract 1 from the hit roll. |
| Frag grenade | 6" | Grenade D6 | 3 | 0 | 1 | - |
| Krak grenade | 6" | Grenade 1 | 6 | -1 | D3 | - |

| WARGEAR OPTIONS | • This model may replace its bolt pistol with a boltgun.<br>• This model may replace its chainsword with an eviscerator or a weapon from the *Melee Weapons* list.<br>• This model may replace either its bolt pistol or its chainsword with a weapon from the *Ranged Weapons* or *Pistols* list. |
|-----------------|---|

| ABILITIES | Acts of Faith, Shield of Faith (pg 90)<br><br>Rosarius: This model has a 4+ invulnerable save. | Lead the Righteous: You can re-roll all hit rolls of 1 for friendly <ORDER> units within 6" of this model. |
|-----------|---|---|

| FACTION KEYWORDS | IMPERIUM, ADEPTUS MINISTORUM, ADEPTA SORORITAS, <ORDER> |
|------------------|---|

| KEYWORDS | CHARACTER, INFANTRY, CANONESS |
|----------|---|

Saint Celestine is a living miracle, an avenging angel sent forth to stir the hearts of the faithful and bring judgment to the damned.

## IMAGIFIER

**2 POWER**

| NAME | M | WS | BS | S | T | W | A | Ld | Sv |
|------|---|-----|-----|---|---|---|---|-----|-----|
| Imagifier | 6" | 3+ | 3+ | 3 | 3 | 4 | 3 | 8 | 3+ |

An Imagifier is a single model equipped with a bolt pistol, boltgun, frag grenades and krak grenades.

| WEAPON | RANGE | TYPE | S | AP | D | ABILITIES |
|--------|-------|------|---|-----|---|-----------|
| Bolt pistol | 12" | Pistol 1 | 4 | 0 | 1 | - |
| Boltgun | 24" | Rapid Fire 1 | 4 | 0 | 1 | - |
| Frag grenade | 6" | Grenade D6 | 3 | 0 | 1 | - |
| Krak grenade | 6" | Grenade 1 | 6 | -1 | D3 | - |

| ABILITIES | Acts of Faith, Shield of Faith (pg 90)<br><br>**Simulacrum Imperialis:** Roll a D6 at the start of each of your turns; on a 4+ you can pick a friendly <ORDER> unit within 6" of this model and perform an Act of Faith with it. This is in addition to the Act of Faith you are normally allowed to use in a turn. |
|-----------|-----------|
| **FACTION KEYWORDS** | IMPERIUM, ADEPTUS MINISTORUM, ADEPTA SORORITAS, <ORDER> |
| **KEYWORDS** | CHARACTER, INFANTRY, IMAGIFIER |

## HOSPITALLER

**2 POWER**

| NAME | M | WS | BS | S | T | W | A | Ld | Sv |
|------|---|-----|-----|---|---|---|---|-----|-----|
| Hospitaller | 6" | 4+ | 3+ | 3 | 3 | 4 | 2 | 8 | 3+ |

A Hospitaller is a single model armed with a chirurgeon's tools.

| WEAPON | RANGE | TYPE | S | AP | D | ABILITIES |
|--------|-------|------|---|-----|---|-----------|
| Chirurgeon's tools | Melee | Melee | User | -1 | 1 | - |

| ABILITIES | Acts of Faith, Shield of Faith (pg 90)<br><br>**Healer:** At the end of your Movement phase a Hospitaller can attempt to heal or revive a single model. Select a friendly ADEPTA SORORITAS INFANTRY unit within 3" of the Hospitaller and roll a D6. On a roll of 4+, one model in the unit recovers D3 lost wounds; if the chosen unit contains no wounded models but one or more of its models have been slain during the battle, then a single slain model is returned to the unit with 1 wound remaining. A unit can only be the target of the Healer ability once in each turn. |
|-----------|-----------|
| **FACTION KEYWORDS** | IMPERIUM, ADEPTUS MINISTORUM, ADEPTA SORORITAS |
| **KEYWORDS** | CHARACTER, INFANTRY, HOSPITALLER |

## DIALOGUS

**1 POWER**

| NAME | M | WS | BS | S | T | W | A | Ld | Sv |
|------|---|-----|-----|---|---|---|---|-----|-----|
| Dialogus | 6" | 4+ | 3+ | 3 | 3 | 4 | 2 | 8 | 6+ |

A Dialogus is a single model armed with a Dialogus staff.

| WEAPON | RANGE | TYPE | S | AP | D | ABILITIES |
|--------|-------|------|---|-----|---|-----------|
| Dialogus staff | Melee | Melee | +1 | 0 | 1 | When attacking with this weapon, you must subtract 1 from the hit roll. |

| ABILITIES | Acts of Faith, Shield of Faith (pg 90)<br><br>**Laud Hailer:** Friendly ADEPTA SORORITAS units within 6" of this model can re-roll failed Morale tests. |
|-----------|-----------|
| **FACTION KEYWORDS** | IMPERIUM, ADEPTUS MINISTORUM, ADEPTA SORORITAS |
| **KEYWORDS** | CHARACTER, INFANTRY, DIALOGUS |

# BATTLE SISTERS SQUAD

| NAME | M | WS | BS | S | T | W | A | Ld | Sv |
|---|---|---|---|---|---|---|---|---|---|
| Battle Sister | 6" | 4+ | 3+ | 3 | 3 | 1 | 1 | 7 | 3+ |
| Sister Superior | 6" | 4+ | 3+ | 3 | 3 | 1 | 2 | 8 | 3+ |

This unit contains 1 Sister Superior and 4 Battle Sisters. It may contain up to 5 additional Battle Sisters (**Power Rating +4**) or up to 10 additional Battle Sisters (**Power Rating +8**). Each model is armed with a bolt pistol, boltgun, frag grenades and krak grenades.

| WEAPON | RANGE | TYPE | S | AP | D | ABILITIES |
|---|---|---|---|---|---|---|
| Bolt pistol | 12" | Pistol 1 | 4 | 0 | 1 | - |
| Boltgun | 24" | Rapid Fire 1 | 4 | 0 | 1 | - |
| Frag grenade | 6" | Grenade D6 | 3 | 0 | 1 | - |
| Krak grenade | 6" | Grenade 1 | 6 | -1 | D3 | - |

| WARGEAR OPTIONS | • One Battle Sister may replace her boltgun with a weapon from the *Special Weapons* list.<br>• One Battle Sister may replace her boltgun with a weapon from the *Special Weapons* or *Heavy Weapons* list.<br>• The Sister Superior may replace her boltgun with a weapon from the *Melee Weapons* or *Ranged Weapons* list.<br>• The Sister Superior may replace her bolt pistol with a weapon from the *Pistols* list. |
|---|---|
| **ABILITIES** | Acts of Faith, Shield of Faith (pg 90) |
| **FACTION KEYWORDS** | IMPERIUM, ADEPTUS MINISTORUM, ADEPTA SORORITAS, <ORDER> |
| **KEYWORDS** | INFANTRY, BATTLE SISTERS SQUAD |

# SERAPHIM SQUAD

| NAME | M | WS | BS | S | T | W | A | Ld | Sv |
|---|---|---|---|---|---|---|---|---|---|
| Seraphim | 12" | 3+ | 3+ | 3 | 3 | 1 | 1 | 7 | 3+ |
| Seraphim Superior | 12" | 3+ | 3+ | 3 | 3 | 1 | 2 | 8 | 3+ |

This unit contains 1 Seraphim Superior and 4 Seraphim. It can include up to 5 additional Seraphim (**Power Rating +4**). Each model is armed with two bolt pistols, frag grenades and krak grenades.

| WEAPON | RANGE | TYPE | S | AP | D | ABILITIES |
|---|---|---|---|---|---|---|
| Bolt pistol | 12" | Pistol 1 | 4 | 0 | 1 | - |
| Hand flamer | 6" | Pistol D6 | 3 | 0 | 1 | This weapon automatically hits its target. |
| Inferno pistol | 6" | Pistol 1 | 8 | -4 | D6 | If the target is within half range of this weapon, roll two dice when inflicting damage with it and discard the lowest result. |
| Frag grenade | 6" | Grenade D6 | 3 | 0 | 1 | - |
| Krak grenade | 6" | Grenade 1 | 6 | -1 | D3 | - |

| WARGEAR OPTIONS | • Up to two Seraphim may replace both their bolt pistols with two hand flamers or two inferno pistols.<br>• The Seraphim Superior may replace one of her bolt pistols with a chainsword or power sword.<br>• The Seraphim Superior may replace her other bolt pistol with a plasma pistol. |
|---|---|

| ABILITIES | Acts of Faith, Shield of Faith (pg 90)<br><br>**Angelic Visage:** Re-roll failed Shield of Faith invulnerable saves for this unit. | **Sky Strike:** During deployment, you can set up a unit of Seraphim high in the sky instead of placing them on the battlefield. At the end of any of your Movement phases the Seraphim can descend from the sky – set them up anywhere on the battlefield that is more than 9" away from any enemy models. |
|---|---|---|
| **FACTION KEYWORDS** | IMPERIUM, ADEPTUS MINISTORUM, ADEPTA SORORITAS, <ORDER> | |
| **KEYWORDS** | INFANTRY, JUMP PACK, FLY, SERAPHIM | |

## CELESTIAN SQUAD

**5** POWER

| NAME | M | WS | BS | S | T | W | A | Ld | Sv |
|---|---|---|---|---|---|---|---|---|---|
| Celestian | 6" | 3+ | 3+ | 3 | 3 | 1 | 2 | 8 | 3+ |
| Celestian Superior | 6" | 3+ | 3+ | 3 | 3 | 1 | 3 | 9 | 3+ |

This unit contains 1 Celestian Superior and 4 Celestians. It may contain up to 5 additional Celestians (**Power Rating +5**). Each model is armed with a bolt pistol, boltgun, frag grenades and krak grenades.

| WEAPON | RANGE | TYPE | S | AP | D | ABILITIES |
|---|---|---|---|---|---|---|
| Bolt pistol | 12" | Pistol 1 | 4 | 0 | 1 | - |
| Boltgun | 24" | Rapid Fire 1 | 4 | 0 | 1 | - |
| Frag grenade | 6" | Grenade D6 | 3 | 0 | 1 | - |
| Krak grenade | 6" | Grenade 1 | 6 | -1 | D3 | - |

| WARGEAR OPTIONS | • One Celestian may replace her boltgun with a weapon from the *Special Weapons* list.<br>• One other Celestian may replace her boltgun with a weapon from the *Special Weapons* or *Heavy Weapons* list.<br>• The Celestian Superior may replace her boltgun with a weapon from the *Melee Weapons* or *Ranged Weapons* list.<br>• The Celestian Superior may replace her bolt pistol with a weapon from the *Pistols* list. |
|---|---|
| ABILITIES | Acts of Faith, Shield of Faith (pg 90)<br><br>**Bodyguard:** Roll a D6 each time a friendly <ORDER> CHARACTER loses a wound whilst they are within 3" of this unit; on a 2+ a model from this unit can intercept that hit – the character does not lose a wound but this unit suffers a mortal wound. |
| FACTION KEYWORDS | IMPERIUM, ADEPTUS MINISTORUM, ADEPTA SORORITAS, <ORDER> |
| KEYWORDS | INFANTRY, CELESTIANS |

## MISTRESS OF REPENTANCE

**2** POWER

| NAME | M | WS | BS | S | T | W | A | Ld | Sv |
|---|---|---|---|---|---|---|---|---|---|
| Mistress of Repentance | 6" | 3+ | 3+ | 3 | 3 | 4 | 3 | 8 | 3+ |

A Mistress of Repentance is a single model armed with neural whips, frag grenades and krak grenades.

| WEAPON | RANGE | TYPE | S | AP | D | ABILITIES |
|---|---|---|---|---|---|---|
| Neural whips | Melee | Melee | User | -2 | 1 | Add 1 to the wound rolls for attacks made with this weapon if the target unit's highest Leadership characteristic is less than 8 (other than VEHICLES). |
| Frag grenade | 6" | Grenade D6 | 3 | 0 | 1 | - |
| Krak grenade | 6" | Grenade 1 | 6 | -1 | D3 | - |

| ABILITIES | Acts of Faith, Shield of Faith (pg 90)<br><br>**Angelic Visage:** Re-roll failed Shield of Faith invulnerable saves for this unit. | **Driven Onwards:** You can re-roll Advance, charge and hit rolls for friendly <ORDER> REPENTIA units that are within 6" of this model. |
|---|---|---|
| FACTION KEYWORDS | IMPERIUM, ADEPTUS MINISTORUM, ADEPTA SORORITAS, <ORDER> | |
| KEYWORDS | CHARACTER, INFANTRY, MISTRESS OF REPENTANCE | |

## REPENTIA SQUAD

| NAME | M | WS | BS | S | T | W | A | Ld | Sv |
|------|---|----|----|---|---|---|---|----|----|
| Sister Repentia | 6" | 3+ | 3+ | 3 | 3 | 1 | 2 | 8 | 7+ |

This unit contains 3 Sisters Repentia. It may contain up to 3 additional Sisters Repentia (**Power Rating +3**) or up to 6 additional Sisters Repentia (**Power Rating +6**). Each model is armed with a penitent eviscerator.

| WEAPON | RANGE | TYPE | S | AP | D | ABILITIES |
|--------|-------|------|---|----|----|-----------|
| Penitent eviscerator | Melee | Melee | x2 | -2 | 2 | When attacking with this weapon, you must subtract 1 from the hit roll. |

| ABILITIES | Acts of Faith, Shield of Faith (pg 90) |
|-----------|----------------------------------------|
| FACTION KEYWORDS | IMPERIUM, ADEPTUS MINISTORUM, ADEPTA SORORITAS, <ORDER> |
| KEYWORDS | INFANTRY, REPENTIA |

## RETRIBUTOR SQUAD

| NAME | M | WS | BS | S | T | W | A | Ld | Sv |
|------|---|----|----|---|---|---|---|----|----|
| Retributor | 6" | 4+ | 3+ | 3 | 3 | 1 | 1 | 7 | 3+ |
| Retributor Superior | 6" | 4+ | 3+ | 3 | 3 | 1 | 2 | 7 | 3+ |

This unit contains 1 Retributor Superior and 4 Retributors. It may contain up to 5 additional Retributors (**Power Rating +4**). Each model is armed with a bolt pistol, a boltgun, frag grenades and krak grenades.

| WEAPON | RANGE | TYPE | S | AP | D | ABILITIES |
|--------|-------|------|---|----|----|-----------|
| Bolt pistol | 12" | Pistol 1 | 4 | 0 | 1 | - |
| Boltgun | 24" | Rapid Fire 1 | 4 | 0 | 1 | - |
| Frag grenade | 6" | Grenade D6 | 3 | 0 | 1 | - |
| Krak grenade | 6" | Grenade 1 | 6 | -1 | D3 | - |

| WARGEAR OPTIONS | • Up to four Retributors may replace their boltgun with a weapon from the *Heavy Weapons* list.<br>• The Retributor Superior may replace her boltgun with a weapon from the *Melee Weapons* or *Ranged Weapons* list.<br>• The Retributor Superior may replace their bolt pistol with a weapon from the *Pistols* list. |
|-----------------|-----------------------------------------------------------------------------------------------------------------------|

| ABILITIES | Acts of Faith, Shield of Faith (pg 90) |
|-----------|----------------------------------------|
| FACTION KEYWORDS | IMPERIUM, ADEPTUS MINISTORUM, ADEPTA SORORITAS, <ORDER> |
| KEYWORDS | INFANTRY, RETRIBUTORS |

Hearts ablaze with devotion to the God-Emperor, the Sisters of Battle purge the faithless and corrupt with bolter and flame.

# DOMINION SQUAD

**5 POWER**

| NAME | M | WS | BS | S | T | W | A | Ld | Sv |
|------|---|----|----|---|---|---|---|----|----|
| Dominion | 6" | 4+ | 3+ | 3 | 3 | 1 | 1 | 7 | 3+ |
| Dominion Superior | 6" | 4+ | 3+ | 3 | 3 | 1 | 2 | 8 | 3+ |

This unit contains 1 Dominion Superior and 4 Dominions. It can include up to 5 additional Dominions (**Power Rating +4**). Each model is armed with a bolt pistol, boltgun, frag grenades and krak grenades.

| WEAPON | RANGE | TYPE | S | AP | D | ABILITIES |
|--------|-------|------|---|----|----|-----------|
| Bolt pistol | 12" | Pistol 1 | 4 | 0 | 1 | - |
| Boltgun | 24" | Rapid Fire 1 | 4 | 0 | 1 | - |
| Frag grenade | 6" | Grenade D6 | 3 | 0 | 1 | - |
| Krak grenade | 6" | Grenade 1 | 6 | -1 | D3 | - |

| WARGEAR OPTIONS | • Up to four Dominions may replace their boltgun with a weapon from the *Special Weapons* list. |
|---|---|
| | • The Dominion Superior may replace her boltgun with a weapon from the *Ranged Weapons* or *Melee Weapons* list. |
| | • The Dominion Superior may replace her bolt pistol with a weapon from the *Pistols* list. |

| ABILITIES | **Acts of Faith, Shield of Faith** (pg 90) |
|---|---|
| | **Vanguard:** Once both sides are deployed but before the first player takes their turn, this unit can move as if it were their Movement phase. If both players have units that can do this, the player who is taking the first turn moves their units first. If all of the models embarked on a transport vehicle have this ability, then the transport vehicle can make the move instead. |

| FACTION KEYWORDS | IMPERIUM, ADEPTUS MINISTORUM, ADEPTA SORORITAS, <ORDER> |
|---|---|
| KEYWORDS | INFANTRY, DOMINIONS |

---

# SORORITAS RHINO

**4 POWER**

| NAME | M | WS | BS | S | T | W | A | Ld | Sv |
|------|---|----|----|---|---|---|---|----|----|
| Sororitas Rhino | * | 6+ | * | 6 | 7 | 10 | * | 8 | 3+ |

A Sororitas Rhino is a single model equipped with a storm bolter.

| WEAPON | RANGE | TYPE | S | AP | D | ABILITIES |
|--------|-------|------|---|----|----|-----------|
| Hunter-killer missile | 48" | Heavy 1 | 8 | -2 | D6 | Each hunter-killer missile can only be fired once per battle. |
| Storm bolter | 24" | Rapid Fire 2 | 4 | 0 | 1 | - |

**DAMAGE**

Some of this model's characteristics change as it suffers damage, as shown below:

| REMAINING W | M | BS | A |
|-------------|---|----|----|
| 6-10+ | 12" | 3+ | 3 |
| 3-5 | 6" | 4+ | D3 |
| 1-2 | 3" | 5+ | 1 |

| WARGEAR OPTIONS | • This model may take a hunter-killer missile. |
|---|---|
| | • This model make take an additional storm bolter. |

| ABILITIES | **Shield of Faith** (pg 90) | **Smoke Launchers:** Once per game, instead of shooting any weapons in the Shooting phase, this model can use its smoke launchers; until your next Shooting phase your opponent must subtract 1 from all hit rolls for ranged weapons that target this vehicle. |
|---|---|---|
| | **Self-repair:** Roll a D6 at the start of each of your turns; on a 6, this model regains one lost wound. | |
| | **Explodes:** If this model is reduced to 0 wounds, roll a D6 before removing it from the battlefield and before any embarked models disembark. On a 6 it explodes, and each unit within 6" suffers D3 mortal wounds. | |

| TRANSPORT | This model can transport 10 ADEPTUS MINISTORUM INFANTRY models. It cannot transport JUMP PACK models or ADEPTA SORORITAS models from a different Order. |
|---|---|
| FACTION KEYWORDS | IMPERIUM, ADEPTUS MINISTORUM, ADEPTA SORORITAS, <ORDER> |
| KEYWORDS | VEHICLE, TRANSPORT, RHINO, SORORITAS RHINO |

## IMMOLATOR

**5 POWER**

| NAME | M | WS | BS | S | T | W | A | Ld | Sv |
|------|---|----|----|---|---|---|---|----|----|
| Immolator | * | 6+ | * | 6 | 7 | 10 | * | 8 | 3+ |

An Immolator is a single model equipped with a immolation flamer.

**DAMAGE**

Some of this model's characteristics change as it suffers damage, as shown below:

| REMAINING W | M | BS | A |
|-------------|---|----|---|
| 6-10+ | 12" | 3+ | 3 |
| 3-5 | 6" | 4+ | D3 |
| 1-2 | 3" | 5+ | 1 |

| WEAPON | RANGE | TYPE | S | AP | D | ABILITIES |
|--------|-------|------|---|----|----|-----------|
| Hunter-killer missile | 48" | Heavy 1 | 8 | -2 | D6 | Each hunter-killer missile can only be fired once per battle. |
| Immolation flamer | 12" | Assault 2D6 | 5 | -1 | 1 | This weapon automatically hits its target. |
| Storm bolter | 24" | Rapid Fire 2 | 4 | 0 | 1 | - |
| Twin heavy bolter | 36" | Heavy 6 | 5 | -1 | 1 | - |
| Twin multi-melta | 24" | Heavy 2 | 8 | -4 | D6 | If the target is within half range of this weapon, roll two dice when inflicting damage with it and discard the lowest result. |

**WARGEAR OPTIONS**
- This model may replace its immolation flamer with a twin heavy bolter or twin multi-melta.
- This model may take a storm bolter.
- This model may take a hunter-killer missile.

**ABILITIES**

Shield of Faith (pg 90)

**Explodes:** If this model is reduced to 0 wounds, roll a D6 before removing it from the battlefield and before any embarked models disembark. On a 6 it explodes, and each unit within 6" suffers D3 mortal wounds.

**Smoke Launchers:** Once per game, instead of shooting any weapons in the Shooting phase, this model can use its smoke launchers; until your next Shooting phase your opponent must subtract 1 from all hit rolls for ranged weapons that target this vehicle.

**TRANSPORT**

This model can transport 6 ADEPTUS MINISTORUM INFANTRY models. It cannot transport JUMP PACK models or ADEPTA SORORITAS models from a different Order.

**FACTION KEYWORDS**

IMPERIUM, ADEPTUS MINISTORUM, ADEPTA SORORITAS, <ORDER>

**KEYWORDS**

VEHICLE, TRANSPORT, IMMOLATOR

---

## EXORCIST

**8 POWER**

| NAME | M | WS | BS | S | T | W | A | Ld | Sv |
|------|---|----|----|---|---|---|---|----|----|
| Exorcist | * | 6+ | * | 7 | 8 | 12 | * | 7 | 3+ |

An Exorcist is a single model equipped with an Exorcist missile launcher.

**DAMAGE**

Some of this model's characteristics change as it suffers damage, as shown below:

| REMAINING W | M | BS | A |
|-------------|---|----|---|
| 7-12+ | 12" | 3+ | 3 |
| 4-6 | 6" | 4+ | D3 |
| 1-3 | 4" | 5+ | 1 |

| WEAPON | RANGE | TYPE | S | AP | D | ABILITIES |
|--------|-------|------|---|----|----|-----------|
| Exorcist missile launcher | 48" | Heavy D6 | 8 | -4 | D3 | - |
| Hunter-killer missile | 48" | Heavy 1 | 8 | -2 | D6 | Each hunter-killer missile can only be fired once per battle. |
| Storm bolter | 24" | Rapid Fire 2 | 4 | 0 | 1 | - |

**WARGEAR OPTIONS**
- This model may take a storm bolter.
- This model may take a hunter-killer missile.

**ABILITIES**

Shield of Faith (pg 90)

**Explodes:** If this model is reduced to 0 wounds, roll a D6 before removing it from the battlefield. On a 6 it explodes, and each unit within 6" suffers D3 mortal wounds.

**Smoke Launchers:** Once per game, instead of shooting any weapons in the Shooting phase, this model can use its smoke launchers; until your next Shooting phase your opponent must subtract 1 from all hit rolls for ranged weapons that target this vehicle.

**FACTION KEYWORDS**

IMPERIUM, ADEPTUS MINISTORUM, ADEPTA SORORITAS, <ORDER>

**KEYWORDS**

VEHICLE, EXORCIST

# ADEPTUS ASTRA TELEPATHICA

**The Imperium is host to untold numbers of psychically active individuals. Left unchecked and unministered, psykers can be extremely dangerous, their talent connecting them to the warp and the terrible creatures that lurk there. As such, the High Lords of Terra seek to recruit, categorise and train them, the better to guide them towards the Emperor's light.**

Over the long course of its history, Humanity has evolved from a race confined to a single world to a galaxy-spanning empire of souls, and its psychic potential has blossomed with its expansion. Although a relatively small minority of humans develop such powers, these numbers are ever on the increase. Over the course of the Time of Ending, reports of psychic phenomena have grown at an exponential rate – where incidents of confirmed psyker activity were once one in a billion, they are now hundreds of times more frequent. Some of these souls are gifted, their destinies lying in the service of the Immortal Emperor of Mankind. Others are cursed beyond measure – their fates only to become the playthings of twisted monsters from the warp.

Many psykers are capable of becoming vital assets to the Imperium, but regardless of their potential, each one poses a significant threat because of their abilities. The denizens of the warp prey upon those with weak wills, and all psykers offer these creatures a conduit via which they can enter reality. The work of the Adeptus Astra Telepathica is therefore vital to the continued survival of the human race. This ancient institution was founded in secrecy, but has become a framework that extends throughout the galaxy, an organisation tasked with the acquisition, grading and training of psykers from every human world.

## BLACK SHIPS

The League of Black Ships is a great armada, second only to the fleets of the Imperial Navy in size. Its captains and landing parties scour the worlds of the Imperium for those who show any signs of psychic aptitude. These individuals are rounded up and stowed in thrice-blessed brigs protected by powerful null auras that can contain all but the most powerful psykers. The constant psychic occlusion and discordant noise broadcast throughout the Black Ships keep those incarcerated in a state of anguish – and hence docility – on the long haul back to Terra.

## SCHOLASTICA PSYKANA

The source of the Imperium's sanctioned psykers, the Scholastica Psykana is an organisation steeped in arcane lore. Upon reaching Terra, prospective psykers are handed to the Scholastica Psykana for assessment. Any determined to be tainted are immediately destroyed – assuming they do not escape detection. Those who show promise in the empyric arts may become Astropaths or Wyrdvane Psykers, whereas those graded as Primary are given five years of harsh and rigorous training. These are the individuals that may become Primaris Psykers, Inquisitors, Librarians and even Grey Knights should they prove truly indomitable.

The vast majority of those brought to Terra by the Black Ships are judged to lack the willpower needed to serve the Emperor, but even then, the Imperium has use for them. These unfortunate acolytes are used to feed the Golden Throne's eldritch machineries, or to line the walls of the Chamber of the Astronomican. There they are slowly devoured by the immense psychic might of the Emperor.

Astropaths are psykers who – through the strange psalms and chorister rituals of their order – can swiftly transmit visionary messages across the interstellar distances that divide one system from another. Without these telepathic links binding the Imperium, the cohesion of Mankind's realm would soon crumble away, leaving only anarchy and disorder behind. Some Astra Militarum regiments in vital war zones have Astropaths assigned to them, the better to coordinate their campaigns with the wider Imperial war machine. These militarised psykers are trained in far more deadly arts than telepathic communication and the reading of the Emperor's Tarot, and are rightly held in fear by the common soldiery as a result. As part of their training, Astropaths undergo the Soul Binding ritual. If they are judged worthy, they will witness the Emperor's glory first hand, and inherit a tiny portion of his power – though this inevitably costs them their sight, which is seared away by the blinding magnificence of the Master of Mankind.

Primaris Psykers possess abilities far beyond those of lesser initiates, and are trusted to operate independently on the battlefield. Though not as powerful as a Space Marine Librarian, their knowledge of their craft is considerable and their extensive military experience makes them a significant asset to Astra Militarum leaders. Wyrdvane Psykers are less adept at controlling their abilities without aid, but rather act in concert to both amplify and guide their energies, drawing on each other's strength to harness the power of the warp.

# ADEPTUS ASTRA TELEPATHICA ARMY LIST

This section contains all of the datasheets that you will need in order to fight battles with your Adeptus Astra Telepathica miniatures. Each datasheet includes the characteristics profiles of the unit it describes, as well as any wargear and abilities it may have. Some rules are common to several Astra Telepathica units – these are described below and referenced on the datasheets.

## PSYKANA DISCIPLINE

Before the battle, generate the psychic powers for **PSYKERS** that can use powers from the Psykana discipline using the table below. You can either roll a D3 to generate their powers randomly (re-roll any duplicate results), or you can select the psychic powers you wish the psyker to have.

| PSYKANA DISCIPLINE | |
|---|---|
| **D3** | **PSYCHIC POWER** |
| 1 | **Terrifying Visions**<br>*Terrifying Visions* has a warp charge value of 7. If manifested, choose an enemy unit within 18" of the psyker. That unit subtracts 2 from its Leadership until the start of your next turn. |
| 2 | **Gaze of the Emperor**<br>*Gaze of the Emperor* has a warp charge value of 6. If manifested, draw a straight line 2D6" long directly away from the psyker. Roll a dice for each model the centre of the line passes over. On a 4+ that model's unit suffers a mortal wound. |
| 3 | **Psychic Barrier**<br>*Psychic Barrier* has a warp charge value of 6. If manifested, select a friendly **ASTRA MILITARUM** unit within 12" of the psyker. Until the start of your next Psychic phase, add 1 to that unit's saving throws. |

# PRIMARIS PSYKER

**2 POWER**

| NAME | M | WS | BS | S | T | W | A | Ld | Sv |
|------|---|----|----|---|---|---|---|----|----|
| Primaris Psyker | 6" | 3+ | 3+ | 3 | 3 | 4 | 3 | 8 | 5+ |

A Primaris Psyker is a single model armed with a laspistol and force stave.

| WEAPON | RANGE | TYPE | S | AP | D | ABILITIES |
|--------|-------|------|---|----|----|-----------|
| Laspistol | 12" | Pistol 1 | 3 | 0 | 1 | - |
| Force stave | Melee | Melee | +2 | -1 | D3 | - |

| ABILITIES | **It's For Your Own Good:** If this model is slain as a result of Perils of the Warp whilst within 6" of a friendly **Commissar**, they are executed before anything untoward can happen – the power they were attempting still fails, but units within 6" of them do not suffer D3 mortal wounds as normal. |
|-----------|---|
| PSYKER | This model can attempt to manifest one psychic power in each friendly Psychic phase, and attempt to deny one psychic power in each enemy Psychic phase. It knows the *Smite* power and two psychic powers from the Psykana discipline (pg 105). |
| FACTION KEYWORDS | **Imperium, Astra Militarum, Astra Telepathica, Scholastica Psykana** |
| KEYWORDS | **Character, Infantry, Psyker, Primaris Psyker** |

Imperial Guardsmen may fear and distrust sanctioned psykers, but they cannot deny the lethal might of a psychic choir in action.

## WYRDVANE PSYKERS

**1 POWER**

| NAME | M | WS | BS | S | T | W | A | Ld | Sv |
|------|---|----|----|---|---|---|---|----|----|
| Wyrdvane Psyker | 6" | 5+ | 4+ | 3 | 3 | 1 | 1 | 7 | 6+ |

This unit contains 3 Wyrdvane Psykers. It may contain up to 3 additional Wyrdvane Psykers (**Power Rating +1**) or up to 6 additional Wyrdvane Psykers (**Power Rating +2**). Each model is armed with a laspistol and a Wyrdvane stave.

| WEAPON | RANGE | TYPE | S | AP | D | ABILITIES |
|--------|-------|------|---|----|----|-----------|
| Laspistol | 12" | Pistol 1 | 3 | 0 | 1 | - |
| Wyrdvane stave | Melee | Melee | +1 | 0 | 1 | - |

| ABILITIES | **Choir of Minds:** Each time you take a Psychic test or Deny the Witch test for this unit, roll 1D6 instead of 2D6. You can add 1 to Psychic tests you make for this unit if it has 3 or more models, or 2 to tests if it has 6 or more models. |
|-----------|---|

| PSYKER | This unit can attempt to manifest one psychic power in each friendly Psychic phase, and attempt to deny one psychic power in each enemy Psychic phase. It knows the *Smite* psychic power and one psychic power from the Psykana discipline (pg 105).<br><br>When manifesting or denying a psychic power, first select a model in the unit – measure range, visibility etc. from this model. If this unit suffers Perils of the Warp, it suffers D3 mortal wounds as described in the core rules, but units within 6" will only suffer damage if the Perils of the Warp causes the last model in the manifesting unit to be slain. |
|--------|---|

| FACTION KEYWORDS | IMPERIUM, ASTRA MILITARUM, ASTRA TELEPATHICA, SCHOLASTICA PSYKANA |
|------------------|---|
| KEYWORDS | INFANTRY, PSYKER, WYRDVANE PSYKERS |

## ASTROPATH

**1 POWER**

| NAME | M | WS | BS | S | T | W | A | Ld | Sv |
|------|---|----|----|---|---|---|---|----|----|
| Astropath | 6" | 5+ | 6+ | 3 | 3 | 3 | 1 | 6 | 6+ |

An Astropath is a single model armed with a telepathica stave.

| WEAPON | RANGE | TYPE | S | AP | D | ABILITIES |
|--------|-------|------|---|----|----|-----------|
| Laspistol | 12" | Pistol 1 | 3 | 0 | 1 | - |
| Telepathica stave | Melee | Melee | +1 | 0 | D3 | - |

| WARGEAR OPTIONS | • This model may replace its telepathica stave with a laspistol. |
|-----------------|---|

| ABILITIES | **Astral Divination:** At the start of your Shooting phase, pick an enemy unit within 18" of this model. For the duration of the phase, the unit you picked gains no bonus to their saving throws for being in cover when it is targeted by attacks made by friendly **ASTRA MILITARUM** units within 6" of this model. | **Telepathic Assault:** Each time you take a Psychic test for this unit when it attempts to manifest *Smite*, roll 1D6 instead of 2D6. |
|-----------|---|---|

| PSYKER | This model can attempt to manifest one psychic power in each friendly Psychic phase, and attempt to deny one psychic power in each enemy Psychic phase. It knows the *Smite* power and one power from the Psykana discipline (pg 105). |
|--------|---|

| FACTION KEYWORDS | IMPERIUM, ASTRA MILITARUM, ASTRA TELEPATHICA, SCHOLASTICA PSYKANA |
|------------------|---|
| KEYWORDS | CHARACTER, INFANTRY, PSYKER, ASTROPATH |

# SISTERS OF SILENCE

Clad in power armour and armed with bolter and blade, the Sisters of Silence make for vicious combatants, but it is their aura of nullification that gives them their legendary status. To a normal human, these witch-hunters are unsettling; to a psyker, even standing near a Sister of Silence is an unbearable ordeal.

Much like the Adeptus Custodes, the Sisters of Silence are the personal elite of the Master of Mankind. Together, the two organisations are often called the Talons of the Emperor, for it is they that rip the dark heart of tyranny from the body of the Imperium. It is the Sisters of Silence who form the foremost defence against the darkness that haunts Mankind's evolution – in many ways they are the truest and most effective weapon ever created in the quest to defy the Dark Gods.

The Pariah gene occurs in perhaps one in a trillion humans. It is well named indeed, for those in whom it germinates are excluded and persecuted by the vast majority of the Imperium's citizenry. Where a normal mortal man or woman has a spiritual core, an ethereal animus that some call a soul, those with the Pariah gene have a sucking void so powerful it casts a shroud over the spirits of those nearby. This manifests as a feeling of unease, disquiet and fear in those who stay in a Pariah's proximity, and causes most to shun their company. Only those who appreciate the very real danger of psychic apocalypse realise that these Pariahs are in fact natural-born weapons that have immeasurable value in the long war against Chaos. The most visionary of these far-sighted scholars was the Emperor.

Even before the dawn of the Imperium, the Emperor was gathering these 'blanks' to his Imperial Palace upon Terra. Much in the same vein as psykers, they were tested, categorised, and given a new life as assets of the Imperium. The most promising male Pariahs would be sent to the Officio Assassinorum, there to be remade as the anti-psychic horrors known as Culexus Assassins. The best of the females were instead given stringent mental and physical testing, reconditioning, and autohypnotic training that shaped them into living weapons against the supernatural enemies of Mankind. It was these warriors, true of heart, strong of mind and absent of soul, that became the first Sisters of Silence.

Upon full induction into their order, the Sisters of Silence swear a vow to speak only with actions instead of words – the forked tongues of the demagogue and the Daemon have led men astray for millennia, so they forsake such tools of deception completely. This vow of fealty is sacred to the Emperor, and there are no records of it having been broken even under the most extreme duress. The Sisters instead communicate via Thoughtmark, a complex system of hand gestures that can be simplified in the heat of battle or translated through interlocutors of lesser rank so the order might better fight alongside the armies of the Imperium. None relish such an alliance; even a hardened veteran of the Astra Militarum will find his skin crawling and his mind aching when he is near these Null-Maidens. In the heat of battle, the Sisters of Silence magnify their disruptive aura through a great effort of will, projecting their unsettling otherness in rippling waves that make it difficult even to look upon them. The psykers they hunt find the raging powers they once wielded with a twitch of their fingertips guttering out, etheric energies draining from their bodies and mental shields stripped away. To become little more than a simple mortal – often clad in no more protective apparel than robes and jewellery – is a horrifying experience for such would-be conquerors. This lesson in humility is swiftly followed by an agonising death as the Sisters of Silence attack. Prosecutor squads unleash storms of bolt rounds as Witchseekers lay down burning promethium infernos, the combined assault enough to break even a frenzied horde of enemies. Those that survive are cut down by the powered greatswords of the Vigilator squads – even the mightiest psykers are unceremoniously beheaded as a lesson to all who would defy the Emperor's rule.

# SISTERS OF SILENCE ARMY LIST

The following section contains all of the datasheets that you will need in order to fight battles with your Sisters of Silence miniatures. Each datasheet includes the characteristics profiles of the unit it describes, as well as any wargear and abilities it may have. Some rules are common to several Sisters of Silence units – these are described below and referenced on the datasheets.

## ABILITIES

The following abilities are common to many Sisters of Silence units:

### WITCH HUNTERS

You can re-roll failed wound rolls for this unit when it attacks **PSYKERS** in the Fight phase.

## PSYCHIC ABOMINATION

This unit can never be targeted or affected by psychic powers in any way. In addition, enemy **PSYKERS** must subtract 1 from any Psychic tests and Deny the Witch tests they take for each unit with this ability that is within 18" of them (to a maximum of -4). Note, however, that this ability has no effect whilst the unit is embarked upon a **TRANSPORT**.

## PROSECUTORS

**3 POWER**

| NAME | M | WS | BS | S | T | W | A | Ld | Sv |
|------|---|----|----|---|---|---|---|----|----|
| Prosecutor | 7" | 3+ | 3+ | 3 | 3 | 1 | 2 | 8 | 3+ |
| Sister Superior | 7" | 3+ | 3+ | 3 | 3 | 1 | 3 | 9 | 3+ |

This unit contains 1 Sister Superior and 4 Prosecutors. It can include up to 5 additional Prosecutors (**Power Rating +3**). Each model is armed with a boltgun and psyk-out grenades.

| WEAPON | RANGE | TYPE | S | AP | D | ABILITIES |
|--------|-------|------|---|----|----|-----------|
| Boltgun | 24" | Rapid Fire 1 | 4 | 0 | 1 | - |
| Psyk-out grenade | 6" | Grenade D3 | 2 | 0 | 1 | Each time you roll a hit roll of 6+ for this weapon when targeting a **Psyker** or **Daemon**, the target suffers a mortal wound instead of the normal damage. |

| ABILITIES | Psychic Abomination, Witch Hunters (pg 109) |
|-----------|---------------------------------------------|
| | **Prosecution Protocols:** Models in this unit can target enemy **Characters** that are **Psykers**, even if they are not the closest enemy unit. |
| FACTION KEYWORDS | IMPERIUM, ASTRA TELEPATHICA, SISTERS OF SILENCE |
| KEYWORDS | INFANTRY, PROSECUTORS |

## VIGILATORS

**4 POWER**

| NAME | M | WS | BS | S | T | W | A | Ld | Sv |
|------|---|----|----|---|---|---|---|----|----|
| Vigilator | 7" | 3+ | 3+ | 3 | 3 | 1 | 2 | 8 | 3+ |
| Sister Superior | 7" | 3+ | 3+ | 3 | 3 | 1 | 3 | 9 | 3+ |

This unit contains 1 Sister Superior and 4 Vigilators. It can include up to 5 additional Vigilators (**Power Rating +4**). Each model is armed with an executioner greatblade and psyk-out grenades.

| WEAPON | RANGE | TYPE | S | AP | D | ABILITIES |
|--------|-------|------|---|----|----|-----------|
| Executioner greatblade | Melee | Melee | +1 | -3 | D3 | - |
| Psyk-out grenade | 6" | Grenade D3 | 2 | 0 | 1 | Each time you roll a hit roll of 6+ for this weapon when targeting a **Psyker** or **Daemon**, the target suffers a mortal wound instead of the normal damage. |

| ABILITIES | Psychic Abomination, Witch Hunters (pg 109) |
|-----------|---------------------------------------------|
| FACTION KEYWORDS | IMPERIUM, ASTRA TELEPATHICA, SISTERS OF SILENCE |
| KEYWORDS | INFANTRY, VIGILATORS |

## WITCHSEEKERS

**5 POWER**

| NAME | M | WS | BS | S | T | W | A | Ld | Sv |
|---|---|---|---|---|---|---|---|---|---|
| Witchseeker | 7" | 3+ | 3+ | 3 | 3 | 1 | 2 | 8 | 3+ |
| Sister Superior | 7" | 3+ | 3+ | 3 | 3 | 1 | 3 | 9 | 3+ |

This unit contains 1 Sister Superior and 4 Witchseekers. It can include up to 5 additional Witchseekers (**Power Rating +5**). Each model is armed with a flamer and psyk-out grenades.

| WEAPON | RANGE | TYPE | S | AP | D | ABILITIES |
|---|---|---|---|---|---|---|
| Flamer | 8" | Assault D6 | 4 | 0 | 1 | This weapon automatically hits its target. |
| Psyk-out grenade | 6" | Grenade D3 | 2 | 0 | 1 | Each time you roll a hit roll of 6+ for this weapon when targeting a **PSYKER** or **DAEMON**, the target suffers a mortal wound instead of the normal damage. |

| ABILITIES | Psychic Abomination, Witch Hunters (pg 109) |
|---|---|
| FACTION KEYWORDS | IMPERIUM, ASTRA TELEPATHICA, SISTERS OF SILENCE |
| KEYWORDS | INFANTRY, WITCHSEEKERS |

---

## NULL-MAIDEN RHINO

**4 POWER**

**DAMAGE**

Some of this model's characteristics change as it suffers damage, as shown below:

| REMAINING W | M | BS | A |
|---|---|---|---|
| 6-10+ | 12" | 3+ | 3 |
| 3-5 | 6" | 4+ | D3 |
| 1-2 | 3" | 5+ | 1 |

| NAME | M | WS | BS | S | T | W | A | Ld | Sv |
|---|---|---|---|---|---|---|---|---|---|
| Null-Maiden Rhino | * | 6+ | * | 6 | 7 | 10 | * | 8 | 3+ |

A Null-Maiden Rhino is a single model equipped with a storm bolter.

| WEAPON | RANGE | TYPE | S | AP | D | ABILITIES |
|---|---|---|---|---|---|---|
| Hunter-killer missile | 48" | Heavy 1 | 8 | -2 | D6 | Each hunter-killer missile can only be fired once per battle. |
| Storm bolter | 24" | Rapid Fire 2 | 4 | 0 | 1 | - |

| WARGEAR OPTIONS | • This model may take a hunter-killer missile. |
|---|---|

| ABILITIES | **Explodes:** If this model is reduced to 0 wounds, roll a D6 before removing it from the battlefield and before any embarked models disembark. On a 6 it explodes, and each unit within 6" suffers D3 mortal wounds. | **Smoke Launchers:** Once per game, instead of shooting any weapons in the Shooting phase, this model can use its smoke launchers; until your next Shooting phase your opponent must subtract 1 from all hit rolls for ranged weapons that target this vehicle. |
|---|---|---|
| | **Self-Repair:** Roll a D6 at the start of each of your turns – on a 6, this model regains one lost wound. | |

| TRANSPORT | This model can transport 10 SISTERS OF SILENCE INFANTRY models. |
|---|---|
| FACTION KEYWORDS | IMPERIUM, ASTRA TELEPATHICA, SISTERS OF SILENCE |
| KEYWORDS | VEHICLE, TRANSPORT, RHINO, NULL-MAIDEN RHINO |

# OFFICIO ASSASSINORUM

The Imperium's armies are vast, but there are times when one well-timed strike can do more to alter the course of a battle than even the largest force. When such services are required, the Imperium turns to the shadowy Officio Assassinorum, calling upon them to unleash their highly trained killers. The assassins are the knife in the dark, the blade that can pierce where other weapons cannot.

The Officio Assassinorum is a clandestine organisation. It is so cloaked in secrecy that many of the highest ranking officials in service to the Imperium have heard nothing of such practices, save perhaps only rumours. Its assassins are a precious resource, their deployment reserved for the direst of targets. Heretic prophets that lead entire star systems into rebellion, xenos leaders that command armies capable of laying waste to whole swathes of Imperial space – these are quarry worthy of assassination. Vast armies are a currency the Imperium is willing to spend, but to assemble and deploy such resources can take years, even decades, and there are times when a foe's momentum must be halted immediately.

There are many different temples within the Officio Assassinorum, each teaching their own unique brand of murder. The most frequently deployed assassins come from the largest temples – Vindicare, Callidus, Eversor and Culexus. Typically, agents of the Assassinorum work unsupported in the field, using whatever means are necessary to complete their mission. There are occasions when a threat is deemed so significant that an Execution Force of assassins from different temples is composed. Ideally, Imperial assassins stay under cover, completing their assignment without ever revealing themselves. However, circumstances are not always optimal. Should an assassin's best route toward completing their mission involve hacking their way through a battlefield or causing catastrophic collateral damage, they will not hesitate to do so.

## CALLIDUS ASSASSIN

Infiltration and deception are the specialties of those agents from the Callidus temple. Using the shape-shifting powers of polymorphine, a Callidus Assassin can assume the identity of anyone, working close to their target before delivering the killing blow. Trained to use their bodies as living weapons, a Callidus also wields a variety of close combat weapons, notably the living metal blade of a phase sword and the formidable neural shredder pistol.

## VINDICARE ASSASSIN

The Vindicare Assassin is a master marksman, a sniper extraordinaire who rains death from afar. Their spymask feeds information directly into their brains, aiding wind calculations, trajectories and dozens of variables, as well as allowing the Assassin to see through smoke, fog or driving snow. Equipped with a powerful exitus rifle, a Vindicare Assassin possesses almost insectile patience, and will spend weeks or months locating the perfect position before triggering their kill-shot with split-second timing. For close-ranged encounters the Vindicare fells their foes with an exitus pistol, gunning them down before making good their escape.

## EVERSOR ASSASSIN

Granted superhuman speed and strength by extensive augmentations and stimms, Eversor Assassins inflict maximum damage with their shock attacks. Armed with toxin-laced weapons, the Eversor is unleashed in a frenetic spree of wanton destruction. Their executioner pistol fires bolts and toxic darts, whilst their melta bombs can blast apart armour, and their power sword and neuro-gauntlet can be used in a berserker fury to rake down even heavily armoured foes. Should they fall, an Eversor remains deadly, their death triggering the overcharged stimulants in their blood to react with the explosive force of a high yield grenade.

## CULEXUS ASSASSIN

Even when concealed by their reality-phasing synskin, the Culexus Assassin fills those nearby with an ancient and nameless fear. Those from the Culexus temple bear the Pariah gene, meaning they are soulless, registering no presence in the warp. They wear a uniquely designed battle-helm – the animus speculum – that can muffle or focus their unique powers to confound or scramble the minds of any nearby. The negative presence of the Culexus Assassin is death personified to psykers, however, and saps away their very life force.

# OFFICIO ASSASSINORUM ARMY LIST

This section contains all of the datasheets that you will need in order to fight battles with your Officio Assassinorum miniatures. Each datasheet includes the characteristics profiles of the unit it describes, as well as any wargear and abilities it has. Some rules are common to several Officio Assassinorum units – these are described here and referenced on the datasheets.

## ABILITIES

The following abilities are common to many Officio Assassinorum units:

### INDEPENDENT OPERATIVE

This model can never have a Warlord Trait. During deployment, you can set this model up in concealment instead of placing it on the battlefield. At the end of any of your Movement phases, this model can reveal its position – set it up anywhere on the battlefield that is more than 9" from any enemy model.

### LIGHTNING REFLEXES

This model has a 4+ invulnerable save.

## VINDICARE ASSASSIN

**5 POWER**

| NAME | M | WS | BS | S | T | W | A | Ld | Sv |
|---|---|---|---|---|---|---|---|---|---|
| Vindicare Assassin | 7" | 2+ | 2+ | 4 | 4 | 5 | 5 | 9 | 6+ |

A Vindicare Assassin is a single model armed with an exitus pistol, an exitus rifle, and blind grenades.

| WEAPON | RANGE | TYPE | S | AP | D | ABILITIES |
|---|---|---|---|---|---|---|
| Exitus pistol | 12" | Pistol 1 | 4 | -3 | D3 | Invulnerable saves cannot be taken against a wound inflicted by this weapon. This weapon wounds **INFANTRY** units on a 2+. |
| Exitus rifle | 72" | Heavy 1 | 5 | -3 | D3 | Invulnerable saves cannot be taken against a wound inflicted by this weapon. This weapon wounds **INFANTRY** units on a 2+. |
| Blind grenade | 12" | Grenade D6 | * | * | * | This weapon does not inflict any damage on the target. Instead, if a unit is hit by any blind grenades, your opponent must subtract 1 from all hit rolls made for that unit until the end of the turn. |

| ABILITIES | Independent Operative, Lightning Reflexes (pg 113)<br><br>**Deadshot:** This model can target a **CHARACTER** even if it is not the closest enemy unit. In addition, each time you roll a wound roll of 6+ for this model in the Shooting phase, the Damage for that attack is D6 rather than D3. | **Spymask:** Enemy models targeted by this model in the Shooting phase do not gain a bonus to their saving throws for being in cover.<br><br>**Stealth Suit:** Your opponent must subtract 1 from hit rolls that target this model in the Shooting phase. If this model is in cover, they must subtract 2 instead. |
|---|---|---|
| **FACTION KEYWORDS** | **IMPERIUM, OFFICIO ASSASSINORUM** | |
| **KEYWORDS** | **INFANTRY, CHARACTER, VINDICARE ASSASSIN** | |

## CALLIDUS ASSASSIN

**5 POWER**

| NAME | M | WS | BS | S | T | W | A | Ld | Sv |
|---|---|---|---|---|---|---|---|---|---|
| Callidus Assassin | 7" | 2+ | 2+ | 4 | 4 | 5 | 5 | 9 | 6+ |

A Callidus Assassin is a single model armed with a neural shredder, a phase sword and poison blades.

| WEAPON | RANGE | TYPE | S | AP | D | ABILITIES |
|---|---|---|---|---|---|---|
| Neural shredder | 9" | Assault 1 | * | * | * | Roll 3D6 if a unit is hit by this weapon; if the roll is equal to or greater than the target unit's highest Leadership characteristic, then it suffers D3 mortal wounds. |
| Phase sword | Melee | Melee | User | -3 | 1 | Invulnerable saves cannot be taken against a wound inflicted by this weapon. |
| Poison blades | Melee | Melee | * | -1 | 1 | Each time the bearer fights, it can make 1 additional attack with this weapon. This weapon wounds on a 3+, unless it is targeting a **VEHICLE**, in which case it wounds on a 6+. |

| ABILITIES | Independent Operative, Lightning Reflexes (pg 113)<br><br>**Polymorphine:** During deployment, you can set up this model in disguise instead of placing it on the battlefield. At the end of any of your Movement phases this model can revert to its true form – set it up anywhere on the battlefield that is more than D6+3" away from any enemy models. For example, if you roll a 4, the model can be set up anywhere that is more than 7" from any enemy model. | **Hit and Run:** This model can Fall Back and still shoot and charge in the same turn.<br><br>**Reign of Confusion:** If you have any Callidus Assassins in your army, then during the first battle round you must roll a dice each time your opponent spends Command Points (CPs) to use a Stratagem. On a 4+, your opponent must spend one extra CP to use that Stratagem, or else it has no effect (the CPs spent so far are lost). This ability cannot effect Stratagems used 'before the battle begins'. |
|---|---|---|
| **FACTION KEYWORDS** | **IMPERIUM, OFFICIO ASSASSINORUM** | |
| **KEYWORDS** | **INFANTRY, CHARACTER, CALLIDUS ASSASSIN** | |

## ⊕ (4) POWER — EVERSOR ASSASSIN

| NAME | M | WS | BS | S | T | W | A | Ld | Sv |
|---|---|---|---|---|---|---|---|---|---|
| Eversor Assassin | 7" | 2+ | 2+ | 4 | 4 | 6 | 6 | 9 | 6+ |

An Eversor Assassin is a single model armed with an executioner pistol, a neuro-gauntlet, a power sword, and melta bombs.

| WEAPON | RANGE | TYPE | S | AP | D | ABILITIES |
|---|---|---|---|---|---|---|
| Executioner pistol | 12" | Pistol 4 | 4 | -1 | 1 | You can re-roll failed wound rolls for this weapon if the target is an INFANTRY model. |
| Neuro-gauntlet | Melee | Melee | +1 | -1 | 1 | You can re-roll failed wound rolls for this weapon. |
| Power sword | Melee | Melee | User | -3 | 1 | - |
| Melta bomb | 4" | Grenade 1 | 8 | -4 | D6 | You can re-roll failed wound rolls for this weapon if the target is a VEHICLE. |

| ABILITIES | Independent Operative, Lightning Reflexes (pg 113)<br><br>**Bio-meltdown:** If this model is reduced to 0 Wounds, roll a D6 for each enemy unit that is within 1" of this model before removing it from the battlefield. On a roll of 4+ the enemy unit suffers D3 mortal wounds. | **Frenzon:** When making a charge roll for this model, roll 3D6 rather than 2D6. In addition, add 2 to this model's Attacks characteristic if they charged in the preceding Charge phase.<br><br>**Sentinel Array:** You can re-roll failed hit rolls for this model when it fires Overwatch. |
|---|---|---|

| FACTION KEYWORDS | IMPERIUM, OFFICIO ASSASSINORUM |
|---|---|
| KEYWORDS | INFANTRY, CHARACTER, EVERSOR ASSASSIN |

## ⊕ (5) POWER — CULEXUS ASSASSIN

| NAME | M | WS | BS | S | T | W | A | Ld | Sv |
|---|---|---|---|---|---|---|---|---|---|
| Culexus Assassin | 7" | 2+ | 2+ | 4 | 4 | 5 | 4 | 9 | 6+ |

A Culexus Assassin is a single model armed with an animus speculum and psyk-out grenades.

| WEAPON | RANGE | TYPE | S | AP | D | ABILITIES |
|---|---|---|---|---|---|---|
| Animus speculum | 18" | Assault D3 | 5 | -4 | 1 | Change this weapon's Type to Assault D6 if there are any enemy PSYKERS within 18" of the bearer. |
| Psyk-out grenade | 6" | Grenade D3 | 2 | 0 | 1 | Each time you roll a hit roll of 6+ for this weapon when targeting a PSYKER or DAEMON, the target suffers a mortal wound instead of the normal damage. |

| ABILITIES | Independent Operative, Lightning Reflexes (pg 113)<br><br>**Abomination:** This model can never be targeted or affected by psychic powers in any way. Enemy PSYKERS that are within 18" of any Culexus Assassins must subtract 2 from Psychic tests and Deny the Witch tests they take.<br><br>**Life Drain:** Armour saves cannot be taken against close combat attacks made by this model. | **Etherium:** Each time an enemy model attacks this model, the attacks are resolved as if the attacker had a Weapon Skill and Ballistic Skill characteristic of 6+.<br><br>**Psychic Assassin:** This model can target a CHARACTER that is a PSYKER, even if it is not the closest enemy unit. In addition, this model can make an attack with a psyk-out grenade in the same Shooting phase that it uses its animus speculum. |
|---|---|---|

| FACTION KEYWORDS: | IMPERIUM, OFFICIO ASSASSINORUM |
|---|---|
| KEYWORDS: | INFANTRY, CHARACTER, CULEXUS ASSASSIN |

# THE INQUISITION

**A highly secretive organisation, the Inquisition is bound by no authority save its own. They are empowered to investigate any potential threat to the Imperium and to take whatever measures they consider appropriate to neutralize the danger. Its agents, the Inquisitors, are the ever-vigilant protectors of the Emperor and, perhaps, Mankind itself.**

The Inquisition is shrouded in mystery, from tales of its founding to its organisational structure, to any true limits of its powers or jurisdictions. The Inquisition's purpose, however, is clear: to root out and identify the myriad dangers that threaten the Imperium and to destroy them. For most, this means by any means necessary. No one, save only the Emperor himself, is beyond the scrutiny and judgement of the Inquisition.

The Inquisition is sometimes referred to as the Holy Ordos of the Inquisition. This is because it is not one unified faction, but is instead composed of many different Ordos, each specializing in a particular kind of threat ranging from alien invaders to internal corruption. There are many dozens of different branches, some so small that their existence has been all but forgotten, or else purposefully hidden from even their own brethren, but at present there are three Ordo Majoris; the Ordo Malleus, the Ordo Hereticus and the Ordo Xenos.

It is not unusual for these different Ordos to work together for the same purpose. It is even more common for the Inquisition to enlist the aid of any number of military branches of the Imperium, such as the Astra Militarum or the Adeptus Astartes. Many Ordos are strongly connected to certain branches, but the galaxy is vast and warp travel is haphazard, so often an Inquisitor will be forced to muster whatever forces can be reached in time. In some circumstances an Inquisitor will temporarily assume command over an army, while in other situations he will merely be attached to other Imperial forces while conducting their own investigations.

Inquisitors are as varied in appearance, manner – and even method – as the worlds of the Imperium that they strive to protect. Inquisitors range from youthful zealots propelled by the righteousness of their cause, to hoary veterans who methodically question even their own motives. Some Inquisitors cover themselves in a shroud of secrecy, never revealing their true purpose so as to better observe all those around them. Other Inquisitors are ostentatious, announcing their presence with fanfare and bearing glaring symbols of their Inquisitorial affiliations upon banner poles. Although they prefer to direct others, Inquisitors are no strangers to battle. Prepared for any situation, Inquisitors can carry a staggeringly wide range of weapons and wargear, from master-crafted artefacts wrought in the foundries of Mars, to mystic items of unknown origin. Many Inquisitors prefer to surround themselves with a retinue. These can range from warrior bodyguards and Death Cult Assassins to xenos techno-savants and even Daemonhosts – warp spirits bound by rite and ceremony within a mortal body.

Across all Ordos there runs a schism. Those of radical beliefs use outlandish weaponry taken from defeated foes, such as Daemon-possessed armaments. To their minds, the only way to defeat the enemy is to use their own weapons against them. Victory by any means is still victory. Conversely, those Inquisitors of more puritanical minds consider such acts as heretical, and prefer to use equipment fabricated exclusively by the Adeptus Mechanicus. At times such debates have escalated into outright conflict, but with the threat levels in the Imperium the highest they have been since the Horus Heresy, the Inquisition have their hands too full to allow much time to continue the age-old debate.

## ORDO HERETICUS

Founded after the corruptions of the Age of Apostasy, the Ordo Hereticus hunts down heretics, mutants and rogue psykers. It is their responsibility to police the Adeptus Ministorum. Their most common ally is the Order Militant of the Ecclesiarchy, the Sisters of Battle.

## ORDO XENOS

The Ordo Xenos is the arm of the Inquisition tasked with defeating the alien in all its loathsome forms. They study their foe, always probing for more information about the weaknesses of the galaxy's myriad denizens. It is their duty to investigate xenos influence over the million settled planets of the Imperium. Their operations see them often working alongside the Space Marines of the Deathwatch.

## ORDO MALLEUS

The Enemy Without, the Order of the Hammer, the Daemonhunters: the Ordo Malleus were established to fight against Mankind's greatest menace – the corrupting powers of Chaos. The Chamber Militant of the Ordo Malleus are the Grey Knights, and often campaign together under a dual command structure.

# INQUISITION ARMY LIST

This section contains all of the datasheets that you will need in order to fight battles with your Inquisition miniatures. Each datasheet includes the characteristics profiles of the unit it describes, as well as any wargear and abilities it may have. Some rules are common to several Inquisition units – these are described below and referenced on the datasheets.

## KEYWORDS

Throughout this section you will come across a keyword that is within angular brackets, specifically <ORDO>. This is shorthand for a keyword of your own choosing, as described below.

## <ORDO>

All members of the Inquisition belong to an Ordo, each of which specialises in combating a particular threat to mankind. Some datasheets specify what Ordo the unit is drawn from (e.g. Inquisitor Coteaz has the ORDO MALLEUS keyword). Other Inquisition datasheets will have the <ORDO> keyword. When you include such a unit in your army, you must nominate which Ordo that unit is from. You then simply replace the <ORDO> keyword in every instance on that unit's datasheet with the name of your chosen Ordo.

## ABILITIES

The following abilities are common to many Inquisition units:

## QUARRY

A unit with this ability gains a bonus when attacking a certain type of enemy. If the unit belongs to the ORDO MALLEUS, the ORDO HERETICUS or the ORDO XENOS, it gains the relevant trait from the table below.

If the unit does not belong to one of these three main Ordos, it belongs to one of the rarer and more specialised Ordos. These Ordos are assumed to be focused upon hunting down specific individuals that pose a threat to the Imperium, and so gain the Specialist trait from the table below.

### ORDOS TRAITS

| ORDO | QUARRY |
|---|---|
| Malleus | You can re-roll hit rolls and wound rolls for ORDO MALLEUS units if the target has the CHAOS or DAEMON keyword. |
| Hereticus | You can re-roll hit rolls and wound rolls for ORDO HERETICUS units if the target has the CHAOS or PSYKER keyword. |
| Xenos | You can re-roll hit rolls and wound rolls of 1 for ORDO XENOS units against targets that do not have the CHAOS, IMPERIUM or UNALIGNED FACTION keywords. |
| Specialist | You can re-roll hit rolls of 1 for Specialist units if the target has the CHARACTER keyword. |

## AUTHORITY OF THE INQUISITION

Units with this ability can embark onto any IMPERIUM TRANSPORT, even though the transport in question might normally only permit models with other Faction keywords to do so. All other restrictions apply normally, and INQUISITOR TERMINATOR models can only embark upon TRANSPORTS that specifically allow Terminator models to do so.

## TELETHESIA DISCIPLINE

Before the battle, generate the psychic powers for PSYKERS that can use powers from the Telethesia discipline using the table below. You can either roll a D3 to generate their powers randomly (re-roll any duplicate results), or you can select the psychic powers you wish the psyker to have.

### TELETHESIA DISCIPLINE

| D3 | PSYCHIC POWER |
|---|---|
| 1 | **Terrify** *Terrify* has a warp charge value of 6. If manifested, select a visible enemy unit within 18" of the psyker. Until the start of your next psychic phase, that unit must subtract 1 from its Leadership characteristic and it cannot fire Overwatch. |
| 2 | **Mental Fortitude** *Mental Fortitude* has a warp charge value of 4. If manifested, select a visible IMPERIUM unit within 18" of the psyker. Until the start of your next psychic phase, that unit automatically passes Morale tests. |
| 3 | **Dominate** *Dominate* has a warp charge value of 7. If manifested, select an enemy CHARACTER within 18" of the psyker. You can force the model to immediately shoot a single weapon or make a single close combat attack at an enemy unit of your choice as if it were part of your army. Models cannot attack themselves, but they can attack other members of their own unit. |

## WARGEAR

### INQUISITION MELEE WEAPONS
- Nemesis Daemon hammer [1]
- Null rod [1]
- Power sword
- Power maul
- Power fist
- Thunder hammer

### INQUISITION RANGED WEAPONS
- Boltgun
- Combi-flamer
- Combi-melta
- Combi-plasma
- Condemnor boltgun [1]
- Flamer
- Hot-shot lasgun

- Incinerator [1]
- Meltagun
- Plasma gun
- Storm bolter

### INQUISITION PISTOL WEAPONS
- Bolt pistol
- Inferno pistol [1]
- Needle pistol
- Plasma pistol

### INQUISITION FORCE WEAPONS
- Force axe
- Force sword
- Force stave

[1] INQUISITOR only.

## INQUISITOR GREYFAX

| NAME | M | WS | BS | S | T | W | A | Ld | Sv |
|---|---|---|---|---|---|---|---|---|---|
| Inquisitor Greyfax | 6" | 3+ | 3+ | 3 | 3 | 5 | 4 | 10 | 3+ |

Inquisitor Greyfax is a single model armed with a master-crafted condemnor boltgun, a master-crafted power sword, frag grenades, krak grenades and psyk-out grenades. Only one of this model can be included in your army.

| WEAPON | RANGE | TYPE | S | AP | D | ABILITIES |
|---|---|---|---|---|---|---|
| Master-crafted condemnor boltgun | 24" | Rapid Fire 1 | 4 | -1 | 1 | If the target is a **Psyker**, increase the Damage of an attack with this weapon from 1 to 3. |
| Master-crafted power sword | Melee | Melee | User | -3 | 2 | - |
| Frag grenade | 6" | Grenade D6 | 3 | 0 | 1 | - |
| Krak grenade | 6" | Grenade 1 | 6 | -1 | D3 | - |
| Psyk-out grenade | 6" | Grenade D3 | 2 | 0 | 1 | Each time you roll a hit roll of 6+ for this weapon when targeting a **Psyker** or **Daemon**, the target suffers a mortal wound instead of the normal damage. |

| ABILITIES | Authority of the Inquisition, Quarry (pg 117)<br><br>**Psyocculum:** Inquisitor Greyfax can target enemy **Characters** that have the **Psyker** or **Daemon** keyword even if they are not the closest enemy unit. | **Indomitable:** Add 1 to the result of the roll for any Deny the Witch tests made for Inquisitor Greyfax.<br><br>**Unquestionable Wisdom:** All friendly **Imperium** units within 6" of Inquisitor Greyfax can use her Leadership characteristic instead of their own. |
|---|---|---|
| PSYKER | Inquisitor Greyfax can attempt to manifest one psychic power in each friendly Psychic phase, and attempt to deny two psychic powers in each enemy Psychic phase. She knows the *Smite* power and one psychic power from the Telethesia discipline (pg 117). | |
| FACTION KEYWORDS | **Imperium, Inquisition, Ordo Hereticus** | |
| KEYWORDS | **Character, Infantry, Inquisitor, Psyker, Greyfax** | |

## INQUISITOR KARAMAZOV

| NAME | M | WS | BS | S | T | W | A | Ld | Sv |
|---|---|---|---|---|---|---|---|---|---|
| Inquisitor Karamazov | 5" | 3+ | 3+ | 5 | 5 | 8 | 4 | 10 | 4+ |

Inquisitor Karamazov is a single model armed with a master-crafted power sword. He sits atop the Throne of Judgement, which is equipped with a master-crafted multi-melta and attacks with its stomping feet. Only one of this model can be included in your army.

| WEAPON | RANGE | TYPE | S | AP | D | ABILITIES |
|---|---|---|---|---|---|---|
| Master-crafted multi-melta | 30" | Assault 1 | 8 | -4 | D6 | If the target is within half range of this weapon, roll two dice when inflicting damage with it and discard the lowest result. |
| Master-crafted power sword | Melee | Melee | User | -3 | 2 | - |
| Throne of Judgement's stomping feet | Melee | Melee | User | 0 | 2 | Each time the bearer fights, it can make 2 additional attacks with this weapon. |

| ABILITIES | Authority of the Inquisition, Quarry (pg 117)<br><br>**Dread Reputation:** Enemy **Psykers** within 12" of Inquisitor Karamazov must subtract 1 from the result of any Psychic tests, and enemy **Infantry** units within 12" of Inquisitor Karamazov in the Morale phase must subtract 1 from their Leadership characteristic.<br><br>**Throne of Judgement:** Inquisitor Karamazov has a 4+ invulnerable save. | **Iron Will:** If an enemy psychic power targets Inquisitor Karamazov, roll 2D6. If the result equals or beats the result of the Psychic test for the psychic power, then the power has no effect upon Inquisitor Karamazov (though any other models that were targeted will be affected normally).<br><br>**Unquestionable Wisdom:** All friendly **Imperium** units within 6" of Inquisitor Karamazov can use his Leadership characteristic instead of their own. |
|---|---|---|
| FACTION KEYWORDS | **Imperium, Inquisition, Ordo Hereticus** | |
| KEYWORDS | **Vehicle, Character, Inquisitor, Karamazov** | |

## INQUISITOR COTEAZ

**4** POWER

| NAME | M | WS | BS | S | T | W | A | Ld | Sv |
|---|---|---|---|---|---|---|---|---|---|
| Inquisitor Coteaz | 6" | 3+ | 3+ | 3 | 3 | 5 | 4 | 10 | 2+ |

Inquisitor Coteaz is a single model armed with a bolt pistol, a master-crafted Nemesis Daemon hammer and a psyber-eagle. Only one of this model can be included in your army.

| WEAPON | RANGE | TYPE | S | AP | D | ABILITIES |
|---|---|---|---|---|---|---|
| Bolt pistol | 12" | Pistol 1 | 4 | 0 | 1 | - |
| Psyber-eagle | 24" | Assault D6 | 4 | 0 | 1 | - |
| Master-crafted Nemesis Daemon hammer | Melee | Melee | x2 | -3 | 3 | - |

| ABILITIES | Authority of the Inquisition, Quarry (pg 117) | Spy Network: If an enemy unit is set up on the battlefield after the game has begun, you can select a friendly ORDO MALLEUS unit within 6" of Inquisitor Coteaz and immediately use it to fire Overwatch on the enemy unit that has just been set up. |
|---|---|---|
| | Unquestionable Wisdom: All friendly IMPERIUM units within 6" of Inquisitor Coteaz can use his Leadership characteristic instead of their own. | |

| PSYKER | Inquisitor Coteaz can attempt to manifest two psychic powers in each friendly Psychic phase, and attempt to deny one psychic power in each enemy Psychic phase. He knows the *Smite* power and one psychic power from the Telethesia discipline (pg 117). |
|---|---|
| FACTION KEYWORDS | IMPERIUM, INQUISITION, ORDO MALLEUS |
| KEYWORDS | CHARACTER, INFANTRY, INQUISITOR, PSYKER, COTEAZ |

Scenting the foul reek of heresy, Inquisitor Coteaz leads a strike force of Blood Angels in a pre-emptive purge.

**5** POWER

# INQUISITOR

| NAME | M | WS | BS | S | T | W | A | Ld | Sv |
|------|---|----|----|----|----|----|----|----|----|
| Inquisitor | 6" | 3+ | 3+ | 3 | 3 | 5 | 4 | 9 | 4+ |

An Inquisitor is a single model armed with a bolt pistol, a chainsword, frag grenades and krak grenades.

| WEAPON | RANGE | TYPE | S | AP | D | ABILITIES |
|--------|-------|------|---|----|----|-----------|
| Bolt pistol | 12" | Pistol 1 | 4 | 0 | 1 | - |
| Chainsword | Melee | Melee | User | 0 | 1 | Each time the bearer fights, it can make 1 additional attack with this weapon. |
| Frag grenade | 6" | Grenade D6 | 3 | 0 | 1 | - |
| Krak grenade | 6" | Grenade 1 | 6 | -1 | D3 | - |

| | |
|---|---|
| **WARGEAR OPTIONS** | • This model may replace its bolt pistol with an item from the *Inquisition Pistol Weapons* list.<br>• This model may replace its chainsword with one item from the *Inquisition Melee Weapons* or *Inquisition Ranged Weapons* lists.<br>• This model may be a psyker. If it is, it gains the **PSYKER** keyword and may replace its chainsword with an item from the *Inquisition Force Weapons* list. If it is not, it has the Iron Will ability (see below). |

| | | |
|---|---|---|
| **ABILITIES** | Authority of the Inquisition, Quarry (pg 117)<br><br>**Unquestionable Wisdom:** All friendly **IMPERIUM** units within 6" of this model can use its Leadership characteristic instead of their own. | **Iron Will:** If an enemy psychic power targets an **INQUISITOR** who is not a **PSYKER**, roll 2D6. If the result equals or beats the result of the Psychic test for the psychic power, then the power has no effect upon that model (though any other models that were targeted will be affected normally). |

| | |
|---|---|
| **PSYKER** | If this model is a **PSYKER**, it can attempt to manifest one psychic power in each friendly Psychic phase, and attempt to deny one psychic power in each enemy Psychic phase. It also knows the *Smite* power and one psychic power from the Telethesia discipline (pg 117). |
| **FACTION KEYWORDS** | **IMPERIUM, INQUISITION, <ORDO>** |
| **KEYWORDS** | **CHARACTER, INFANTRY, INQUISITOR** |

The mandate of an Inquisitor is limitless. Even the notoriously secretive Adeptus Mechanicus must comply.

# ORDO MALLEUS INQUISITOR
## IN TERMINATOR ARMOUR

| NAME | M | WS | BS | S | T | W | A | Ld | Sv |
|------|---|----|----|----|---|---|---|----|----|
| Ordo Malleus Inquisitor in Terminator Armour | 6" | 3+ | 3+ | 3 | 3 | 6 | 5 | 9 | 2+ |

An Ordo Malleus Inquisitor in Terminator Armour is a single model armed with a storm bolter, a Nemesis Daemon hammer and psyk-out grenades.

| WEAPON | RANGE | TYPE | S | AP | D | ABILITIES |
|--------|-------|------|---|----|----|-----------|
| Combi-flamer | | When attacking with this weapon, choose one or both of the profiles below. If you choose both, subtract 1 from all hit rolls for this weapon. | | | | |
| - Boltgun | 24" | Rapid Fire 1 | 4 | 0 | 1 | - |
| - Flamer | 8" | Assault D6 | 4 | 0 | 1 | This weapon automatically hits its target. |
| Combi-melta | | When attacking with this weapon, choose one or both of the profiles below. If you choose both, subtract 1 from all hit rolls for this weapon. | | | | |
| - Boltgun | 24" | Rapid Fire 1 | 4 | 0 | 1 | - |
| - Meltagun | 12" | Assault 1 | 8 | -4 | D6 | If the target is within half range of this weapon, roll two dice when inflicting damage with it and discard the lowest result. |
| Combi-plasma | | When attacking with this weapon, choose one or both of the profiles below. If you choose both, subtract 1 from all hit rolls for this weapon. | | | | |
| - Boltgun | 24" | Rapid Fire 1 | 4 | 0 | 1 | - |
| - Plasma gun | 24" | Rapid Fire 1 | 7 | -3 | 1 | This weapon can be supercharged by the bearer before firing. If they do so, increase the Strength and Damage of the weapon by 1 this turn. On any hit rolls of 1 when firing supercharge, the bearer is slain after all of the weapon's shots have been resolved. |
| Psycannon | 24" | Heavy 4 | 7 | -1 | 1 | - |
| Storm bolter | 24" | Rapid Fire 2 | 4 | 0 | 1 | - |
| Nemesis Daemon hammer | Melee | Melee | x2 | -3 | 3 | When attacking with this weapon, you must subtract 1 from the hit roll. |
| Psyk-out grenade | 6" | Grenade D3 | 2 | 0 | 1 | Each time you roll a hit roll of 6+ for this weapon when targeting a PSYKER or DAEMON, the target suffers a mortal wound instead of the normal damage. |

| WARGEAR OPTIONS | |
|-----------------|--|
| | • This model may replace its storm bolter with a combi-flamer, combi-melta, combi-plasma or psycannon. |
| | • This model may be a psyker. If it is, it gains the **PSYKER** keyword and may replace its Nemesis Daemon hammer with an item from the *Inquisition Force Weapons* list. If it is not, it has the Iron Will ability (see below). |

| ABILITIES | |
|-----------|--|
| | **Authority of the Inquisition, Quarry** (pg 117) |

**Iron Will:** If an enemy psychic power targets an **INQUISITOR** who is not a **PSYKER**, roll 2D6. If the result equals or beats the result of the Psychic test for the psychic power, then the power has no effect upon that model (though any other models that were targeted will be affected normally).

**Terminator Armour:** Ordo Malleus Inquisitors in Terminator Armour have a 5+ invulnerable save.

**Teleport Strike:** During deployment, you can set up this model in a teleportarium chamber instead of placing it on the battlefield. At the end of any of your Movement phases this model can teleport into battle – set it up anywhere on the battlefield that is more than 9" away from any enemy models.

**Unquestionable Wisdom:** All friendly **IMPERIUM** units within 6" of this model can use its Leadership characteristic instead of their own.

| PSYKER | |
|--------|--|
| | If this model is a **PSYKER**, it can attempt to manifest one psychic power in each friendly Psychic phase, and attempt to deny one psychic power in each enemy Psychic phase. It also knows the *Smite* power and one psychic power from the Telethesia discipline (pg 117). |

| FACTION KEYWORDS | **IMPERIUM, INQUISITION, ORDO MALLEUS** |
|------------------|------------------------------------------|
| KEYWORDS | **CHARACTER, INFANTRY, TERMINATOR, INQUISITOR** |

## ACOLYTES

**1 POWER**

| NAME | M | WS | BS | S | T | W | A | Ld | Sv |
|------|---|----|----|---|---|---|---|----|----|
| Acolyte | 6" | 4+ | 4+ | 3 | 3 | 3 | 2 | 7 | 5+ |

This unit contains 1 Acolyte. It can include up to 5 additional Acolytes (**Power Rating + 1 per Acolyte**). Each Acolyte is armed with a laspistol and a chainsword.

| WEAPON | RANGE | TYPE | S | AP | D | ABILITIES |
|--------|-------|------|---|----|----|-----------|
| Laspistol | 12" | Pistol 1 | 3 | 0 | 1 | - |
| Chainsword | Melee | Melee | User | 0 | 1 | Each time the bearer fights, it can make 1 additional attack with this weapon. |

| WARGEAR OPTIONS | • Any model may replace its laspistol with an item from the *Inquisition Pistol Weapons* list. <br> • Any model may replace its chainsword with an item from the *Inquisition Melee Weapons* or *Inquisition Ranged Weapons* lists. |
|---|---|
| **ABILITIES** | **Authority of the Inquisition, Quarry** (pg 117) <br><br> **Loyal Servant:** Roll a D6 each time a friendly **<ORDO> INQUISITOR** loses a wound whilst they are within 3" of this unit; on a 2+ a model from this unit can intercept that hit – the character does not lose a wound but the Acolyte suffers a mortal wound. |
| **FACTION KEYWORDS** | **IMPERIUM, INQUISITION, <ORDO>** |
| **KEYWORDS** | **INFANTRY, ACOLYTE** |

## DAEMONHOST

**1 POWER**

| NAME | M | WS | BS | S | T | W | A | Ld | Sv |
|------|---|----|----|---|---|---|---|----|----|
| Daemonhost | 6" | 4+ | 4+ | 4 | 4 | 3 | 2 | 7 | 7+ |

A Daemonhost is a single model. It attacks with its unholy gaze and warp grasp.

| WEAPON | RANGE | TYPE | S | AP | D | ABILITIES |
|--------|-------|------|---|----|----|-----------|
| Unholy gaze | 12" | Assault 1 | 8 | -1 | 1 | Each time you make a wound roll of 6+ for this weapon, that hit is resolved with a Damage of 3 instead of 1. |
| Warp grasp | Melee | Melee | User | -3 | 1 | - |

| ABILITIES | **Daemonic Power:** Roll a D6 for this model at the start of its Movement phase, and look up the result of the roll on the following table. |
|---|---|

| D6 | Result |
|----|--------|
| 1-2 | **Daemonic Speed:** The model has a Move of 12" and can **FLY** for the rest of the Movement phase. |
| 3-4 | **Re-knit Host Form:** Remove any wounds suffered by this model earlier in the battle. |
| 5-6 | **Energy Torrent:** Roll a D6 for each enemy unit within 3" of this model; on a roll of 2+ the enemy unit suffers D3 mortal wounds. |

**Daemonic:** This model has a 5+ invulnerable save.

| FACTION KEYWORDS | **IMPERIUM, INQUISITION** |
|---|---|
| **KEYWORDS** | **INFANTRY, DAEMON, DAEMONHOST** |

# JOKAERO WEAPONSMITH

| NAME | M | WS | BS | S | T | W | A | Ld | Sv |
|------|---|----|----|---|---|---|---|----|----|
| Jokaero Weaponsmith | 6" | 6+ | 4+ | 2 | 3 | 3 | 2 | 7 | 7+ |

A Jokaero Weaponsmith is a single model armed with digital weapons.

| WEAPON | RANGE | TYPE | S | AP | D | ABILITIES |
|--------|-------|------|---|----|----|-----------|
| Digital weapons | When attacking with this weapon, choose one of the profiles below. | | | | | |
| - Focused strike | 24" | Heavy 1 | 7 | -3 | D3 | - |
| - Scatter shot | 12" | Assault 5 | 4 | -1 | 1 | - |

| ABILITIES | |
|-----------|---|
| | **Defence Orbs:** This model has a 5+ invulnerable save. |
| | **Inconceivable Customisation:** At the start of the Shooting phase, you can roll a D6 for one friendly <Ordo> unit within 3" of this model, and apply the result from the following table to that unit for the remainder of the phase: |

| D6 | Result |
|----|--------|
| 1-2 | **Augmented Targeting:** The unit can re-roll failed hit rolls. |
| 3-4 | **Augmented Penetration:** The unit can re-roll failed wound rolls. |
| 5-6 | **The Works:** The unit can re-roll failed hit and wound rolls. |

| FACTION KEYWORDS | IMPERIUM, JOKAERO, INQUISITION, <ORDO> |
|------------------|----------------------------------------|
| KEYWORDS | INFANTRY, JOKAERO WEAPONSMITH |

Some Inquisitors will make use of xenos and bound Daemons in the fight to save the Imperium, even if it costs them their souls.

# ADEPTUS CUSTODES

**The shining golden warriors known as the Adeptus Custodes are the elite bodyguard of the Emperor himself. Their word is law and their might in battle unsurpassed, even amongst the ranks of the Space Marines. Striding resplendent and fearless through the fog of war, they bring hope to the embattled civilisations of Mankind and swift death to their enemies.**

It is said that as the Space Marines are forged from the gene-seed of the Primarchs, the Custodian Guard are fashioned from that of the Emperor. His greatness runs in their veins, gives them stature and strength far beyond human limits. A portion of his inviolable willpower is bequeathed to them, steeling their minds against the corruption of Chaos. So trusted and respected are these warriors that those who fell during the Great Crusade had their names inscribed on the interior surfaces of the Emperor's armour. These are warriors entrusted with more authority than any other Imperial agent – save perhaps the High Lords and the most senior of Inquisitors – for they speak on behalf of the Imperial Palace. Small wonder these are figures of legend and awe in the armies of the Imperium, and that even Space Marines kneel in their presence.

Each of the Custodian Guard is a champion possessed of incredible martial skill and garbed in the finest personal wargear the Imperium can provide. He fights as an army of one, more than capable of cutting down a squad of Heretic Astartes or a charging mob of Orks over the course of a few blood-soaked minutes. The guardian spears and sentinel blades used by these golden warriors incorporate not only powerful disruption fields that can cleave adamantium, but also inbuilt bolters that can shatter a battle line at range. Their baroque armour can turn aside powered blades and vorpal talons alike, for each represents the pinnacle of the tech-artificer's art. On the rare occasions one of these warriors is laid low, he may then be interred in a mighty Contemptor Dreadnought, a walking effigy of destruction that can rip open the war machines of the enemy with powered fist and blazing cannon. The Custodian Guard typically deploy straight into battle via the most blessed of teleportarium arrays, appearing in a blaze of pure white light to strike with the force of a lighting storm, but when they need to redeploy at speed, they use ancient Land Raiders that have served the Imperium faithfully for millennia. A single Custodian Guard can rip through an enemy fortification on a killing rampage; a whole army can collapse an entire battlefront. Heroes all, they engage the champions and sorcerers of the most heinous foes without a flicker of doubt, for they know that righteousness, strength and indomitable will can overcome even the direst threat.

For all their magnificence, there is a hereditary blight on the otherwise glorious history of the Adeptus Custodes, a scar of disgrace that can never truly heal. At the end of the Horus Heresy, the Warmaster Horus all but slew the Master of Mankind as he was slain in his turn – the Custodian Guard, though they fought with every iota of their strength and bravery, failed in their duty. They took to wearing cloaks of black cloth in order to mark that mournful day, and for thousands of years bore the stain of defeat without as well as within. However, since the return of the Primarch Guilliman, the remit of the Adeptus Custodes has changed. Although they will ever be the Emperor's guardians, now their duty lies at his gates and beyond. Many of the Adeptus Custodes have sallied forth into the galaxy once more, reforging their legend by smiting those who would bring harm to Holy Terra before they have even taken to their ships.

## THE TOWER OF HEROES

There is a jutting and mountainous spire in the Emperor's Palace called the Tower of Heroes. At its summit hangs the Bell of Lost Souls. It is an ancient thing, massive as a building and adorned with dark runes, its peal like the scream of an anguished god. It is tolled but once when a great hero of the Imperium dies. Its wailing moan of grief lasts long and reaches the ears of millions, and its tones penetrate the unifying aether of Humanity, turning the thoughts of countless billions towards Mankind's loss.

## CUSTODIAN GUARD

**14** POWER

| NAME | M | WS | BS | S | T | W | A | Ld | Sv |
|---|---|---|---|---|---|---|---|---|---|
| Custodian | 6" | 2+ | 3+ | 5 | 5 | 3 | 3 | 8 | 2+ |
| Shield-Captain | 6" | 2+ | 2+ | 5 | 5 | 3 | 4 | 9 | 2+ |

This unit contains 1 Shield-Captain and 4 Custodians. It can include up to 5 additional Custodians (**Power Rating +13**). Each model is armed with a guardian spear.

| WEAPON | RANGE | TYPE | S | AP | D | ABILITIES |
|---|---|---|---|---|---|---|
| Guardian spear (shooting) | 24" | Rapid Fire 1 | 4 | -1 | 2 | - |
| Sentinel blade (shooting) | 12" | Pistol 2 | 4 | 0 | 1 | - |
| Guardian spear (melee) | Melee | Melee | +1 | -3 | D3 | - |
| Power knife | Melee | Melee | User | -2 | 1 | A model equipped with a sentinel blade and power knife can make 1 additional attack each time it fights. |
| Sentinel blade (melee) | Melee | Melee | User | -3 | D3 | - |

| WARGEAR OPTIONS | • Any model may replace its guardian spear with a sentinel blade.<br>• One Custodian in the unit may replace its guardian spear with a Custodes vexilla and a power knife. Note that only one Custodian Guard unit per Detachment can take a Custodes vexilla.<br>• Any Custodian not armed with a guardian spear may take a storm shield.<br>• A Shield-Captain armed with a sentinel blade may take a storm shield or a power knife. |
|---|---|

| ABILITIES | **Aegis of the Emperor:** Models in this unit have a 5+ invulnerable save.<br><br>**Storm Shield:** A model equipped with a storm shield has a 3+ invulnerable save. | **Custodes Vexilla:** You can re-roll failed Morale tests for friendly **IMPERIUM** units within 6" of a model equipped with a Custodes vexilla. In addition, you can make 1 additional attack in the Fight phase for all models in this unit whilst it has a Custodes vexilla. |
|---|---|---|

| FACTION KEYWORDS | **IMPERIUM, ADEPTUS CUSTODES** |
|---|---|
| KEYWORDS | **INFANTRY, CUSTODIAN GUARD** |

## VENERABLE CONTEMPTOR DREADNOUGHT

**8** POWER

| NAME | M | WS | BS | S | T | W | A | Ld | Sv |
|---|---|---|---|---|---|---|---|---|---|
| Venerable Contemptor Dreadnought | * | * | * | 7 | 7 | 10 | 4 | 8 | 3+ |

A Venerable Contemptor Dreadnought is a single model equipped with a Dreadnought combat weapon, a multi-melta and a combi-bolter.

**DAMAGE**

Some of this model's characteristics change as it suffers damage, as shown below:

| REMAINING W | M | WS | BS |
|---|---|---|---|
| 6-10+ | 9" | 2+ | 2+ |
| 3-5 | 6" | 3+ | 3+ |
| 1-2 | 4" | 4+ | 4+ |

| WEAPON | RANGE | TYPE | S | AP | D | ABILITIES |
|---|---|---|---|---|---|---|
| Combi-bolter | 24" | Rapid Fire 2 | 4 | 0 | 1 | - |
| Kheres pattern assault cannon | 24" | Heavy 6 | 7 | -1 | 1 | - |
| Multi-melta | 24" | Heavy 1 | 8 | -4 | D6 | If the target is within half range of this weapon, roll two dice when inflicting damage with it and discard the lowest result. |
| Dreadnought combat weapon | Melee | Melee | x2 | -3 | 3 | - |

| WARGEAR OPTIONS | • This model may replace its multi-melta with a Kheres pattern assault cannon. |
|---|---|

| ABILITIES | **Aegis of the Emperor:** This model has a 5+ invulnerable save.<br><br>**Unyielding Ancient:** Roll a D6 each time this model loses a wound; on a 6 the damage is ignored and that wound is not lost. | **Explodes:** If this model is reduced to 0 wounds, roll a D6 before removing it from the battlefield. On a 6 it explodes, and each unit within 6" suffers D3 mortal wounds. |
|---|---|---|

| FACTION KEYWORDS | **IMPERIUM, ADEPTUS CUSTODES** |
|---|---|
| KEYWORDS | **VEHICLE, DREADNOUGHT, VENERABLE CONTEMPTOR DREADNOUGHT** |

# VENERABLE LAND RAIDER

**19 POWER**

| NAME | M | WS | BS | S | T | W | A | Ld | Sv |
|------|---|----|----|---|---|---|---|----|----|
| Venerable Land Raider | ✴ | 6+ | ✴ | 8 | 8 | 16 | ✴ | 9 | 2+ |

**DAMAGE**

Some of this model's characteristics change as it suffers damage, as shown below:

| REMAINING W | M | BS | A |
|-------------|---|----|----|
| 9-16+ | 10" | 2+ | 6 |
| 5-8 | 5" | 3+ | D6 |
| 1-4 | 3" | 4+ | 1 |

A Venerable Land Raider is a single model equipped with twin heavy bolters and two twin lascannons.

| WEAPON | RANGE | TYPE | S | AP | D | ABILITIES |
|--------|-------|------|---|----|----|-----------|
| Hunter-killer missile | 48" | Heavy 1 | 8 | -2 | D6 | A model can only fire each of its hunter-killer missiles once per battle. |
| Storm bolter | 24" | Rapid Fire 2 | 4 | 0 | 1 | - |
| Twin heavy bolter | 36" | Heavy 6 | 5 | -1 | 1 | - |
| Twin lascannon | 48" | Heavy 2 | 9 | -3 | D6 | - |

| WARGEAR OPTIONS | • This model may take a hunter-killer missile.<br>• This model may take a storm bolter. |
|-----------------|---|

**ABILITIES**

**Aegis of the Emperor:** This model has a 5+ invulnerable save.

**Power of the Machine Spirit:** This model does not suffer the penalty to hit rolls for moving and firing Heavy weapons.

**Unyielding Ancient:** Roll a D6 each time this model loses a wound; on a 6 the damage is ignored and that wound is not lost.

**Explodes:** If this model is reduced to 0 wounds, roll a D6 before removing it from the battlefield and before any embarked models disembark. On a 6 it explodes, and each unit within 6" suffers D6 mortal wounds.

**Smoke Launchers:** Once per game, instead of shooting any weapons in the Shooting phase, this model can use its smoke launchers; until your next Shooting phase your opponent must subtract 1 from all hit rolls for ranged weapons that target this vehicle.

| TRANSPORT | A Venerable Land Raider can transport 5 **ADEPTUS CUSTODES INFANTRY** models. |
|-----------|---|
| FACTION KEYWORDS | **IMPERIUM, ADEPTUS CUSTODES** |
| KEYWORDS | **VEHICLE, LAND RAIDER, VENERABLE LAND RAIDER** |

The ancient machine spirits of Venerable Land Raiders are fierce and proud, and delight in the obliteration of the Imperium's foes.

# FORTIFICATIONS

As darkness deepens across the galaxy, every world of the Imperium finds itself besieged. At such a dire time, the importance of solid walls and tireless guns is greater than ever. The fortresses and strongholds of the Imperium are nigh-impregnable and bristling with defensive weaponry. The tides of heretic and xenos armies break against them like surf on the shore.

Upon the ornate cartologues of the Adeptus Terra, the Emperor's realm appears as a unified fastness, fancifully illuminated with gothic flourishes and proud aquilas. Commanders and savants casting their gaze over these miles-wide star maps would be forgiven for envisioning Mankind stood shoulder-to-shoulder across the stars, a resolute wall of faith against which the most tireless of their numerous foes must surely dash themselves to ruin.

Sadly for Humanity, the reality is rather different.

The Imperium is immense, but it is also scattered. Many Imperial star systems are virtually isolated by distance and the turbulent channels of the warp. Rather than a unified whole, the Imperium is more akin to thousands of vassal nations, linked only by their faith and surrounded on all sides by the dangerous darkness of the void.

Conscious of the terrors that may fall upon them at any moment, all but the most neglectful of Imperial governors raise fortifications and planetary defence garrisons. So have the Emperor's worlds ever looked to their own defence in the face of piratical raids, xenos invasions or the nefarious and sinister attentions of heretics.

With the coming of the Great Rift, such defences have become more crucial than ever before. The deranged servants of Chaos spill from the warp in endless waves, battering at the Imperial defences in an endless, frenzied assault. Xenos incursions become ever more common as alien races prey upon weakened worlds, or else flee en masse from the coming of yet worse things at their backs. Madness, heresy and despair run rife, leading world after world down the dark road to insurrection and civil war.

Faced with such threats, the warriors of the Imperium gather behind their defences, fighting to repel wave after wave of pitiless attackers even as their engineers and castellans shore up the barricades and raise monolithic new fortresses to hold back the foe. For many Imperial strongholds it has become an endless, grinding siege in which victory is simple survival, and defences must be raised as swiftly as they are brought crashing down. Fortunately for the myriad worlds of the Imperium, the standard template defensive structures raised for their protection are mighty indeed.

Built from plasteel and reinforced ferrocrete, wreathed in crackling force fields and clouds of blessed incense, the fortifications of the Imperium stand obstinate and inviolate against any who would see their inhabitants slaughtered. Many boast emplaced heavy weaponry, murderous guns fed from armoured hoppers and directed either by the warriors sheltering within the fortification, or else by servitor-brain components and auto-targeting machine spirits wired directly into the weapons themselves. To advance upon such towering bastions is to face a wall of overlapping firepower that makes a mockery of cover. Victims are channelled into carefully calculated killing grounds, where tanks are reduced to smouldering wreckage and soldiers to bullet-riddled corpses.

Simplest of these defences are the prefabricated barricades of the Aegis Defence Lines, and the corpse-shored trench networks of the Wall of Martyrs. In both cases, such obstructions give shelter to infantrymen, artillery teams and the like that hunker behind them, their reinforced structures durable enough to shrug off all but the most ferocious enemy fire. Imperial engineers or Adeptus Mechanicus servitors can raise such defences with swift efficiency. On many Imperial war fronts these barricades and trench lines can stretch for mile upon mile, deployed in ablative layers that reach back from the front, spreading out from larger fortifications like fractal webs.

Bunkers and bastions are also common sights on many Imperial worlds, their stark silhouettes rising over lurking minefields and rusting nests of razor wire. Whether they be lone fortifications, raised to guard outlying highways and passes, or networks of towers and bunkers constructed by the dozen around crucial strategic assets, these slab-sided fastnesses offer protection to Imperial soldiery and death to their foes. Fire support elements such as Space Marine Devastators and Astra Militarum Heavy Weapon Squads often favour Imperial Bastions, making the most of their improved protection and commanding sight-lines, while officers and command sections regularly quarter themselves in Imperial Bunkers, where they can spread out maps and charts, and endure the worst bombardments that the foe can hurl their way.

The armies of the Imperium also deploy larger and rarer fortifications, many being air-dropped into war zones in prefabricated sections to allow for swift assembly and auto-sanctification. Firestorm Redoubts and Vengeance Weapon Batteries provide heavy fire support as well as armoured durability. Their guns blast enemy aircraft from the skies, and mow down the infantry and armour of the foe with an array of servitor-guided guns. Vast weapons emplacements such as the Plasma Obliterator and the Macro-cannon Aquila Strongpoint dominate battlefields, unleashing firepower of a magnitude that hurls Titans from their feet, or punching shots up through the atmosphere to tear the guts from enemy spacecraft. Most terrifying of all is the Vortex Missile Aquila Strongpoint, whose intercontinental empyric destabilisation warheads are fired only as a last resort to unleash the unbound fury of the warp upon the foe.

Finally, there are those structures that provide exceptional support to defending armies. Void Shield Generators use arcane and ineffable technologies to project thrumming force fields that ward away incoming firepower and render nearby friendly warriors inviolate to harm. Meanwhile, Skyshield Landing Pads provide forward staging posts for squadrons of Imperial aircraft, allowing them to land, repair, refuel and re-arm without needing to return to the Imperial rear lines or orbiting spacecraft. This extends the range of such aerial assets enormously, while in extremis the armoured barricades that ring the landing pad can be raised, providing protection to craft and defenders alike should the enemy forces break through and attack.

# AEGIS DEFENCE LINE

| NAME | M | WS | BS | S | T | W | A | Ld | Sv |
|------|---|----|----|---|---|---|---|----|----|
| Gun Emplacement | - | - | 5+ | - | 7 | 3 | - | - | 4+ |

An Aegis Defence Line consists of 4 large shield sections and 4 small shield sections. It may also include one gun emplacement. All shield sections of an Aegis Defence Line must be set up so that they are in end-to-end contact with at least one other shield section, while the gun emplacement must be set up within 6" of any shield section. The gun emplacement is equipped with an Icarus lascannon.

| WEAPON | RANGE | TYPE | S | AP | D | ABILITIES |
|--------|-------|------|---|----|----|-----------|
| Icarus lascannon | 96" | Heavy 1 | 9 | -3 | D6 | Add 1 to hit rolls made for this weapon against targets that can **FLY**. Subtract 1 from hit rolls made for this weapon against all other targets. |
| Quad-gun | 48" | Heavy 8 | 7 | -1 | 1 | Add 1 to hit rolls made for this weapon against targets that can **FLY**. Subtract 1 from hit rolls made for this weapon against all other targets. |

| WARGEAR OPTIONS | • The gun emplacement may replace its Icarus lascannon with a quad-gun. |
|-----------------|-------------------------------------------------------------------------|

| ABILITIES | **Static Defence Network:** After it is set up, an Aegis Defence Line (excluding its gun emplacement, if any) is treated as a terrain feature. It cannot move for any reason, is not treated as a friendly or enemy model, and cannot be targeted or affected by any attacks or abilities.<br><br>**Immobile:** This model cannot move for any reason, nor can it fight in the Fight phase. Enemy models automatically hit this model in the Fight phase – do not make hit rolls. However, this model can still shoot if there are enemy models within 1" of it, and friendly units can still target enemy units that are within 1" of this model. | **Automated Weapons:** Unless a friendly **INFANTRY** model is within 1" of a gun emplacement, it can only target the nearest visible enemy unit. If two units are equally close, you may chose which is targeted.<br><br>**Defence Line: INFANTRY** units within 1" of an Aegis Defence Line, and behind it from the point of view of the firing unit, receive the benefit of cover.<br><br>When charging a unit on the opposite side of an Aegis Defence Line, the charge is successful if the charging unit can move within 2" of that unit. When resolving fights between units on opposite sides of an Aegis Defence Line, units can be chosen to fight and make their attacks if the enemy is within 2" instead of the normal 1". |
|-----------|---|---|

| FACTION KEYWORDS | **UNALIGNED** |
|------------------|---------------|
| KEYWORDS (DEFENCE LINE) | **AEGIS DEFENCE LINE** |
| KEYWORDS (GUN EMPLACEMENT) | **VEHICLE, GUN EMPLACEMENT** |

An Imperial regiment prepares to fend off a planetary invasion, presenting a bristling wall of lasguns and artillery to the foe.

# IMPERIAL BASTION

| NAME | M | WS | BS | S | T | W | A | Ld | Sv |
|------|---|----|----|----|---|---|---|----|----|
| Imperial Bastion | - | - | 5+ | - | 9 | 20 | - | - | 3+ |

An Imperial Bastion is a single model equipped with four heavy bolters.

| WEAPON | RANGE | TYPE | S | AP | D | ABILITIES |
|--------|-------|------|---|----|----|-----------|
| Heavy bolter | 36" | Heavy 3 | 5 | -1 | 1 | - |
| Icarus lascannon | 96" | Heavy 1 | 9 | -3 | D6 | Add 1 to hit rolls made for this weapon against targets that can **FLY**. Subtract 1 from hit rolls made for this weapon against all other targets. |
| Quad-gun | 48" | Heavy 8 | 7 | -1 | 1 | Add 1 to hit rolls made for this weapon against targets that can **FLY**. Subtract 1 from hit rolls made for this weapon against all other targets. |

| | |
|---|---|
| **WARGEAR OPTIONS** | • This model may take an Icarus lascannon or a quad-gun. |
| **ABILITIES** | **Immobile:** This model cannot move for any reason, nor can it fight in the Fight phase. Enemy models automatically hit this model in the Fight phase – do not make hit rolls. However, this model can still shoot if there are enemy models within 1" of it, and friendly units can still target enemy units that are within 1" of this model. |
| | **Automated Weapons:** Unless a friendly unit is embarked inside this model, each of its weapons can only target the nearest visible enemy. If two units are equally close, you may choose which is targeted. |
| | **Fire Points:** 10 models embarked in this model can shoot in their Shooting phase, measuring range and drawing line of sight from any point on this model. They can do this even if enemy models are within 1" of this model. |
| | **Magazine Explosion:** If this model is reduced to 0 wounds, roll a D6 before removing it from the battlefield and before any embarked models disembark. On a 6 its magazine explodes, and each unit within 2D6" suffers D3 mortal wounds. |
| | **Designer's Note:** *If you cannot physically remove this model from your battlefield when it is destroyed (because, for example, it is glued to the surface) then regardless of whether its magazine explodes or not, it is wrecked – from that point on, models can no longer embark inside it, it can no longer shoot etc.* |
| **TRANSPORT** | This model can transport any number of **INFANTRY CHARACTERS** and one other **INFANTRY** unit, up to a maximum of 20 models. |
| | **Designer's Note:** *When you embark models onto an Imperial Bastion, you may find it useful to place some of them on the battlements to remind you which unit(s) are inside the fortification.* |
| **FACTION KEYWORDS** | **UNALIGNED** |
| **KEYWORDS** | **BUILDING, VEHICLE, TRANSPORT, IMPERIAL BASTION** |

# IMPERIAL DEFENCE LINE

An Imperial Defence Line consists of 2 trench sections and up to 4 end sections, or 3 defence emplacement sections and up to 2 additional end sections. All sections must be set up so that they are in end-to-end contact with at least one other **WALL OF MARTYRS** model.

| | |
|---|---|
| **ABILITIES** | **Static Defence Network:** After it is set up, an Imperial Defence Line is treated as a terrain feature. It cannot move for any reason, is not treated as a friendly or enemy model, and cannot be targeted or affected by any attacks or abilities. |

**Stalwart Defence: IMPERIUM INFANTRY** units add 1 to their Leadership whilst they are within an Imperial Defence Line.

**Defence Line: INFANTRY** units within an Imperial Defence Line, and behind it from the point of view of the firing unit, receive the benefit of cover.

When charging a unit within an Imperial Defence Line, the charge is successful if the charging unit can move within 2" of that unit. When resolving fights between units on opposite sides of an Imperial Defence Line, units can be chosen to fight and make their attacks if the enemy is within 2" instead of the normal 1".

| | |
|---|---|
| **FACTION KEYWORDS** | **UNALIGNED** |
| **KEYWORDS** | **WALL OF MARTYRS, IMPERIAL DEFENCE LINE** |

# IMPERIAL BUNKER

**5 POWER**

| NAME | M | WS | BS | S | T | W | A | Ld | Sv |
|------|---|----|----|---|---|---|---|----|----|
| Imperial Bunker | - | | 5+ | - | 8 | 12 | - | - | 3+ |

An Imperial Bunker is a single model.

| WEAPON | RANGE | TYPE | S | AP | D | ABILITIES |
|--------|-------|------|---|----|----|-----------|
| Icarus lascannon | 96" | Heavy 1 | 9 | -3 | D6 | Add 1 to hit rolls made for this weapon against targets that can **FLY**. Subtract 1 from hit rolls made for this weapon against all other targets. |
| Quad-gun | 48" | Heavy 8 | 7 | -1 | 1 | Add 1 to hit rolls made for this weapon against targets that can **FLY**. Subtract 1 from hit rolls made for this weapon against all other targets. |

| WARGEAR OPTIONS | • This model may take an Icarus lascannon or a quad-gun. |
|-----------------|----------------------------------------------------------|

| ABILITIES | |
|-----------|---|
| | **Immobile:** This model cannot move for any reason, nor can it fight in the Fight phase. Enemy models automatically hit this model in the Fight phase – do not make hit rolls. However, this model can still shoot if there are enemy models within 1" of it, and friendly units can still target enemy units that are within 1" of this model. <br><br> **Designer's Note:** *If you cannot physically remove this model from your battlefield when it is destroyed (because, for example, it is glued to the surface) then regardless of whether it explodes or not, it is wrecked – from that point on, models can no longer embark inside it, it can no longer shoot etc.* | **Fire Points:** 5 models embarked in this model can shoot in their Shooting phase, measuring range and drawing line of sight from any point on this model. They can do this even if enemy models are within 1" of this model. <br><br> **Explodes:** If this model is reduced to 0 wounds, roll a D6 before removing it from the battlefield and before any embarked models disembark. On a 6 it explodes, and each unit within D6" suffers D3 mortal wounds. <br><br> **Automated Weapons:** Unless a friendly unit is embarked inside this model, each of its weapons can only target the nearest visible enemy. If two units are equally close, you may choose which is targeted. |

| TRANSPORT | This model can transport any number of **INFANTRY CHARACTERS** and one other **INFANTRY** unit, up to a maximum of 10 models. | **Designer's Note:** *When you embark models onto an Imperial Bunker, you may find it useful to place some of them on the battlements to remind you which unit(s) are inside the fortification.* |
|-----------|---|---|

| FACTION KEYWORDS | **UNALIGNED** |
|------------------|---------------|

| KEYWORDS | **BUILDING, VEHICLE, TRANSPORT, WALL OF MARTYRS, IMPERIAL BUNKER** |
|----------|------------------------------------------------------------------|

# VENGEANCE WEAPON BATTERIES

**6** POWER

| NAME | M | WS | BS | S | T | W | A | Ld | Sv |
|------|---|----|----|---|---|---|---|----|----|
| Vengeance Weapon Battery | - | - | 5+ | - | 8 | 10 | - | - | 3+ |

A Vengeance Weapon Battery is a single model equipped with a punisher gatling cannon. It can include 1 additional Vengeance Weapon Battery (**Power Rating +6**).

| WEAPON | RANGE | TYPE | S | AP | D | ABILITIES |
|--------|-------|------|---|----|----|-----------|
| Battle cannon | 72" | Heavy D6 | 8 | -2 | D3 | - |
| Punisher gatling cannon | 24" | Heavy 20 | 5 | 0 | 1 | - |
| Quad Icarus lascannon | 96" | Heavy 4 | 9 | -3 | D6 | Add 1 to all hit rolls made for this weapon against targets that can **FLY**. Subtract 1 from the hit rolls made for this weapon against all other targets. |

| WARGEAR OPTIONS | • This model may replace its punisher gatling cannon with a battle cannon or a quad Icarus lascannon. |
|-----------------|-----|

| ABILITIES | **Immobile:** This model cannot move for any reason, nor can it fight in the Fight phase. Enemy models automatically hit this model in the Fight phase – do not make hit rolls. However, this model can still shoot if there are enemy models within 1" of it, and friendly units can still target enemy units that are within 1" of this model.<br><br>**Fully Automated Weapons:** This model's weapons can only target the nearest visible enemy. Quad Icarus lascannons can instead choose to target the nearest visible enemy that can **FLY**. In either case, if two units are equally close, you may choose which is targeted. | **Magazine Explosion:** If this model is reduced to 0 wounds, roll a D6 before removing it from the battlefield. On a 6 its magazine explodes, and each unit within 2D6" suffers D3 mortal wounds.<br><br>**Designer's Note:** *If you cannot physically remove this model from your battlefield when it is destroyed (because, for example, it is glued to the surface) then regardless of whether its magazine explodes or not, it is wrecked – from that point on, models can no longer target it, it can no longer shoot etc.* |
|---|---|---|

| FACTION KEYWORDS | UNALIGNED |
|------------------|-----------|
| KEYWORDS | BUILDING, VEHICLE, WALL OF MARTYRS, VENGEANCE WEAPON BATTERIES |

# FIRESTORM REDOUBT

| NAME | M | WS | BS | S | T | W | A | Ld | Sv |
|------|---|----|----|----|----|----|----|----|----|
| Firestorm Redoubt | - | - | 5+ | - | 8 | 20 | - | - | 3+ |

A Firestorm Redoubt is a single model equipped with two quad Icarus lascannons.

| WEAPON | RANGE | TYPE | S | AP | D | ABILITIES |
|--------|-------|------|---|----|----|-----------|
| Battle cannon | 72" | Heavy D6 | 8 | -2 | D3 | - |
| Punisher gatling cannon | 24" | Heavy 20 | 5 | 0 | 1 | - |
| Quad Icarus lascannon | 96" | Heavy 4 | 9 | -3 | D6 | Add 1 to all hit rolls made for this weapon against targets that can FLY. Subtract 1 from the hit rolls made for this weapon against all other targets. |

| | |
|---|---|
| **WARGEAR OPTIONS** | • This model may replace each quad Icarus lascannon with a battle cannon or a punisher gatling cannon. |
| **ABILITIES** | **Automated Weapons:** Unless a friendly unit is embarked inside this model, this model's weapons can only target the nearest visible enemy. Quad Icarus lascannons can instead choose to target the nearest visible enemy that can FLY. In either case, if two units are equally close, you may choose which is targeted.<br><br>**Magazine Explosion:** If this model is reduced to 0 wounds, roll a D6 before removing it from the battlefield and before any embarked models disembark. On a 6 its magazine explodes, and each unit within 2D6" suffers D3 mortal wounds.<br><br>**Fire Points:** 10 models embarked in this model can shoot in their Shooting phase, measuring range and drawing line of sight from any point on this model. They can do this even if enemy models are within 1" of this model. | **Immobile:** This model cannot move for any reason, nor can it fight in the Fight phase. Enemy models automatically hit this model in the Fight phase – do not make hit rolls. However, this model can still shoot if there are enemy models within 1" of it, and friendly units can still target enemy units that are within 1" of this model.<br><br>**Designer's Note:** *If you cannot physically remove this model from your battlefield when it is destroyed (because, for example, it is glued to the surface) then regardless of whether its magazine explodes or not, it is wrecked – from that point on, models can no longer embark inside it, it can no longer shoot etc.* |
| **TRANSPORT** | This model can transport any number of **INFANTRY CHARACTERS** and one other **INFANTRY** unit, up to a maximum of 20 models.<br><br>**Designer's Note:** *When you embark models onto a Firestorm Redoubt, you may find it useful to place some of them on the battlements to remind you which unit(s) are inside the fortification.* |
| **FACTION KEYWORDS** | **UNALIGNED** |
| **KEYWORDS** | **BUILDING, VEHICLE, TRANSPORT, WALL OF MARTYRS, FIRESTORM REDOUBT** |

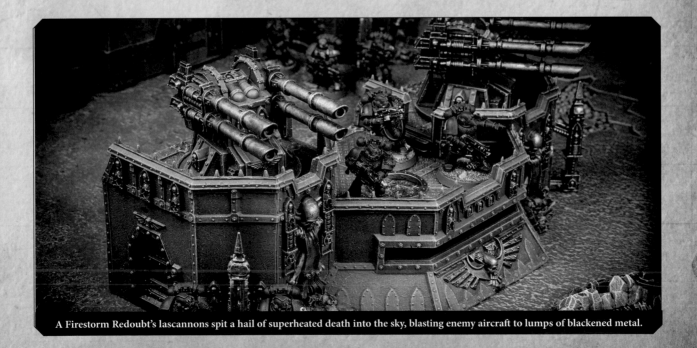

A Firestorm Redoubt's lascannons spit a hail of superheated death into the sky, blasting enemy aircraft to lumps of blackened metal.

# PLASMA OBLITERATOR

**9 POWER**

| NAME | M | WS | BS | S | T | W | A | Ld | Sv |
|------|---|----|----|---|---|---|---|----|----|
| Plasma Obliterator | - | - | 5+ | - | 9 | 20 | - | - | 3+ |

A Plasma Obliterator is a single model equipped with a plasma obliterator.

| WEAPON | RANGE | TYPE | S | AP | D | ABILITIES |
|--------|-------|------|---|----|----|-----------|
| Plasma obliterator | 72" | Heavy 2D6 | 8 | -3 | 2 | Each time you roll a hit roll of 1 when firing this weapon, this model suffers a mortal wound after all of its shots have been resolved. |

| ABILITIES | |
|-----------|---|
| **Immobile:** This model cannot move for any reason, nor can it fight in the Fight phase. Enemy models automatically hit this model in the Fight phase – do not make hit rolls. However, this model can still shoot if there are enemy models within 1" of it, and friendly units can still target enemy units that are within 1" of this model.<br><br>**Automated Weapons:** Unless a friendly unit is embarked inside this model, each of its weapons can only target the nearest visible enemy. If two units are equally close, you may choose which is targeted. | **Fire Points:** 10 models embarked in this model can shoot in their Shooting phase, measuring range and drawing line of sight from any point on this model. They can do this even if enemy models are within 1" of this model.<br><br>**Plasma Explosion:** If this model is reduced to 0 wounds, roll a D6 before removing it from the battlefield and before any embarked models disembark. On a 4+ its plasma core explodes, and each unit within D6" suffers D6 mortal wounds. |

| TRANSPORT | This model can transport any number of **Infantry Characters** and one other **Infantry** unit, up to a maximum of 20 models. |
|-----------|---|
| **FACTION KEYWORDS** | **Unaligned** |
| **KEYWORDS** | **Building, Vehicle, Transport, Plasma Obliterator** |

# MACRO-CANNON
# AQUILA STRONGPOINT

| NAME | M | WS | BS | S | T | W | A | Ld | Sv |
|------|---|----|----|----|----|----|----|----|----|
| Macro-cannon Aquila Strongpoint | - | - | 5+ | - | 10 | 30 | - | - | 3+ |

A Macro-cannon Aquila Strongpoint is a single model equipped with an Aquila macro-cannon.

| WEAPON | RANGE | TYPE | S | AP | D | ABILITIES |
|--------|-------|------|---|----|----|-----------|
| Aquila macro-cannon | When attacking with this weapon, choose one of the profiles below. | | | | | |
| - Macro shell | 72" | Heavy D6 | 14 | -3 | D6 | Treat any Damage rolls of 1 or 2 made for this weapon as 3 instead. |
| - Quake shell | 180" | Heavy 2D6 | 9 | -2 | D3 | - |
| Heavy bolter | 36" | Heavy 3 | 5 | -1 | 1 | - |

| WARGEAR OPTIONS | • This model may take up to four heavy bolters. |
|-----------------|-------------------------------------------------|

| ABILITIES | |
|-----------|---|
| | **Immobile:** This model cannot move for any reason, nor can it fight in the Fight phase. Enemy models automatically hit this model in the Fight phase – do not make hit rolls. However, this model can still shoot if there are enemy models within 1" of it, and friendly units can still target enemy units that are within 1" of this model. <br><br> **Designer's Note:** *If you cannot physically remove this model from your battlefield when it is destroyed (because, for example, it is glued to the surface) then regardless of whether its magazine explodes or not, it is wrecked – from that point on, models can no longer embark inside it, it can no longer shoot etc.* | **Fire Points:** 15 models embarked in this model can shoot in their Shooting phase, measuring range and drawing line of sight from any point on this model. They can do this even if enemy models are within 1" of this model. <br><br> **Magazine Explosion:** If this model is reduced to 0 wounds, roll a D6 before removing it from the battlefield and before any embarked models disembark. On a 6 its magazine explodes, and each unit within 2D6" suffers D6 mortal wounds. <br><br> **Automated Weapons:** Unless a friendly unit is embarked inside this model, each of its weapons can only target the nearest visible enemy. If two units are equally close, you may choose which is targeted. |

| TRANSPORT | This model can transport any number of **INFANTRY CHARACTERS** and one other **INFANTRY** unit, up to a maximum of 30 models. <br><br> **Designer's Note:** *When you embark models onto a Macro-cannon Aquila Strongpoint, you may find it useful to place some of them on the battlements to remind you which unit(s) are inside the fortification.* |
|-----------|---|

| FACTION KEYWORDS | **UNALIGNED** |
|------------------|---------------|

| KEYWORDS | **BUILDING, VEHICLE, TRANSPORT, WALL OF MARTYRS, AQUILA STRONGPOINT, MACRO-CANNON** |
|----------|---|

An Aquila Strongpoint is designed to obliterate enemy super-heavy armour with its fearsome macro-cannon.

## 21 POWER ⟐ VORTEX MISSILE AQUILA STRONGPOINT

| NAME | M | WS | BS | S | T | W | A | Ld | Sv |
|------|---|----|----|----|----|----|----|----|----|
| Vortex Missile Aquila Strongpoint | - | - | 5+ | - | 10 | 30 | - | - | 3+ |

A Vortex Missile Aquila Strongpoint is a single model equipped with a vortex missile battery.

| WEAPON | RANGE | TYPE | S | AP | D | ABILITIES |
|--------|-------|------|---|----|----|-----------|
| Heavy bolter | 36" | Heavy 3 | 5 | -1 | 1 | - |
| Vortex missile battery | 180" | Heavy D6 | - | - | - | This weapon may target units that are not visible to the bearer, even when firing in accordance with the Automated Weapons ability. Each time you hit the target with this weapon it suffers D6 mortal wounds. If a model is wounded but not slain by the attack, roll another dice; on a 6, the model suffers a further D6 mortal wounds. |

| WARGEAR OPTIONS | • This model may take up to four heavy bolters. |
|-----------------|-------------------------------------------------|

**ABILITIES**

**Containment Failure:** If this model is reduced to 0 wounds, before removing it from the battlefield and before any embarked models disembark, its vortex missiles explode. Each unit within 2D6" suffers D6 mortal wounds. If a model is wounded but not slain in this manner, roll another dice; on a roll of a 6, the model is sucked into the swirling vortex and slain.

**Designer's Note:** *If you cannot physically remove this model from your battlefield when it is destroyed (because, for example, it is glued to the surface) then it is wrecked – from that point on, models can no longer embark inside it, it can no longer shoot etc.*

**Automated Weapons:** Unless a friendly unit is embarked inside this model, each of its weapons can only target the nearest visible enemy. If two units are equally close, you may choose which is targeted.

**Fire Points:** 15 models embarked in this model can shoot in their Shooting phase, measuring range and drawing line of sight from any point on this model. They can do this even if enemy models are within 1" of this model.

**Immobile:** This model cannot move for any reason, nor can it fight in the Fight phase. Enemy models automatically hit this model in the Fight phase – do not make hit rolls. However, this model can still shoot if there are enemy models within 1" of it, and friendly units can still target enemy units that are within 1" of this model.

**TRANSPORT**

This model can transport any number of **INFANTRY CHARACTERS** and one other **INFANTRY** unit, up to a maximum of 30 models.

**Designer's Note:** *When you embark models onto a Vortex Missile Aquila Strongpoint, you may find it useful to place some of them on the battlements to remind you which unit(s) are inside the fortification.*

| FACTION KEYWORDS | UNALIGNED |
|------------------|-----------|
| KEYWORDS | BUILDING, VEHICLE, TRANSPORT, WALL OF MARTYRS, AQUILA STRONGPOINT, VORTEX MISSILE |

---

## 9 POWER ⟐ VOID SHIELD GENERATOR

| NAME | M | WS | BS | S | T | W | A | Ld | Sv |
|------|---|----|----|----|----|----|----|----|----|
| Void Shield Generator | - | - | - | - | 8 | 18 | - | - | 4+ |

**DAMAGE**

The effectiveness of the void shield changes as this model suffers damage, as shown below:

| REMAINING W | INVULNERABLE SAVE |
|-------------|-------------------|
| 10-18+ | 4+ |
| 5-9 | 5+ |
| 1-4 | 6+ |

A Void Shield Generator is a single model.

**ABILITIES**

**Immobile:** This model cannot move for any reason, nor can it fight in the Fight phase. Enemy models automatically hit this model in the Fight phase – do not make hit rolls. Friendly units can still target enemy units that are within 1" of this model.

**Projected Void Shields:** All models wholly within 12" of a Void Shield Generator receive an invulnerable save against any attacks made in the Shooting phase (unless the firing model is also wholly within 12" of the Void Shield Generator). The value of the invulnerable save is shown in the damage table above.

| FACTION KEYWORDS | UNALIGNED |
|------------------|-----------|
| KEYWORDS | BUILDING, VEHICLE, VOID SHIELD GENERATOR |

# SKYSHIELD LANDING PAD

**6** POWER

| NAME | M | WS | BS | S | T | W | A | Ld | Sv |
|------|---|----|----|---|---|---|---|----|----|
| Skyshield Landing Pad | - | - | - | - | 8 | 20 | - | - | 4+ |

A Skyshield Landing Pad is a single model.

| | |
|---|---|
| **ABILITIES** | **Landing Pad Configuration:** At the start of your turn, if there are no enemy models within 1" of the Skyshield Landing Pad, a friendly model within 1" of it can change the Skyshield Landing Pad's configuration to one of the following: |
| | • **Shielded:** All models (friend or foe) that are on top of the Skyshield Landing Pad in this configuration receive a 5+ invulnerable save against any attacks made in the Shooting phase (unless the firing model is also on top of the Skyshield Landing Pad). Note, however, that the Skyshield Landing Pad itself does not receive an invulnerable save in this manner. |
| | • **Unfurled:** Any friendly unit with the Flyer Battlefield Role that spends its entire turn on top of a Skyshield Landing Pad in this configuration regains D3 lost wounds at the end of the turn as a result of the landing pad's auto-repair systems. |
| | **Immobile:** This model cannot move for any reason, nor can it fight in the Fight phase. Enemy models automatically hit this model in the Fight phase – do not make hit rolls. Friendly units can still target enemy units that are within 1" of this model. |
| **FACTION KEYWORDS** | UNALIGNED |
| **KEYWORDS** | BUILDING, VEHICLE, SKYSHIELD LANDING PAD |

Tempestus warriors disembark onto a Skyshield Landing Pad, ready to unleash their weapons into the oncoming enemy.

# BATTLE-FORGED ARMIES

When picking a Battle-forged army for matched play, you will need to record the details of your army on a piece of paper (your Army Roster). Here we show one example of how you can do this; using several Detachment Rosters, at least one for each Detachment in your army, and the summarising main Army Roster itself. Over the page are blank rosters you can photocopy.

## DETACHMENT ROSTERS

Each Detachment Roster details all the units it includes. Each unit has a small entry of its own where you can write down the name and type of unit, its Battlefield Role, the number of models it contains, and the weapons each model in the unit is equipped with. Details of how many models make up each unit and what weapons, options and upgrades each can take can be found on that unit's datasheet.

The points value of each unit's models and each individual weapon is then noted down by referencing the points lists in the appendix (pg 142-167), and added together to give a points cost for the unit. The points cost of the entire Detachment is simply then the sum of the points costs of its units. This can be noted down alongside other useful information, such as the number of Command Points (if any) the Detachment gives you (see the *Warhammer 40,000* rulebook for more on Command Points).

### Unit Champions

Many units are led by a champion of some kind such as a Sergeant. Unit champions often have better characteristics and weapon options than the models they command. All the champions in this book have the same points cost as the other models in their unit.

### Under-strength Units

Sometimes you may find that you do not have enough models to field a minimum-sized unit; if this is the case, you can still include one unit of that type in your army with as many models as you have available. In matched play games, you only pay the points for the models you actually have in an under-strength unit (and any weapons they are equipped with). An under-strength unit still takes the appropriate slot in a Detachment.

## ARMY ROSTER

Once you have filled in all of your Detachment Rosters, you can then fill out the main Army Roster. The name and points value of each Detachment is noted down here for reference. The total points cost of your army is the sum of all the Detachment points costs in your army plus any reinforcement points you have chosen to put aside (see below). The points cost of your army should not exceed the points limit you are using for the battle.

There are lots of other useful things to write down on your main Army Roster, such as who the army's Warlord is (this should be done at the start of the battle) and the number of Command Points available to your army. Remember that all Battle-forged armies start with 3 Command Points, but certain Detachments, and occasionally certain models, can change this total.

### Reinforcement Points

Sometimes an ability will allow you to add units to your army, or replace units that have been destroyed. You must set aside some of your points in order to use these units. The points you set aside are called your reinforcement points, and need to be recorded on your army roster. Each time a unit is added to an army during battle, subtract the number of points the unit would cost from your pool of reinforcement points.

---

## ARMY ROSTER

| PLAYER NAME: | Alex Smith | ARMY FACTION: | Astra Militarum |
|---|---|---|---|
| ARMY NAME: | Battle Group Iron Fist | WARLORD: | Colonel Lourgant |

| DETACHMENT NAME | TYPE | CPS | POINTS |
|---|---|---|---|
| Kappic Eagles Recon Team | Patrol | 0 | 382 |
| Cadian 243rd Armoured | Spearhead | 1 | 1116 |
| Shadowsword 'Titan's Bane' | Super-heavy Auxiliary | 0 | 502 |

| WARLORD TRAIT | | |
|---|---|---|
| FILL IN AT SET-UP: | | |

| | |
|---|---|
| Total Command Points: | 4 |
| Reinforcement Points: | 0 |
| TOTAL POINTS: | 2000 |

# DETACHMENT ROSTER

| NAME: | Kappic Eagles Recon Team | TYPE: | Patrol |
|-------|--------------------------|-------|--------|

## UNIT

| UNIT TITLE: | BATTLEFIELD ROLE: | NO. OF MODELS: | POINTS (MODELS): |
|-------------|-------------------|----------------|------------------|
| Tempestor Prime | HQ | 1 | 40 |

| WARGEAR: | POINTS (WARGEAR): |
|----------|-------------------|
| Plasma pistol (5), frag and krak grenades (0) | 5 |

| | TOTAL POINTS (UNIT): | 45 |
|---|---|---|

## UNIT

| UNIT TITLE: | BATTLEFIELD ROLE: | NO. OF MODELS: | POINTS (MODELS): |
|-------------|-------------------|----------------|------------------|
| Militarum Tempestus Command Squad | Elites | 4 | 36 |

| WARGEAR: | POINTS (WARGEAR): |
|----------|-------------------|
| 2 x hot-shot laspistol (2), hot-shot lasgun (1), grenade launcher (5), platoon standard (5), medi-pack (10), vox-caster (5), 4 x frag and krak grenades (0) | 28 |

| | TOTAL POINTS (UNIT): | 64 |
|---|---|---|

## UNIT

| UNIT TITLE: | BATTLEFIELD ROLE: | NO. OF MODELS: | POINTS (MODELS): |
|-------------|-------------------|----------------|------------------|
| Militarum Tempestus Scions | Troops | 10 | 90 |

| WARGEAR: | POINTS (WARGEAR): |
|----------|-------------------|
| Chainsword (0), 2 x hot-shot laspistols (2), hot-shot volley gun (9), plasma gun (7), 2 x flamers (14), 4 x hot-shot lasguns (4), vox-caster (5) 10 x frag and krak grenades (0) | 41 |

| | TOTAL POINTS (UNIT): | 131 |
|---|---|---|

## UNIT

| UNIT TITLE: | BATTLEFIELD ROLE: | NO. OF MODELS: | POINTS (MODELS): |
|-------------|-------------------|----------------|------------------|
| Taurox Prime | Dedicated Transport | 1 | 60 |

| WARGEAR: | POINTS (WARGEAR): |
|----------|-------------------|
| Taurox missile launcher (50), 2 x autocannons (30), storm bolter (2) | 82 |

| | TOTAL POINTS (UNIT): | 142 |
|---|---|---|

| Total Points (Detachment): | 382 | Command Points: | 0 |
|-----------------------------|-----|-----------------|---|

| NOTES: |
|--------|
| |

# ARMY ROSTER

**PLAYER NAME:**

**ARMY FACTION:**

**ARMY NAME:**

**WARLORD:**

| DETACHMENT NAME | TYPE | CPS | POINTS |
|---|---|---|---|
| | | | |
| | | | |
| | | | |
| | | | |
| | | | |
| | | | |
| | | | |
| | | | |
| | | | |
| | | | |
| | | | |
| | | | |
| | | | |
| | | | |
| | | | |
| | | | |
| | | | |
| | | | |
| | | | |
| | | | |

## WARLORD TRAIT

FILL IN AT SET-UP:

| | |
|---|---|
| **Total Command Points:** | |
| **Reinforcement Points:** | |
| **TOTAL POINTS:** | |

# DETACHMENT ROSTER

**NAME:** | **TYPE:**

## UNIT

| UNIT TITLE: | BATTLEFIELD ROLE: | NO. OF MODELS: | POINTS (MODELS): |
|---|---|---|---|
| WARGEAR: | | | POINTS (WARGEAR): |
| | | TOTAL POINTS (UNIT): | |

## UNIT

| UNIT TITLE: | BATTLEFIELD ROLE: | NO. OF MODELS: | POINTS (MODELS): |
|---|---|---|---|
| WARGEAR: | | | POINTS (WARGEAR): |
| | | TOTAL POINTS (UNIT): | |

## UNIT

| UNIT TITLE: | BATTLEFIELD ROLE: | NO. OF MODELS: | POINTS (MODELS): |
|---|---|---|---|
| WARGEAR: | | | POINTS (WARGEAR): |
| | | TOTAL POINTS (UNIT): | |

## UNIT

| UNIT TITLE: | BATTLEFIELD ROLE: | NO. OF MODELS: | POINTS (MODELS): |
|---|---|---|---|
| WARGEAR: | | | POINTS (WARGEAR): |
| | | TOTAL POINTS (UNIT): | |

**Total Points (Detachment):** | **Command Points:**

**NOTES:**

# ASTRA MILITARUM POINTS VALUES

If you are playing a matched play game, or a game that uses a points limit, you can use the following lists to determine the total points cost of your army. Simply add together the points costs of all your models and the wargear they are equipped with to determine your army's total points value.

## UNITS

| UNIT | MODELS PER UNIT | POINTS PER MODEL (Does not include wargear) |
| --- | --- | --- |
| Armoured Sentinels | 1-3 | 40 |
| Baneblade | 1 | 430 |
| Banehammer | 1 | 410 |
| Banesword | 1 | 390 |
| Basilisks | 1-3 | 100 |
| Bullgryns | 3-9 | 35 |
| Chimera | 1 | 75 |
| Command Squad | 4 | 6 |
| Commissar | 1 | 30 |
| Company Commander | 1 | 30 |
| Conscripts | 20-50 | 3 |
| Deathstrike | 1 | 155 |
| Doomhammer | 1 | 420 |
| Heavy Weapons Squad | 3 | 4 |
| Hellhammer | 1 | 450 |
| Hellhounds | 1-3 | 73 |
| Hydras | 1-3 | 115 |
| Infantry Squad | 10 | 4 |
| Knight Commander Pask | 1 | 177 |
| Leman Russ Battle Tanks | 1-3 | 132 |
| Leman Russ Demolishers | 1-3 | 132 |
| Lord Commissar | 1 | 50 |
| Manticore | 1 | 125 |
| Master of Ordnance | 1 | 38 |
| Militarum Tempestus Command Squad | 4 | 9 |
| Militarum Tempestus Scions | 5-10 | 9 |
| Officer of the Fleet | 1 | 25 |
| Ogryns | 3-9 | 30 |
| Platoon Commander | 1 | 20 |
| Ratlings | 5-10 | 5 |
| Rough Riders | 5-10 | 8 |
| Scout Sentinels | 1-3 | 35 |
| Shadowsword | 1 | 430 |
| Special Weapons Squad | 6 | 4 |
| Stormlord | 1 | 430 |
| Stormsword | 1 | 390 |
| Tank Commander | 1 | 167 |
| Taurox | 1 | 55 |
| Taurox Prime | 1 | 60 |
| Tempestor Prime | 1 | 40 |
| Valkyries | 1-3 | 130 |
| Veterans | 10 | 6 |
| Wyverns | 1-3 | 85 |

## UNITS

| UNIT | MODELS PER UNIT | POINTS PER MODEL (Including wargear) |
| --- | --- | --- |
| Colonel 'Iron Hand' Straken | 1 | 90 |
| Colour Sergeant Kell | 1 | 50 |
| Commissar Yarrick | 1 | 130 |
| Lord Castellan Creed | 1 | 70 |
| Nork Deddog | 1 | 80 |
| Sergeant Harker | 1 | 50 |

## RANGED WEAPONS

| WEAPON | POINTS PER WEAPON |
| --- | --- |
| Artillery barrage | 0 |
| Autocannon | 15 |
| Baneblade cannon | 0 |
| Battle cannon | 22 |
| Bolt pistol | 1 |
| Boltgun | 1 |
| Chem cannon | 15 |
| Deathstrike missile | 0 |
| Demolisher cannon | 40 |
| Demolition charge | 5 |
| Earthshaker cannon | 0 |
| Eradicator nova cannon | 25 |
| Executioner plasma cannon | 20 |
| Exterminator autocannon | 25 |
| Flamer | 7 |
| Frag bomb | 0 |
| Frag grenade | 0 |
| Grenade launcher | 5 |
| Grenadier gauntlet | 10 |
| Heavy bolter | 8 |
| Heavy flamer | 17 |
| Heavy stubber | 4 |
| Hellhammer cannon | 0 |
| Hellstrike missiles | 20 |
| Hot-shot lasgun | 1 |
| Hot-shot laspistol | 1 |
| Hot-shot volley gun | 9 |
| Hunter-killer missile | 6 |
| Hydra quad autocannon | 0 |
| Inferno cannon | 20 |
| Krak grenade | 0 |
| Lascannon | 20 |
| Lasgun | 0 |
| Lasgun array | 0 |
| Laspistol | 0 |

## RANGED WEAPONS

| WEAPON | POINTS PER WEAPON |
|---|---|
| Magma cannon | 0 |
| Melta cannon | 35 |
| Meltagun | 12 |
| Missile launcher | 20 |
| Mortar | 5 |
| Multi-laser | 10 |
| Multi-melta | 20 |
| Multiple rocket pod | 11 |
| Plasma cannon | 15 |
| Plasma gun | 7 |
| Plasma pistol | 5 |
| Punisher gatling cannon | 20 |
| Quake cannon | 0 |
| Ripper gun | 0 |
| Shotgun | 0 |
| Sniper rifle | 2 |
| Storm bolter | 2 |
| Storm eagle rockets | 0 |
| Stormsword siege cannon | 0 |
| Taurox battle cannon | 28 |
| Taurox gatling cannon | 18 |
| Taurox missile launcher | 50 |
| Tremor cannon | 0 |
| Twin heavy bolter | 14 |
| Twin heavy flamer | 30 |
| Vanquisher battle cannon | 25 |
| Volcano cannon | 0 |
| Vulcan mega-bolter | 0 |
| Wyvern quad stormshard mortar | 0 |

## MELEE WEAPONS

| WEAPON | POINTS PER WEAPON |
|---|---|
| Adamantium tracks | 0 |
| Bullgryn maul | 7 |
| Chainsword | 0 |
| Hunting lance | 2 |
| Power axe | 5 |
| Power fist | 10 |
| Power lance | 4 |
| Power maul | 4 |
| Power sword | 4 |
| Sentinel chainsaw | 2 |
| Trampling hooves | 0 |

## OTHER WARGEAR

| WARGEAR | POINTS PER ITEM |
|---|---|
| Brute shield | 0 |
| Medi-pack | 10 |
| Platoon standard | 5 |
| Regimental standard | 5 |
| Slabshield | 0 |
| Tempestus command rod | 0 |
| Vox-caster | 5 |

# ASTRA MILITARUM WARGEAR

## RANGED WEAPONS

| WEAPON | RANGE | TYPE | S | AP | D | ABILITIES |
|---|---|---|---|---|---|---|
| Artillery barrage | 100" | Heavy D6 | 8 | -2 | D3 | This weapon can only be fired once per battle, and cannot be used if the bearer moves. This weapon can target units that are not visible to the bearer (when doing so, subtract 1 from the hit rolls). You may only use one artillery barrage per turn, regardless of how many Masters of Ordnance you have in your army. |
| Autocannon | 48" | Heavy 2 | 7 | -1 | 2 | - |
| Bale Eye | 6" | Pistol 1 | 3 | -2 | 1 | - |
| Baneblade cannon | 72" | Heavy 2D6 | 9 | -3 | 3 | - |
| Battle cannon | 72" | Heavy D6 | 8 | -2 | D3 | - |
| Bolt pistol | 12" | Pistol 1 | 4 | 0 | 1 | - |
| Boltgun | 24" | Rapid Fire 1 | 4 | 0 | 1 | - |
| Chem cannon | 8" | Heavy D6 | * | -3 | 1 | This weapon automatically hits its target. In addition, it wounds on a 2+, unless it is targeting a VEHICLE, in which case it wounds on a 6+. |
| Deathstrike missile | 200" | Heavy 3D6 | * | * | * | This weapon can only be fired once per battle. This weapon can target units that are not visible to the bearer. Each time you hit the target with this weapon it suffers a mortal wound. After resolving all damage on the unit, roll a D6 for every other unit within 6" of the target unit – on a 4+ that unit also suffers D3 mortal wounds. |
| Demolisher cannon | 24" | Heavy D3 | 10 | -3 | D6 | When attacking units with 10 or more models, change this weapon's Type to Heavy D6. |
| Demolition charge | 6" | Grenade D6 | 8 | -3 | D3 | Each demolition charge can only be used once per battle. |
| Earthshaker cannon | 240" | Heavy D6 | 9 | -2 | D3 | Roll two dice for the number of attacks when firing this weapon and discard the lowest result. This weapon can target units that are not visible to the bearer. |
| Eradicator nova cannon | 36" | Heavy D6 | 6 | -2 | D3 | Units attacked by this weapon do not gain any bonus to their saving throws for being in cover. |
| Executioner plasma cannon | When attacking with this weapon, choose one of the profiles below. | | | | | |
| - Standard | 36" | Heavy D6 | 7 | -3 | 1 | - |
| - Supercharge | 36" | Heavy D6 | 8 | -3 | 2 | If you make one or more hit rolls of 1, the bearer suffers D6 mortal wounds after all of this weapon's shots have been resolved. |
| Exterminator autocannon | 48" | Heavy 4 | 7 | -1 | 2 | - |
| Flamer | 8" | Assault D6 | 4 | 0 | 1 | This weapon automatically hits its target. |
| Frag bomb | 6" | Grenade D6 | 4 | 0 | 1 | - |
| Frag grenade | 6" | Grenade D6 | 3 | 0 | 1 | - |
| Grenade launcher | When attacking with this weapon, choose one of the profiles below. | | | | | |
| - Frag grenade | 24" | Assault D6 | 3 | 0 | 1 | - |
| - Krak grenade | 24" | Assault 1 | 6 | -1 | D3 | - |
| Grenadier gauntlet | 12" | Assault D6 | 4 | 0 | 1 | - |
| Heavy bolter | 36" | Heavy 3 | 5 | -1 | 1 | - |
| Heavy flamer | 8" | Heavy D6 | 5 | -1 | 1 | This weapon automatically hits its target. |
| Heavy stubber | 36" | Heavy 3 | 4 | 0 | 1 | - |
| Hellhammer cannon | 36" | Heavy 2D6 | 10 | -4 | 3 | Units attacked by this weapon do not gain any bonus to their saving throws for being in cover. |
| Hellstrike missiles | 72" | Heavy 1 | 8 | -2 | D6 | Roll two dice when inflicting damage with this weapon and discard the lowest result. |
| Hot-shot lasgun | 18" | Rapid Fire 1 | 3 | -2 | 1 | - |
| Hot-shot laspistol | 6" | Pistol 1 | 3 | -2 | 1 | - |
| Hot-shot volley gun | 24" | Heavy 4 | 4 | -2 | 1 | - |
| Hunter-killer missile | 48" | Heavy 1 | 8 | -2 | D6 | Each hunter-killer missile can only be fired once per battle. |
| Hydra quad autocannon | 72" | Heavy 8 | 7 | -1 | 2 | Add 1 to all hit rolls made for this weapon against targets that can FLY. Subtract 1 from the hit rolls made for this weapon against all other targets. |
| Inferno cannon | 16" | Heavy D6 | 6 | -1 | 2 | This weapon automatically hits its target. |

## RANGED WEAPONS

| WEAPON | RANGE | TYPE | S | AP | D | ABILITIES |
|---|---|---|---|---|---|---|
| Krak grenade | 6" | Grenade 1 | 6 | -1 | D3 | - |
| Lascannon | 48" | Heavy 1 | 9 | -3 | D6 | - |
| Lasgun | 24" | Rapid Fire 1 | 3 | 0 | 1 | - |
| Lasgun array | 24" | Rapid Fire 3 | 3 | 0 | 1 | This weapon can only be fired if a unit is embarked upon the vehicle equipped with it. |
| Laspistol | 12" | Pistol 1 | 3 | 0 | 1 | - |
| Magma cannon | 60" | Heavy D6 | 10 | -5 | D6 | Units attacked by this weapon do not gain any bonus to their saving throws for being in cover. In addition, if the target is within half range of this weapon, roll two dice when inflicting damage with it and discard the lowest result. |
| Melta cannon | 24" | Heavy D3 | 8 | -4 | D6 | If the target is within half range of this weapon, roll two dice when inflicting damage with it and discard the lowest result. |
| Meltagun | 12" | Assault 1 | 8 | -4 | D6 | If the target is within half range of this weapon, roll two dice when inflicting damage with it and discard the lowest result. |
| Missile launcher | When attacking with this weapon, choose one of the profiles below. | | | | | |
| - Frag missile | 48" | Heavy D6 | 4 | 0 | 1 | - |
| - Krak missile | 48" | Heavy 1 | 8 | -2 | D6 | - |
| Mortar | 48" | Heavy D6 | 4 | 0 | 1 | This weapon can target units that are not visible to the bearer. |
| Multi-laser | 36" | Heavy 3 | 6 | 0 | 1 | - |
| Multi-melta | 24" | Heavy 1 | 8 | -4 | D6 | If the target is within half range of this weapon, roll two dice when inflicting damage with it and discard the lowest result. |
| Multiple rocket pod | 36" | Heavy D6 | 5 | -1 | 1 | - |
| Payback | 36" | Assault 3 | 5 | -2 | 1 | - |
| Plasma cannon | When attacking with this weapon, choose one of the profiles below. | | | | | |
| - Standard | 36" | Heavy D3 | 7 | -3 | 1 | - |
| - Supercharge | 36" | Heavy D3 | 8 | -3 | 2 | On a hit roll of 1, the bearer is slain after all of this weapon's shots have been resolved. |
| Plasma gun | When attacking with this weapon, choose one of the profiles below. | | | | | |
| - Standard | 24" | Rapid Fire 1 | 7 | -3 | 1 | - |
| - Supercharge | 24" | Rapid Fire 1 | 8 | -3 | 2 | On a hit roll of 1, the bearer is slain after all of this weapon's shots have been resolved. |
| Plasma pistol | When attacking with this weapon, choose one of the profiles below. | | | | | |
| - Standard | 12" | Pistol 1 | 7 | -3 | 1 | - |
| - Supercharge | 12" | Pistol 1 | 8 | -3 | 2 | On a hit roll of 1, the bearer is slain. |
| Punisher gatling cannon | 24" | Heavy 20 | 5 | 0 | 1 | - |
| Quake cannon | 140" | Heavy D6 | 14 | -4 | D6 | When rolling for this weapon's damage, treat any rolls of 1 or 2 as 3 instead. |
| Ripper gun | 12" | Assault 3 | 5 | 0 | 1 | - |
| Shotgun | 12" | Assault 2 | 3 | 0 | 1 | If the target is within half range, add 1 to this weapon's Strength. |
| Sniper rifle | 36" | Heavy 1 | 4 | 0 | 1 | A model firing a sniper weapon can target an enemy **Character** even if they are not the closest enemy unit. If you roll a wound roll of 6+ for this weapon, it inflicts a mortal wound in addition to its normal damage. |
| Storm bolter | 24" | Rapid Fire 2 | 4 | 0 | 1 | - |
| Storm eagle rockets | 120" | Heavy 2D6 | 10 | -2 | D3 | This weapon can target units that are not visible to the bearer. A model can only fire a single storm eagle rocket per turn. Each storm eagle rocket can only be fired once per battle. |
| Stormsword siege cannon | 36" | Heavy D6 | 10 | -4 | D6 | Roll two dice for the number of attacks when firing this weapon and discard the lowest result. Units attacked by this weapon do not gain any bonus to their saving throws for being in cover. Re-roll damage rolls of 1 for this weapon. |
| Taurox battle cannon | 48" | Heavy D6 | 7 | -1 | D3 | - |
| Taurox gatling cannon | 24" | Heavy 20 | 4 | 0 | 1 | - |
| Taurox missile launcher | When attacking with this weapon, choose one of the profiles below. | | | | | |
| - Frag missile | 48" | Heavy 2D6 | 4 | 0 | 1 | - |
| - Krak missile | 48" | Heavy 2 | 8 | -2 | D6 | - |
| Tremor cannon | 60" | Heavy 2D6 | 8 | -2 | 3 | If a unit is hit by this weapon, in their following Movement phase they must halve their Move characteristic and cannot Advance. |

## RANGED WEAPONS

| WEAPON | RANGE | TYPE | S | AP | D | ABILITIES |
|---|---|---|---|---|---|---|
| Twin heavy bolter | 36" | Heavy 6 | 5 | -1 | 1 | - |
| Twin heavy flamer | 8" | Heavy 2D6 | 5 | -1 | 1 | This weapon automatically hits its target. |
| Vanquisher battle cannon | 72" | Heavy 1 | 8 | -3 | D6 | Roll two dice when inflicting damage with this weapon and discard the lowest result. |
| Volcano cannon | 120" | Heavy D6 | 16 | -5 | 2D6 | You can re-roll failed wound rolls when targeting TITANIC units with this weapon. |
| Vulcan mega-bolter | 60" | Heavy 20 | 6 | -2 | 2 | - |
| Wyvern quad stormshard mortar | 48" | Heavy 4D6 | 4 | 0 | 1 | This weapon can target units that are not visible to the bearer. You can re-roll failed wound rolls for this weapon. |

## MELEE WEAPONS

| WEAPON | RANGE | TYPE | S | AP | D | ABILITIES |
|---|---|---|---|---|---|---|
| Adamantium tracks | Melee | Melee | User | -2 | D3 | - |
| Bionic arm with devil's claw | Melee | Melee | User | -1 | 2 | - |
| Bullgryn maul | Melee | Melee | +2 | -1 | 2 | - |
| Chainsword | Melee | Melee | User | 0 | 1 | Each time the bearer fights, it can make 1 additional attack with this weapon. |
| Huge knife | Melee | Melee | User | -1 | 2 | - |
| Hunting lance | Melee | Melee | +2 | -2 | D3 | A model may only attack with this weapon on a turn in which it has charged. |
| Power axe | Melee | Melee | +1 | -2 | 1 | - |
| Power fist | Melee | Melee | x2 | -3 | D3 | When attacking with this weapon, you must subtract 1 from the hit roll. |
| Power klaw | Melee | Melee | x2 | -3 | D3 | When attacking with this weapon, you must subtract 1 from the hit roll. |
| Power lance | Melee | Melee | +2 | -1 | 1 | - |
| Power maul | Melee | Melee | +2 | -1 | 1 | - |
| Power sword | Melee | Melee | User | -3 | 1 | - |
| Sentinel chainsaw | Melee | Melee | User | -1 | 1 | - |
| Thunderous headbutt | Melee | Melee | +3 | -2 | D3 | Nork can only make a single thunderous headbutt attack each time he fights. |
| Trampling hooves | Melee | Melee | User | 0 | 1 | After a model on this mount makes its close combat attacks, you can attack with its mount. Make 1 additional attack, using this weapon profile. |

# ADEPTUS MECHANICUS POINTS VALUES

If you are playing a matched play game, or a game that uses a points limit, you can use the following lists to determine the total points cost of your army. Simply add together the points costs of all your models and the wargear they are equipped with to determine your army's total points value.

## UNITS

| UNIT | MODELS PER UNIT | POINTS PER MODEL (Does not include wargear) |
|---|---|---|
| Corpuscarii Electro-Priests | 5-20 | 14 |
| Cybernetica Datasmith | 1 | 22 |
| Fulgurite Electro-Priests | 5-20 | 16 |
| Ironstrider Ballistarii | 1-6 | 50 |
| Kastelan Robots | 2-6 | 65 |
| Kataphron Breachers | 3-12 | 35 |
| Kataphron Destroyers | 3-12 | 35 |
| Onager Dunecrawler | 1 | 90 |
| Servitors | 4 | 2 |
| Sicarian Infiltrators | 5-10 | 18 |
| Sicarian Ruststalkers | 5-10 | 15 |
| Skitarii Rangers | 5-10 | 10 |
| Skitarii Vanguard | 5-10 | 10 |
| Sydonian Dragoons | 1-6 | 59 |
| Tech-Priest Dominus | 1 | 125 |
| Tech-Priest Enginseer | 1 | 40 |

## BELISARIUS CAWL

| UNIT | MODELS PER UNIT | POINTS PER MODEL (Including wargear) |
|---|---|---|
| Belisarius Cawl | 1 | 250 |

## MELEE WEAPONS

| WEAPON | POINTS PER WEAPON |
|---|---|
| Arc claw | 4 |
| Arc maul | 5 |
| Chordclaw | 3 |
| Electroleech stave | 0 |
| Electrostatic gauntlets | 0 |
| Hydraulic claw | 8 |
| Kastelan fists | 35 |
| Omnissian axe | 0 |
| Power fist | 20 |
| Power sword | 4 |
| Servo-arm | 12 |
| Taser goad | 6 |
| Taser lance | 9 |
| Transonic blades | 7 |
| Transonic razor | 2 |

## RANGED WEAPONS

| WEAPON | POINTS PER WEAPON |
|---|---|
| Arc pistol | 3 |
| Arc rifle | 4 |
| Cognis flamer | 11 |
| Cognis heavy stubber | 8 |
| Eradication beamer | 30 |
| Eradication ray | 14 |
| Flechette blaster | 2 |
| Galvanic rifle | 0 |
| Gamma pistol | 10 |
| Heavy arc rifle | 18 |
| Heavy bolter | 10 |
| Heavy grav-cannon | 30 |
| Heavy phosphor blaster | 15 |
| Icarus array | 40 |
| Incendine combustor | 21 |
| Laspistol | 0 |
| Macrostubber | 2 |
| Multi-melta | 27 |
| Neutron laser | 45 |
| Phosphor blast pistol | 4 |
| Phosphor blaster | 8 |
| Phosphor serpenta | 6 |
| Plasma caliver | 14 |
| Plasma cannon | 21 |
| Plasma culverin | 27 |
| Radium carbine | 0 |
| Radium jezzail | 4 |
| Radium pistol | 1 |
| Stubcarbine | 2 |
| Torsion cannon | 22 |
| Transuranic arquebus | 25 |
| Twin cognis autocannon | 25 |
| Twin cognis lascannon | 45 |
| Twin heavy phosphor blaster | 30 |
| Volkite blaster | 8 |

## OTHER WARGEAR

| WARGEAR | POINTS PER ITEM |
|---|---|
| Broad spectrum data-tether | 0 |
| Enhanced data-tether | 9 |
| Omnispex | 7 |
| Smoke launchers | 0 |

# ADEPTUS MECHANICUS WARGEAR

## RANGED WEAPONS

| WEAPON | RANGE | TYPE | S | AP | D | ABILITIES |
|---|---|---|---|---|---|---|
| Arc pistol | 12" | Pistol 1 | 6 | -1 | 1 | When attacking a VEHICLE, this weapon has a Damage of D3. |
| Arc rifle | 24" | Rapid Fire 1 | 6 | -1 | 1 | When attacking a VEHICLE, this weapon has a Damage of D3. |
| Cognis flamer | 8" | Assault D6 | 4 | 0 | 1 | This weapon automatically hits its target. In addition, when firing Overwatch with this weapon, roll two dice when determining how many attacks it makes and discard the lowest result. |
| Cognis heavy stubber | 36" | Heavy 3 | 4 | 0 | 1 | You may fire this weapon even if the firing model Advanced but you must subtract 2 from any hit rolls if you do so. |
| Electrostatic gauntlets (shooting) | 12" | Assault 3 | 5 | 0 | 1 | Each hit roll of 6+ with this weapon causes 3 hits rather than 1. |
| Eradication beamer | 36" | Heavy D6 | 8 | -2 | D3 | When attacking units within 12", change this weapon's Type to Heavy D3, but resolve the shots with an AP of -4 and a Damage of D6. |
| Eradication ray | 24" | Heavy D3 | 6 | -2 | 1 | Attacks from this weapon that target enemies at 8" or less are resolved with an AP of -4 and a Damage of D3. |
| Flechette blaster | 12" | Pistol 5 | 3 | 0 | 1 | - |
| Galvanic rifle | 30" | Rapid Fire 1 | 4 | 0 | 1 | Each time you make a wound roll of 6+ for this weapon, that hit is resolved with an AP of -1. |
| Gamma pistol | 12" | Pistol 1 | 6 | -3 | 2 | You can re-roll failed wound rolls for this weapon when attacking a VEHICLE. |
| Heavy arc rifle | 36" | Heavy 2 | 6 | -2 | D3 | When attacking a VEHICLE, this weapon has a Damage of D6. |
| Heavy bolter | 36" | Heavy 3 | 5 | -1 | 1 | - |
| Heavy grav-cannon | 30" | Heavy 5 | 5 | -3 | 1 | If the target has a Save characteristic of 3+ or better, this weapon has a Damage characteristic of D3. |
| Heavy phosphor blaster | 36" | Heavy 3 | 6 | -2 | 1 | Units attacked by this weapon do not gain any bonus to their saving throws for being in cover. |
| Icarus array | When attacking with this weapon, you can fire all three of the profiles below. | | | | | |
| - Daedalus missile launcher | 48" | Heavy 1 | 7 | -3 | D6 | |
| - Gatling rocket launcher | 48" | Heavy 5 | 6 | -2 | 1 | Add 1 to all hit rolls made for this weapon against targets that can FLY. Subtract 1 from hit rolls against all other targets. |
| - Twin Icarus autocannon | 48" | Heavy 4 | 7 | -1 | 2 | |
| Incendine combustor | 12" | Heavy D6 | 5 | -1 | 1 | This weapon automatically hits its target. |
| Laspistol | 12" | Pistol 1 | 3 | 0 | 1 | - |
| Macrostubber | 12" | Pistol 5 | 4 | 0 | 1 | - |
| Multi-melta | 24" | Heavy 1 | 8 | -4 | D6 | If the target is within half range of this weapon, roll two dice when inflicting damage with it and discard the lowest result. |
| Neutron laser | 48" | Heavy D3 | 10 | -4 | D6 | Treat damage rolls of 1 or 2 made by this weapon as 3 instead. |
| Phosphor blast pistol | 12" | Pistol 1 | 5 | -1 | 1 | Units attacked by this weapon do not gain any bonus to their saving throws for being in cover. |
| Phosphor blaster | 24" | Rapid Fire 1 | 5 | -1 | 1 | Units attacked by this weapon do not gain any bonus to their saving throws for being in cover. |
| Phosphor serpenta | 18" | Assault 1 | 5 | -1 | 1 | Units attacked by this weapon do not gain any bonus to their saving throws for being in cover. |
| Plasma caliver | When attacking with this weapon, choose one of the profiles below. | | | | | |
| - Standard | 18" | Assault 2 | 7 | -3 | 1 | - |
| - Supercharge | 18" | Assault 2 | 8 | -3 | 2 | On a hit roll of 1, the bearer is slain after all of this weapon's shots have been resolved. |
| Plasma cannon | When attacking with this weapon, choose one of the profiles below. | | | | | |
| - Standard | 36" | Heavy D3 | 7 | -3 | 1 | - |
| - Supercharge | 36" | Heavy D3 | 8 | -3 | 2 | On a hit roll of 1, the bearer is slain after all of this weapon's shots have been resolved. |
| Plasma culverin | When attacking with this weapon, choose one of the profiles below. | | | | | |
| - Standard | 36" | Heavy D6 | 7 | -3 | 1 | - |
| - Supercharge | 36" | Heavy D6 | 8 | -3 | 2 | On a hit roll of 1, the bearer is slain after all of this weapon's shots have been resolved. |

## RANGED WEAPONS

| WEAPON | RANGE | TYPE | S | AP | D | ABILITIES |
|---|---|---|---|---|---|---|
| Radium carbine | 18" | Assault 3 | 3 | 0 | 1 | Each time you make a wound roll of 6+ for this weapon, that hit inflicts 2 damage instead of 1. |
| Radium jezzail | 30" | Heavy 2 | 5 | 0 | 1 | This weapon may target a CHARACTER even if it is not the closest enemy unit. Each time you make a wound roll of 6+ for this weapon, it inflicts a mortal wound in addition to its normal damage. |
| Radium pistol | 12" | Pistol 1 | 3 | 0 | 1 | Each time you make a wound roll of 6+ for this weapon, that hit inflicts 2 damage instead of 1. |
| Solar atomiser | 12" | Assault D3 | 10 | -4 | D3 | If the target is within half range of this weapon, it has a Damage of D6. |
| Stubcarbine | 18" | Pistol 3 | 4 | 0 | 1 | - |
| Torsion cannon | 24" | Heavy 1 | 8 | -4 | D6 | - |
| Transuranic arquebus | 60" | Heavy 1 | 7 | -2 | D3 | This weapon cannot be fired if the firing model moved during the Movement phase. This weapon may target a CHARACTER even if it is not the closest enemy unit. Each time you make a wound roll of 6+ for this weapon, it inflicts a mortal wound in addition to its normal damage. |
| Twin cognis autocannon | 48" | Heavy 4 | 7 | -1 | 2 | You may fire this weapon even if the firing model Advanced but you must subtract 2 from any hit rolls if you do so. |
| Twin cognis lascannon | 48" | Heavy 2 | 9 | -3 | D6 | You may fire this weapon even if the firing model Advanced but you must subtract 2 from any hit rolls if you do so. |
| Twin heavy phosphor blaster | 36" | Heavy 6 | 6 | -2 | 1 | Units attacked by this weapon do not gain any bonus to their saving throws for being in cover. |
| Volkite blaster | 24" | Heavy 3 | 6 | 0 | 1 | Each time you make a wound roll of 6+ for this weapon, the target suffers a mortal wound in addition to any other damage. |

## MELEE WEAPONS

| WEAPON | RANGE | TYPE | S | AP | D | ABILITIES |
|---|---|---|---|---|---|---|
| Arc claw | Melee | Melee | +1 | -1 | 1 | When attacking a VEHICLE, this weapon has a Damage of D3. |
| Arc maul | Melee | Melee | +2 | -1 | 1 | When attacking a VEHICLE, this weapon has a Damage of D3. |
| Arc scourge | Melee | Melee | x2 | -1 | 1 | When attacking a VEHICLE, this weapon has a Damage of D3. |
| Chordclaw | Melee | Melee | User | 0 | D3 | A chordclaw can only be used to make one attack each time this model fights. Each time you make a wound roll of 6+ with this weapon, the target suffers D3 mortal wounds instead of the normal damage. |
| Electroleech stave | Melee | Melee | +2 | -2 | D3 | Each time you make a wound roll of 6+ with this weapon, the target suffers D3 mortal wounds instead of the normal damage. |
| Electrostatic gauntlets (melee) | Melee | Melee | 5 | 0 | 1 | Each hit roll of 6+ with this weapon causes 3 hits rather than 1. |
| Hydraulic claw | Melee | Melee | x2 | -1 | D3 | When attacking with this weapon, you must subtract 1 from the hit roll. |
| Kastelan fists | Melee | Melee | +4 | -3 | 3 | - |
| Mechadendrite hive | Melee | Melee | User | 0 | 1 | Each time Belisarius Cawl fights, he can make 2D6 additional attacks with this weapon. |
| Omnissian axe | Melee | Melee | +1 | -2 | 2 | - |
| Power fist | Melee | Melee | x2 | -3 | D3 | When attacking with this weapon, you must subtract 1 from the hit roll. |
| Power sword | Melee | Melee | User | -3 | 1 | - |
| Servo-arm | Melee | Melee | x2 | -2 | 3 | Each servo-arm can only be used to make one attack each time this model fights. When a model attacks with this weapon, you must subtract 1 from the hit roll. |
| Taser goad | Melee | Melee | +2 | 0 | 1 | Each hit roll of 6+ with this weapon causes 3 hits rather than 1. |
| Taser lance | Melee | Melee | +3 | 0 | 2 | Each hit roll of 6+ with this weapon causes 3 hits rather than 1. |
| Transonic blades | Melee | Melee | +1 | 0 | 1 | Each time you make a wound roll of 6+ with this weapon, the target suffers a mortal wound instead of the normal damage. |
| Transonic razor | Melee | Melee | User | 0 | 1 | Each time you make a wound roll of 6+ with this weapon, the target suffers a mortal wound instead of the normal damage. |

# QUESTOR IMPERIALIS POINTS VALUES

If you are playing a matched play game, or a game that uses a points limit, you can use the following lists to determine the total points cost of your army. Simply add together the points costs of all your models, as well as the wargear they are equipped with, to determine your army's total points value.

## MELEE WEAPONS

| WEAPON | POINTS PER WEAPON |
|---|---|
| Reaper chainsword | 30 |
| Thunderstrike gauntlet | 35 |
| Titanic feet | 0 |

## RANGED WEAPONS

| WEAPON | POINTS PER WEAPON |
|---|---|
| Avenger gatling cannon | 95 |
| Heavy flamer | 17 |
| Heavy stubber | 4 |
| Ironstorm missile pod | 16 |
| Meltagun | 17 |
| Rapid-fire battle cannon | 100 |
| Stormspear rocket pod | 45 |
| Thermal cannon | 76 |
| Twin Icarus autocannon | 30 |

## UNITS

| UNIT | MODELS PER UNIT | POINTS PER MODEL (Does not include wargear) |
|---|---|---|
| Knight Crusader | 1 | 320 |
| Knight Errant | 1 | 320 |
| Knight Gallant | 1 | 320 |
| Knight Paladin | 1 | 320 |
| Knight Warden | 1 | 320 |

# QUESTOR IMPERIALIS WARGEAR

## RANGED WEAPONS

| WEAPON | RANGE | TYPE | S | AP | D | ABILITIES |
|---|---|---|---|---|---|---|
| Avenger gatling cannon | 36" | Heavy 12 | 6 | -2 | 2 | - |
| Heavy flamer | 8" | Heavy D6 | 5 | -1 | 1 | This weapon automatically hits its target. |
| Heavy stubber | 36" | Heavy 3 | 4 | 0 | 1 | - |
| Ironstorm missile pod | 72" | Heavy D6 | 5 | -1 | 2 | This weapon can target units that are not visible to the bearer. |
| Meltagun | 12" | Assault 1 | 8 | -4 | D6 | If the target is within half range of this weapon, roll two dice when inflicting damage with it and discard the lowest result. |
| Rapid-fire battle cannon | 72" | Heavy 2D6 | 8 | -2 | D3 | - |
| Stormspear rocket pod | 48" | Heavy 3 | 8 | -2 | D6 | - |
| Thermal cannon | 36" | Heavy D3 | 9 | -4 | D6 | When targeting units with 5 or more models, change this weapon's Type to Heavy D6. If the target is within half range of this weapon, roll two dice when inflicting damage with it and discard the lowest result. |
| Twin Icarus autocannon | 48" | Heavy 4 | 7 | -1 | 2 | Add 1 to all hit rolls made for this weapon against targets that can FLY. Subtract 1 from the hit rolls made for this weapon against all other targets. |

## MELEE WEAPONS

| WEAPON | TYPE | S | AP | D | ABILITIES |
|---|---|---|---|---|---|
| Reaper chainsword | Melee | +4 | -3 | 6 | - |
| Thunderstrike gauntlet | Melee | x2 | -4 | 6 | When attacking with this weapon, you must subtract 1 from the hit roll. If a VEHICLE or MONSTER is slain by this weapon, pick an enemy unit within 9" of the bearer and roll a D6. On a 4+ that unit suffers D3 mortal wounds. |
| Titanic feet | Melee | User | -2 | D3 | Make 3 hit rolls for each attack made with this weapon, instead of 1. |

# ADEPTUS MINISTORUM POINTS VALUES

If you are playing a matched play game, or a game that uses a points limit, you can use the following lists to determine the total points cost of your army. Simply add together the points costs of all your models and the wargear they are equipped with to determine your army's total points value.

## UNITS

| UNIT | MODELS PER UNIT | POINTS PER MODEL (Does not include wargear) |
|---|---|---|
| Arco-flagellants | 3-9 | 15 |
| Battle Sisters Squad | 5-15 | 9 |
| Canoness | 1 | 45 |
| Celestian Squad | 5-10 | 11 |
| Crusaders | 2-10 | 11 |
| Death Cult Assassins | 2-10 | 17 |
| Dialogus | 1 | 15 |
| Dominion Squad | 5-10 | 10 |
| Exorcist | 1 | 160 |
| Hospitaller | 1 | 30 |
| Imagifier | 1 | 40 |
| Immolator | 1 | 68 |
| Ministorum Priest | 1 | 35 |
| Mistress of Repentance | 1 | 35 |
| Penitent Engines | 1-3 | 55 |
| Repentia Squad | 3-9 | 17 |
| Retributor Squad | 5-10 | 9 |
| Seraphim Squad | 5-10 | 11 |
| Sororitas Rhino | 1 | 73 |

## UNITS

| UNIT | MODELS PER UNIT | POINTS PER MODEL (Including wargear) |
|---|---|---|
| Celestine | 1 | 150 |
| - Geminae Superia | 0-2 | 50 |
| Uriah Jacobus | 1 | 100 |

## MELEE WEAPONS

| WEAPON | POINTS PER WEAPON |
|---|---|
| Arco-flails | 0 |
| Chainsword | 0 |
| Chirurgeon's tools | 0 |
| Death Cult power blades | 0 |
| Dialogus staff | 0 |
| Eviscerator | 22 |
| Neural whips | 3 |
| Penitent buzz-blades | 40 |
| Penitent eviscerator | 0 |
| Power axe | 5 |
| Power maul | 4 |
| Power sword | 4 |

## RANGED WEAPONS

| WEAPON | POINTS PER WEAPON |
|---|---|
| Autogun | 0 |
| Bolt pistol | 0 |
| Boltgun | 0 |
| Combi-flamer | 11 |
| Combi-melta | 19 |
| Combi-plasma | 15 |
| Condemnor boltgun | 1 |
| Exorcist missile launcher | 0 |
| Flamer | 9 |
| Frag grenade | 0 |
| Hand flamer | 6 |
| Heavy bolter | 10 |
| Heavy flamer | 17 |
| Hunter-killer missile | 6 |
| Immolation flamer | 35 |
| Inferno pistol | 12 |
| Krak grenade | 0 |
| Laspistol | 0 |
| Meltagun | 17 |
| Multi-melta | 27 |
| Plasma gun | 13 |
| Plasma pistol | 7 |
| Shotgun | 0 |
| Storm bolter | 4 |
| Twin heavy bolter | 17 |
| Twin multi-melta | 54 |

## OTHER WARGEAR

| WEAPON | POINTS PER WEAPON |
|---|---|
| Storm shield | 0 |

# ADEPTUS MINISTORUM WARGEAR

## RANGED WEAPONS

| WEAPON | RANGE | TYPE | S | AP | D | ABILITIES |
|---|---|---|---|---|---|---|
| The Ardent Blade (shooting) | 8" | Assault D6 | 5 | -1 | 1 | This weapon automatically hits its target. |
| Autogun | 24" | Rapid Fire 1 | 3 | 0 | 1 | - |
| Bolt pistol | 12" | Pistol 1 | 4 | 0 | 1 | - |
| Boltgun | 24" | Rapid Fire 1 | 4 | 0 | 1 | - |
| Combi-flamer | | When attacking with this weapon, choose one or both of the profiles below. If you choose both, subtract 1 from all hit rolls for this weapon. | | | | |
| - Boltgun | 24" | Rapid Fire 1 | 4 | 0 | 1 | - |
| - Flamer | 8" | Assault D6 | 4 | 0 | 1 | This weapon automatically hits its target. |
| Combi-melta | | When attacking with this weapon, choose one or both of the profiles below. If you choose both, subtract 1 from all hit rolls for this weapon. | | | | |
| - Boltgun | 24" | Rapid Fire 1 | 4 | 0 | 1 | - |
| - Meltagun | 12" | Assault 1 | 8 | -4 | D6 | If the target is within half range of this weapon, roll two dice when inflicting damage with it and discard the lowest result. |
| Combi-plasma | | When attacking with this weapon, choose one or both of the profiles below. If you choose both, subtract 1 from all hit rolls for this weapon. | | | | |
| - Boltgun | 24" | Rapid Fire 1 | 4 | 0 | 1 | - |
| - Plasma gun | 24" | Rapid Fire 1 | 7 | -3 | 1 | *See plasma gun* |
| Condemnor boltgun | 24" | Rapid Fire 1 | 4 | 0 | 1 | When attacking a **PSYKER**, this weapon has a Damage of D3. |
| Exorcist missile launcher | 48" | Heavy D6 | 8 | -4 | D3 | - |
| Flamer | 8" | Assault D6 | 4 | 0 | 1 | This weapon automatically hits its target. |
| Frag grenade | 6" | Grenade D6 | 3 | 0 | 1 | - |
| Hand flamer | 6" | Pistol D6 | 3 | 0 | 1 | This weapon automatically hits its target. |
| Heavy bolter | 36" | Heavy 3 | 5 | -1 | 1 | - |
| Heavy flamer | 8" | Heavy D6 | 5 | -1 | 1 | This weapon automatically hits its target. |
| Hunter-killer missile | 48" | Heavy 1 | 8 | -2 | D6 | Each hunter-killer missile can only be fired once per battle. |
| Immolation flamer | 12" | Assault 2D6 | 5 | -1 | 1 | This weapon automatically hits its target. |
| Inferno pistol | 6" | Pistol 1 | 8 | -4 | D6 | If the target is within half range of this weapon, roll two dice when inflicting damage with it and discard the lowest result. |
| Krak grenade | 6" | Grenade 1 | 6 | -1 | D3 | - |
| Laspistol | 12" | Pistol 1 | 3 | 0 | 1 | - |
| Meltagun | 12" | Assault 1 | 8 | -4 | D6 | If the target is within half range of this weapon, roll two dice when inflicting damage with it and discard the lowest result. |
| Multi-melta | 24" | Heavy 1 | 8 | -4 | D6 | If the target is within half range of this weapon, roll two dice when inflicting damage with it and discard the lowest result. |
| Plasma gun | | When attacking with this weapon, choose one of the profiles below. | | | | |
| - Standard | 24" | Rapid Fire 1 | 7 | -3 | 1 | - |
| - Supercharge | 24" | Rapid Fire 1 | 8 | -3 | 2 | On a hit roll of 1, the bearer is slain after all of this weapon's shots have been resolved. |
| Plasma pistol | | When attacking with this weapon, choose one of the profiles below. | | | | |
| - Standard | 12" | Pistol 1 | 7 | -3 | 1 | - |
| - Supercharge | 12" | Pistol 1 | 8 | -3 | 2 | On a hit roll of 1, the bearer is slain. |
| The Redeemer | 24" | Assault 2 | 4 | -1 | 1 | Any attacks with a wound roll of 6+ for this weapon have a Damage characteristic of 2 instead of 1. |
| Shotgun | 12" | Assault 2 | 3 | 0 | 1 | If the target is within half range, add 1 to this weapon's Strength. |
| Storm bolter | 24" | Rapid Fire 2 | 4 | 0 | 1 | - |
| Twin heavy bolter | 36" | Heavy 6 | 5 | -1 | 1 | - |
| Twin multi-melta | 24" | Heavy 2 | 8 | -4 | D6 | - |

## MELEE WEAPONS

| WEAPON | RANGE | TYPE | S | AP | D | ABILITIES |
|--------|-------|------|---|----|----|-----------|
| Arco-flails | Melee | Melee | +1 | 0 | 1 | When you make an attack with this weapon, roll D3 dice instead of 1. |
| The Ardent Blade (melee) | Melee | Melee | +4 | -3 | 2 | - |
| Chainsword | Melee | Melee | User | 0 | 1 | Each time the bearer fights, it can make 1 additional attack with this weapon. |
| Chirurgeon's tools | Melee | Melee | User | -1 | 1 | - |
| Death Cult power blades | Melee | Melee | User | -2 | 1 | - |
| Dialogus staff | Melee | Melee | +1 | 0 | 1 | When attacking with this weapon, you must subtract 1 from the hit roll. |
| Eviscerator | Melee | Melee | x2 | -4 | D3 | When attacking with this weapon, you must subtract 1 from the hit roll. |
| Neural whips | Melee | Melee | User | -2 | 1 | Add 1 to the wound rolls for attacks made with this weapon if the target unit's highest Leadership characteristic is less than 8 (other than VEHICLES). |
| Penitent buzz-blades | Melee | Melee | x2 | -3 | 3 | - |
| Penitent eviscerator | Melee | Melee | x2 | -2 | 2 | When attacking with this weapon, you must subtract 1 from the hit roll. |
| Power axe | Melee | Melee | +1 | -2 | 1 | - |
| Power maul | Melee | Melee | +2 | -1 | 1 | - |
| Power sword | Melee | Melee | User | -3 | 1 | - |

# ASTRA TELEPATHICA POINTS VALUES

If you are playing a matched play game, or a game that uses a points limit, you can use the following lists to determine the total points cost of your army. Simply add together the points costs of all your models and the wargear they are equipped with to determine your army's total points value.

## UNITS

| UNIT | MODELS PER UNIT | POINTS PER MODEL (Does not include wargear) |
|---|---|---|
| Astropath | 1 | 15 |
| Primaris Psyker | 1 | 28 |
| Wyrdvane Psykers | 3-9 | 8 |

## RANGED WEAPONS

| WEAPON | POINTS PER WEAPON |
|---|---|
| Laspistol | 0 |

## MELEE WEAPONS

| WEAPON | POINTS PER WEAPON |
|---|---|
| Force stave | 12 |
| Telepathica stave | 6 |
| Wyrdvane stave | 0 |

# ASTRA TELEPATHICA WARGEAR

## RANGED AND MELEE WEAPONS

| WEAPON | RANGE | TYPE | S | AP | D | ABILITIES |
|---|---|---|---|---|---|---|
| Force stave | Melee | Melee | +2 | -1 | D3 | - |
| Laspistol | 12" | Pistol 1 | 3 | 0 | 1 | - |
| Telepathica stave | Melee | Melee | +1 | 0 | D3 | - |
| Wyrdvane stave | Melee | Melee | +1 | 0 | 1 | - |

# SISTERS OF SILENCE POINTS VALUES

If you are playing a matched play game, or a game that uses a points limit, you can use the following lists to determine the total points cost of your army. Simply add together the points costs of all your models and the wargear they are equipped with to determine your army's total points value.

## UNITS

| UNIT | MODELS PER UNIT | POINTS PER MODEL (Does not include wargear) |
|---|---|---|
| Null-Maiden Rhino | 1 | 70 |
| Prosecutors | 5-10 | 12 |
| Vigilators | 5-10 | 11 |
| Witchseekers | 5-10 | 11 |

## MELEE WEAPONS

| WEAPON | POINTS PER WEAPON |
|---|---|
| Executioner greatblade | 8 |

## RANGED WEAPONS

| WEAPON | POINTS PER WEAPON |
|---|---|
| Boltgun | 0 |
| Flamer | 9 |
| Hunter-killer missile | 6 |
| Psyk-out grenades | 0 |
| Storm bolter | 2 |

# SISTERS OF SILENCE WARGEAR

## RANGED WEAPONS

| WEAPON | RANGE | TYPE | S | AP | D | ABILITIES |
|---|---|---|---|---|---|---|
| Boltgun | 24" | Rapid Fire 1 | 4 | 0 | 1 | - |
| Flamer | 8" | Assault D6 | 4 | 0 | 1 | This weapon automatically hits its target. |
| Hunter-killer missile | 48" | Heavy 1 | 8 | -2 | D6 | This weapon can only be fired once per battle. |
| Psyk-out grenade | 6" | Grenade D3 | 2 | 0 | 1 | Each time you roll a hit roll of 6+ for this weapon when targeting a **PSYKER** or **DAEMON**, the target suffers a mortal wound instead of the normal damage. |
| Storm bolter | 24" | Rapid Fire 2 | 4 | 0 | 1 | - |

## MELEE WEAPONS

| WEAPON | RANGE | TYPE | S | AP | D | ABILITIES |
|---|---|---|---|---|---|---|
| Executioner greatblade | Melee | Melee | +1 | -3 | D3 | - |

# OFFICIO ASSASSINORUM POINTS VALUES

If you are playing a matched play game, or a game that uses a points limit, you can use the following lists to determine the total points cost of your army. Simply add together the points costs of all your models and the wargear they are equipped with to determine your army's total points value.

## UNITS

| UNIT | MODELS PER UNIT | POINTS PER MODEL (Includes wargear) |
|------|-----------------|-------------------------------------|
| Callidus Assassin | 1 | 80 |
| Culexus Assassin | 1 | 85 |
| Eversor Assassin | 1 | 70 |
| Vindicare Assassin | 1 | 90 |

# OFFICIO ASSASSINORUM WARGEAR

## RANGED WEAPONS

| WEAPON | RANGE | TYPE | S | AP | D | ABILITIES |
|--------|-------|------|---|----|----|-----------|
| Animus speculum | 18" | Assault D3 | 5 | -4 | 1 | Change this weapon's Type to Assault D6 if there are any enemy **PSYKERS** within 18" of the bearer. |
| Blind grenade | 12" | Grenade D6 | * | * | * | This weapon does not inflict any damage on the target. Instead, if a unit is hit by any blind grenades, your opponent must subtract 1 from all hit rolls made for that unit until the end of the turn. |
| Executioner pistol | 12" | Pistol 4 | 4 | -1 | 1 | You can re-roll failed wound rolls for this weapon if the target is an **INFANTRY** model. |
| Exitus pistol | 12" | Pistol 1 | 4 | -3 | D3 | Invulnerable saves cannot be taken against a wound inflicted by this weapon. This weapon wounds **INFANTRY** units on a 2+. |
| Exitus rifle | 72" | Heavy 1 | 5 | -3 | D3 | Invulnerable saves cannot be taken against a wound inflicted by this weapon. This weapon wounds **INFANTRY** units on a 2+. |
| Melta bomb | 4" | Grenade 1 | 8 | -4 | D6 | You can re-roll failed wound rolls for this weapon if the target is a **VEHICLE**. |
| Neural shredder | 9" | Assault 1 | * | * | * | Roll 3D6 if a unit is hit by this weapon; if the roll is equal to or greater than the target unit's highest Leadership characteristic, then it suffers D3 mortal wounds. |
| Psyk-out grenade | 6" | Grenade D3 | 2 | 0 | 1 | Each time you roll a hit roll of 6+ for this weapon when targeting a **PSYKER** or **DAEMON**, the target suffers a mortal wound instead of the normal damage. |

## MELEE WEAPONS

| WEAPON | RANGE | TYPE | S | AP | D | ABILITIES |
|--------|-------|------|---|----|----|-----------|
| Neuro-gauntlet | Melee | Melee | +1 | -1 | 1 | You can re-roll failed wound rolls for this weapon. |
| Phase sword | Melee | Melee | User | -3 | 1 | Invulnerable saves cannot be taken against a wound inflicted by this weapon. |
| Poison blades | Melee | Melee | * | -1 | 1 | Each time the bearer fights, it can make 1 additional attack with this weapon. This weapon wounds on a 3+, unless it is targeting a **VEHICLE**, in which case it wounds on a 6+. |
| Power sword | Melee | Melee | User | -3 | 1 | - |

# INQUISITION POINTS VALUES

If you are playing a matched play game, or a game that uses a points limit, you can use the following lists to determine the total points cost of your army. Simply add together the points costs of all your models and the wargear they are equipped with to determine your army's total points value.

## UNITS

| UNIT | MODELS PER UNIT | POINTS PER MODEL (Does not include wargear) |
|---|---|---|
| Acolytes | 1-6 | 8 |
| Daemonhost | 1 | 25 |
| Inquisitor | 1 | 55 |
| Jokaero Weaponsmith | 1 | 18 |
| Ordo Malleus Inquisitor in Terminator Armour | 1 | 91 |
| Inquisitor Coteaz | 1 | 100 |
| Inquisitor Greyfax | 1 | 85 |
| Inquisitor Karamazov | 1 | 150 |

## MELEE WEAPONS

| WEAPON | POINTS PER WEAPON |
|---|---|
| Chainsword | 0 |
| Force axe | 16 |
| Force stave | 14 |
| Force sword | 12 |
| Master-crafted Nemesis Daemon hammer | 0 |
| Master-crafted power sword | 0 |
| Nemesis Daemon hammer | 25 |
| Null rod | 4 |
| Power fist | 20 |
| Power maul | 4 |
| Power sword | 4 |
| Throne of Judgement's stomping feet | 0 |
| Thunder hammer | 25 |
| Warp grasp | 0 |

## RANGED WEAPONS

| WEAPON | POINTS PER WEAPON |
|---|---|
| Bolt pistol | 0 |
| Boltgun | 0 |
| Combi-flamer | 11 |
| Combi-melta | 19 |
| Combi-plasma | 15 |
| Condemnor boltgun | 1 |
| Digital weapons | 20 |
| Flamer | 9 |
| Frag grenade | 0 |
| Hot-shot lasgun | 4 |
| Incinerator | 20 |
| Inferno pistol | 12 |
| Laspistol | 0 |
| Krak grenade | 0 |
| Master-crafted condemnor boltgun | 0 |
| Master-crafted multi-melta | 0 |
| Meltagun | 17 |
| Needle pistol | 2 |
| Plasma gun | 13 |
| Plasma pistol | 7 |
| Psyber eagle | 0 |
| Psycannon | 20 |
| Psyk-out grenade | 0 |
| Storm bolter | 2 |
| Unholy gaze | 0 |

# INQUISITION WARGEAR

## RANGED WEAPONS

| WEAPON | RANGE | TYPE | S | AP | D | ABILITIES |
|---|---|---|---|---|---|---|
| Bolt pistol | 12" | Pistol 1 | 4 | 0 | 1 | - |
| Boltgun | 24" | Rapid Fire 1 | 4 | 0 | 1 | - |
| Combi-flamer | | When attacking with this weapon, choose one or both of the profiles below. If you choose both, subtract 1 from all hit rolls for this weapon. | | | | |
| - Boltgun | 24" | Rapid Fire 1 | 4 | 0 | 1 | - |
| - Flamer | 8" | Assault D6 | 4 | 0 | 1 | This weapon automatically hits its target. |
| Combi-melta | | When attacking with this weapon, choose one or both of the profiles below. If you choose both, subtract 1 from all hit rolls for this weapon. | | | | |
| - Boltgun | 24" | Rapid Fire 1 | 4 | 0 | 1 | - |
| - Meltagun | 12" | Assault 1 | 8 | -4 | D6 | If the target is within half range of this weapon, roll two dice when inflicting damage with it and discard the lowest result. |
| Combi-plasma | | When attacking with this weapon, choose one or both of the profiles below. If you choose both, subtract 1 from all hit rolls for this weapon. | | | | |
| - Boltgun | 24" | Rapid Fire 1 | 4 | 0 | 1 | - |
| - Plasma gun | 24" | Rapid Fire 1 | 7 | -3 | 1 | *See plasma gun* |
| Condemnor boltgun | 24" | Rapid Fire 1 | 4 | 0 | 1 | If the target is a **Psyker**, increase the Damage of an attack with a condemnor boltgun from 1 to D3. |
| Digital weapons | | When attacking with this weapon, choose one of the profiles below. | | | | |
| - Focused strike | 24" | Heavy 1 | 7 | -3 | D3 | - |
| - Scatter shot | 12" | Assault 5 | 4 | -1 | 1 | |
| Flamer | 8" | Assault D6 | 4 | 0 | 1 | This weapon automatically hits its target. |
| Frag grenade | 6" | Grenade D6 | 3 | 0 | 1 | - |
| Hot-shot lasgun | 18" | Rapid Fire 1 | 3 | -2 | 1 | - |
| Incinerator | 8" | Assault D6 | 6 | -1 | 1 | This weapon automatically hits its target. |
| Inferno pistol | 6" | Pistol 1 | 8 | -4 | D6 | If the target is within half range of this weapon, roll two dice when inflicting damage with it and discard the lowest result. |
| Laspistol | 12" | Pistol 1 | 3 | 0 | 1 | - |
| Krak grenade | 6" | Grenade 1 | 6 | -1 | D3 | - |
| Master-crafted condemnor boltgun | 24" | Rapid Fire 1 | 4 | -1 | 1 | If the target is a **Psyker**, increase the Damage of an attack with this weapon from 1 to 3. |
| Master-crafted multi-melta | 30" | Assault 1 | 8 | -4 | D6 | If the target is within half range of this weapon, roll two dice when inflicting damage with it and discard the lowest result. |
| Meltagun | 12" | Assault 1 | 8 | -4 | D6 | If the target is within half range of this weapon, roll two dice when inflicting damage with it and discard the lowest result. |
| Needle pistol | 12" | Pistol 1 | 1 | 0 | 1 | A needle pistol always wounds on a 2+ unless the target model is a **Vehicle**. |
| Plasma gun | | When attacking with this weapon, choose one of the profiles below. | | | | |
| - Standard | 24" | Rapid Fire 1 | 7 | -3 | 1 | - |
| - Supercharge | 24" | Rapid Fire 1 | 8 | -3 | 2 | On a hit roll of 1, the bearer is slain after all of this weapon's shots have been resolved. |
| Plasma pistol | | When attacking with this weapon, choose one of the profiles below. | | | | |
| - Standard | 12" | Pistol 1 | 7 | -3 | 1 | - |
| - Supercharge | 12" | Pistol 1 | 8 | -3 | 2 | On a hit roll of 1, the bearer is slain. |
| Psyber-eagle | 24" | Assault D6 | 4 | 0 | 1 | - |
| Psycannon | 24" | Heavy 4 | 7 | -1 | 1 | - |
| Psyk-out grenade | 6" | Grenade D3 | 2 | 0 | 1 | Each time you roll a hit roll of 6+ for this weapon when targeting a **Psyker** or **Daemon**, the target suffers a mortal wound instead of the normal damage. |
| Storm bolter | 24" | Rapid Fire 2 | 4 | 0 | 1 | - |
| Unholy gaze | 12" | Assault 1 | 8 | -1 | 1 | Each time you make a wound roll of 6+ for this weapon, that hit is resolved with a Damage of 3 instead of 1. |

## MELEE WEAPONS

| WEAPON | RANGE | TYPE | S | AP | D | ABILITIES |
|---|---|---|---|---|---|---|
| Chainsword | Melee | Melee | User | 0 | 1 | Each time the bearer fights, it can make 1 additional attack with this weapon. |
| Force axe | Melee | Melee | +1 | -2 | D3 | - |
| Force stave | Melee | Melee | +2 | -1 | D3 | - |
| Force sword | Melee | Melee | User | -3 | D3 | - |
| Master-crafted Nemesis Daemon hammer | Melee | Melee | x2 | -3 | 3 | - |
| Master-crafted power sword | Melee | Melee | User | -3 | 2 | - |
| Nemesis Daemon hammer | Melee | Melee | x2 | -3 | 3 | When attacking with this weapon, you must subtract 1 from the hit roll. |
| Null rod | Melee | Melee | User | -2 | 1 | If the target is a PSYKER, increase the Damage of an attack with this weapon from 1 to D3. |
| Power fist | Melee | Melee | x2 | -3 | D3 | When attacking with this weapon, you must subtract 1 from the hit roll. |
| Power maul | Melee | Melee | +2 | -1 | 1 | - |
| Power sword | Melee | Melee | User | -3 | 1 | - |
| Throne of Judgement's stomping feet | Melee | Melee | User | 0 | 2 | Each time the bearer fights, it can make 2 additional attacks with this weapon. |
| Thunder hammer | Melee | Melee | x2 | -3 | 3 | When attacking with this weapon, you must subtract 1 from the hit roll. |
| Warp grasp | Melee | Melee | User | -3 | 1 | - |

# ADEPTUS CUSTODES POINTS VALUES

If you are playing a matched play game, or a game that uses a points limit, you can use the following lists to determine the total points cost of your army. Simply add together the points costs of all your models and the wargear they are equipped with to determine your army's total points value.

## UNITS

| UNIT | MODELS PER UNIT | POINTS PER MODEL (Does not include wargear) |
|---|---|---|
| Custodian Guard | 5-10 | 40 |
| Venerable Contemptor Dreadnought | 1 | 100 |
| Venerable Land Raider | 1 | 241 |

## RANGED WEAPONS

| WEAPON | POINTS PER WEAPON |
|---|---|
| Combi-bolter | 2 |
| Hunter-killer missile | 6 |
| Kheres pattern assault cannon | 25 |
| Multi-melta | 27 |
| Storm bolter | 2 |
| Twin heavy bolter | 23 |
| Twin lascannon | 50 |

## MELEE WEAPONS

| WEAPON | POINTS PER WEAPON |
|---|---|
| Dreadnought combat weapon | 40 |
| Guardian spear | 12 |
| Power knife | 5 |
| Sentinel blade | 9 |

## OTHER WARGEAR

| WEAPON | POINTS PER WEAPON |
|---|---|
| Custodes vexilla | 25 |
| Storm shield | 5 |

# ADEPTUS CUSTODES WARGEAR

## RANGED WEAPONS

| WEAPON | RANGE | TYPE | S | AP | D | ABILITIES |
|---|---|---|---|---|---|---|
| Combi-bolter | 24" | Rapid Fire 2 | 4 | 0 | 1 | - |
| Guardian spear (shooting) | 24" | Rapid Fire 1 | 4 | -1 | 2 | - |
| Hunter-killer missile | 48" | Heavy 1 | 8 | -2 | D6 | A model can only fire each of its hunter-killer missiles once per battle. |
| Kheres pattern assault cannon | 24" | Heavy 6 | 7 | -1 | 1 | - |
| Multi-melta | 24" | Assault 1 | 8 | -4 | D6 | If the target is within half range of this weapon, roll two dice when inflicting damage with it and discard the lowest result. |
| Sentinel blade (shooting) | 12" | Pistol 2 | 4 | 0 | 1 | - |
| Storm bolter | 24" | Rapid Fire 2 | 4 | 0 | 1 | - |
| Twin heavy bolter | 36" | Heavy 6 | 5 | -1 | 1 | - |
| Twin lascannon | 48" | Heavy 2 | 9 | -3 | D6 | - |

## MELEE WEAPONS

| WEAPON | RANGE | TYPE | S | AP | D | ABILITIES |
|---|---|---|---|---|---|---|
| Dreadnought combat weapon | Melee | Melee | x2 | -3 | 3 | - |
| Guardian spear (melee) | Melee | Melee | +1 | -3 | D3 | - |
| Power knife | Melee | Melee | User | -2 | 1 | A model equipped with a sentinel blade and power knife can make 1 additional attack each time it fights. |
| Sentinel blade (melee) | Melee | Melee | User | -3 | D3 | - |

# FORTIFICATIONS POINTS VALUES

If you are playing a matched play game, or a game that uses a points limit, you can use the following lists to determine the total points cost of your army. Simply add together the points costs of all your models and the wargear they are equipped with to determine your army's total points value.

## UNITS

| UNIT | MODELS PER UNIT | POINTS PER MODEL (Does not include wargear) |
|---|---|---|
| Aegis Defence Line | 1 | 75 |
| Firestorm Redoubt | 1 | 160 |
| Imperial Bastion | 1 | 160 |
| Imperial Bunker | 1 | 100 |
| Imperial Defence Line | 1 | 85 |
| Macro-cannon Aquila Strongpoint | 1 | 330 |
| Plasma Obliterator | 1 | 150 |
| Skyshield Landing Pad | 1 | 110 |
| Vengeance Weapon Batteries | 1-2 | 80 |
| Void Shield Generator | 1 | 190 |
| Vortex Missile Aquila Strongpoint | 1 | 330 |

## RANGED WEAPONS

| UNIT | POINTS PER WEAPON |
|---|---|
| Aquila macro-cannon | 80 |
| Battle cannon | 30 |
| Heavy bolter | 8 |
| Icarus lascannon | 25 |
| Plasma obliterator | 40 |
| Punisher gatling cannon | 20 |
| Quad-gun | 30 |
| Quad Icarus lascannon | 70 |
| Vortex missile battery | 100 |

# FORTIFICATIONS WARGEAR

## RANGED WEAPONS

| WEAPON | RANGE | TYPE | S | AP | D | ABILITIES |
|---|---|---|---|---|---|---|
| Aquila macro-cannon | When attacking with this weapon, choose one of the profiles below. | | | | | |
| - Macro shell | 72" | Heavy D6 | 14 | -3 | D6 | Treat any Damage rolls of 1 or 2 made for this weapon as 3 instead. |
| - Quake shell | 180" | Heavy 2D6 | 9 | -2 | D3 | - |
| Battle cannon | 72" | Heavy D6 | 8 | -2 | D3 | - |
| Heavy bolter | 36" | Heavy 3 | 5 | -1 | 1 | - |
| Icarus lascannon | 96" | Heavy 1 | 9 | -3 | D6 | Add 1 to all hit rolls made for this weapon against targets that can FLY. Subtract 1 from the hit rolls made for this weapon against all other targets. |
| Plasma obliterator | 72" | Heavy 2D6 | 8 | -3 | 2 | Each time you roll a hit roll of 1 when firing this weapon, this model suffers a mortal wound after all of its shots have been resolved. |
| Punisher gatling cannon | 24" | Heavy 20 | 5 | 0 | 1 | - |
| Quad-gun | 48" | Heavy 8 | 7 | -1 | 1 | Add 1 to all hit rolls made for this weapon against targets that can FLY. Subtract 1 from the hit rolls made for this weapon against all other targets. |
| Quad Icarus lascannon | 96" | Heavy 4 | 9 | -3 | D6 | Add 1 to all hit rolls made for this weapon against targets that can FLY. Subtract 1 from the hit rolls made for this weapon against all other targets. |
| Vortex missile battery | 180" | Heavy D6 | - | - | - | This weapon may target units that are not visible to the bearer, even when firing in accordance with the Automated Weapons ability. Each time you hit the target with this weapon it suffers D6 mortal wounds. If a model is wounded but not slain by the attack, roll another dice; on a 6, the model suffers a further D6 mortal wounds. |